Matt
With Best Regards
Steve Blaha

The Life Cycle of Civilizations

Some Other Books By Stephen Blaha

Cosmos and Consciousness Second Edition (ISBN: 0972079548, Pingree-Hill Publishing, Auburn, NH, 2002)

A Scientific Inquiry into the Nature of God, the Spiritual, and Near Death Experiences (ISBN: 0972079521, Pingree-Hill Publishing, Auburn, NH, 2002)

A Java™ Programming Introductory and Intermediate Course Second Edition (ISBN: 097207953X, Pingree-Hill Publishing, Auburn, NH, 2002)

C++ for Professional Programming With PC and Unix Applications (ISBN: 1850328013, International Thomson Publishing, Boston, 1995)

The Reluctant Prophets: Has Science Found God? (ISBN: 0759663041, 1stBooks Library, Bloomington, IN, 2001)

The Rhythms of History: A Universal Theory of Civilizations (ISBN: 0972079572, Pingree-Hill Publishing, Auburn, NH, 2002)

A Renormalizable, Unified Quantum Field Theory of the Known Forces of Nature (ISBN: 0972079599, Pingree-Hill Publishing, Auburn, NH, 2003, in preparation)

Available on bn.com and amazon.com as well as bookstores (please tell clerk to order these Print On Demand books from Ingram distributors).

Cover Credits
The front cover depicts various symbols from civilizations: the Aztec Calendar stone, the Giza Sphinx and the Great Pyramid, the Kamakura Buddha (Japan), the White House (Washington DC), the Dome of the Rock Al-Aqsa Mosque (Jerusalem), and the NASA Space Shuttle (courtesy of the NASA Space Program). The back cover shows a galaxy courtesy of NASA.

Cover Design by Stephen Blaha © 2002.

The Life Cycle of Civilizations

By

Stephen Blaha Ph.D.

Pingree-Hill Publishing

Copyright © 2001-2002 by Stephen Blaha
All rights reserved.

This book is an expanded version of *The Rhythms of History*, which was first published in May, 2002. No part of this book may be reproduced, stored in a retrieval system, or transmitted by any means, electronic, mechanical, photocopying, recording, or otherwise, without written permission from the author except for quotations embodied in reviews or critical articles. For additional information write to:

Pingree-Hill Publishing
P. O. Box 368
Auburn, NH 03032

ISBN: 0-9720795-8-0

This book is printed on acid free paper.

rev. 00/00/01

To Margaret

CONTENTS

PREFACE	**XIII**
1. THE IMPORTANCE OF UNDERSTANDING CIVILIZATIONS	**1**
WESTERN CIVILIZATION VS. ISLAMIC CIVILIZATION	1
GROWTH OF ISLAM	2
THE CURRENT SITUATION	2
IMPORTANT CURRENT FACTORS	4
THE OIL WEAPON	4
MUSLIM IMMIGRATION TO THE WEST	7
THE ISRAELI-PALESTINIAN CONFLICT	8
POSSIBLE FUTURES FOR ISLAM AND THE WEST	9
CHINA RESURGENT	12
THE NEED FOR A DEEPER UNDERSTANDING OF CIVILIZATIONS	12
2. TOYNBEE'S THEORY OF CIVILIZATIONS	**13**
SOCIETAL UNITS	13
WHAT IS A CIVILIZATION?	13
GENEALOGY OF HUMAN CIVILIZATIONS	15
TOYNBEE'S THEORY OF CIVILIZATIONS	16
PRIMARY PATTERNS OF CIVILIZATION	16
LIFE CYCLE OF A CIVILIZATION	18
GROWTH OF A CIVILIZATION	20
THE PLAYERS IN THE EVOLUTION OF A CIVILIZATION	22

CREATIVE MINORITY	22
DOMINANT MINORITY	24
INTERNAL PROLETARIAT	24
EXTERNAL PROLETARIAT	24
BREAKDOWN OF GROWTH	**25**
DISINTEGRATION OF A CIVILIZATION	**28**
THE TIME OF TROUBLES	29
A UNIVERSAL STATE	29
THE TRIUMPH OF BARBARISM AND RELIGION	29
THE CIVILIZATIONS OF MAN	**31**

3. THE EMERGENCE OF CIVILIZATIONS — 33

WHY DID CIVILIZATIONS EMERGE?	**33**
FROM 150,000 BC TO 40,000 BC – STATIC SOCIAL GROUPS	34
FROM 40,000 BC TO 8,000 BC – A CREATIVE BURST	35
A GENE MUTATION IN 40,000 BC	37
DID THE CREATIVE MINORITY EMERGED GENETICALLY?	38
CLIMATIC CONDITIONS DELAYED THE EMERGENCE OF CIVILIZATIONS	39
THE NATURE OF A THEORY OF CIVILIZATIONS	**40**

4. THE GENERAL THEORY OF CIVILIZATION — 42

THE APPROACH	**42**
STATIC SOCIETIES	**46**
THE STANDARD PATTERN OF CIVILIZATIONS	**46**
A DYNAMICAL LAW OF CIVILIZATIONS	**48**
THE TOLLING BELLS OF CIVILIZATIONS	48
SOLUTIONS FOR CIVILIZATIONS	49
DETERMINATION OF PARAMETERS OF THEORY FROM HISTORY	**50**

COMPARISON OF THEORY WITH CIVILIZATIONS	59
COMMENTS ON THE SUCCESSFUL MATCH WITH HISTORY	64
THE INITIAL GROWTH SPURT OF CIVILIZATIONS – THE STARTUP PHASE	64
THE VALUE OF S	65
WHY A 267 YEAR PERIOD?	65
RELATION OF THE END OF A CIVILIZATION TO ITS BEGINNING	65
ADDITIONAL COMMENTS	66

5. ARRESTED CIVILIZATIONS 67

ARRESTED CIVILIZATIONS	67

6. SUCCESSIVE CIVILIZATIONS 70

SUCCESSIVE ISOLATED CIVILIZATIONS	70
DIRAC DELTA-FUNCTION HAMMER BLOW TO A CIVILIZATION	73
STEP FUNCTION	73
THE FORCE OF THE HYKSOS CONQUEST	73
JAPANESE CIVILIZATIONS	76

7. THE CONTINUITY OF CIVILIZATIONS 80

CONTINUITY OF CONSECUTIVE CIVILIZATIONS	80
SINIC AND FAR EASTERN (CHINA) CIVILIZATIONS	82
HELLENIC AND WESTERN CIVILIZATIONS	87
SYRAIC AND ARAB ISLAMIC CIVILIZATIONS	92
SYRAIC AND IRANIAN ISLAMIC CIVILIZATIONS	94
INDIC AND HINDU CIVILIZATIONS	100
HELLENIC AND ORTHODOX CHRISTIAN (MAIN BODY)	102
HELLENIC AND ORTHODOX CHRISTIAN (RUSSIAN)	105

GENERAL FEATURES OF THE THEORY'S PARAMETERS	107

8. GENERAL CONSIDERATIONS ON THE THEORY OF CIVILIZATIONS — 112

WHAT IS WAVING?	112
ORIGIN OF THE PERIODIC OSCILLATIONS	113
THE LENGTH OF A CYCLE	113
THE REASON FOR THE PERIODICITY	116
UNIVERSALITY OF THE PERIODIC OSCILLATIONS	118
THEORY APPLIED TO THE ROMAN CATHOLIC CHURCH	118
MULTI-GENERATION SOCIAL EFFECTS	122
A MODEL OF WORLD HISTORY	122

9. IMPLICATIONS FOR THE FUTURE OF CIVILIZATIONS — 123

THE IMMEDIATE FUTURE OF CURRENT CIVILIZATIONS	123
WESTERN TECHNOLOGICAL (TECHNIC) CIVILIZATION	125
CONTEMPORARY JAPANESE CIVILIZATION	125
CONTEMPORARY CHINESE CIVILIZATION	126
CONTEMPORARY INDIAN CIVILIZATION	126
CONTEMPORARY ARAB ISLAMIC CIVILIZATION	127
CONTEMPORARY RUSSIAN CIVILIZATION	127
THE MIX OF CONTEMPORARY CIVILIZATIONS 2002	128
THE MIX OF CONTEMPORARY CIVILIZATIONS 2050	130
THE MIX OF CONTEMPORARY CIVILIZATIONS 2100	131
WILL IT EVER END?	131

10. THE EFFECT OF SHOCKS ON CIVILIZATIONS — 132

THE EFFECT OF SHOCKS ON CIVILIZATIONS	132

MINOAN CIVILIZATION	133
THE G COUPLING CONSTANTS AND THEIR RELATION TO THE INITIAL STARTUP OF A CIVILIZATION	135

11. THE EFFECT OF TECHNOLOGY ON CIVILIZATIONS   136

TECHNICAL PROGRESS AS A DRIVING FORCE FOR CIVILIZATION	136
A CONSTANT TECHNOLOGICAL DRIVING FORCE	139
A LINEARLY INCREASING TECHNOLOGICAL DRIVING FORCE	140
A BOUNDED EXPONENTIAL TECHNOLOGICAL DRIVING FORCE	141

12. BARBARIANS AND CIVILIZATIONS   145

BARBARIANS AND CIVILIZATIONS	145
GOTHIC BARBARIANS AND HELLENIC CIVILIZATION	147

13. INTERACTIONS BETWEEN HUMAN CIVILIZATIONS   150

INTERACTING CIVILIZATIONS	150
INTERACTION BETWEEN HELLENIC AND EGYPTAIC CIVILIZATIONS	152

14. INTERACTIONS WITH POSSIBLE EXTRATERRESTRIAL CIVILIZATIONS   158

EXTRATERRESTRIAL CIVILIZATIONS	158
NEW SEARCHES FOR EXTRATERRESTRIAL LIFE	158
COMMUNICATING WITH EXTRATERRESTRIAL CIVILIZATIONS	159
FORMS OF EXTRATERRESTRIAL CIVILIZATIONS	160
SETTING THE PARAMETERS OF EXTRATERRESTRIAL CIVILIZATIONS	161
EXTRATERRESTRIAL CIVILIZATION INTERACTING WITH A HUMAN CIVILIZATION	166
THE RESULTING RAPID RISE OF HUMAN CIVILIZATIONS	172

DOMINANT TERM IN SOCIETAL LEVEL TRANSITION 173
STIMULUS VIA AN EXTRATERRESTRIAL INFORMATION BURST 173

15. UNIVERSALITY OF INTERACTIONS BETWEEN CIVILIZATIONS 175

A UNIVERSAL INTERACTION CONSTANT 175

16. HUMAN PROGRESS THROUGH THE PROGRESSION OF CIVILIZATIONS 177

THE SOCIETAL PROGRESS OF MANKIND 177
A QUANTITATIVE DEFINITION OF PROGRESS 178
THE CALCULATION OF MANKIND'S PROGRESS 179
A FORMULA FOR THE CUMULATIVE PROGRESS OF MANKIND 187
A HUMAN SUPERCIVILIZATION? 187

17. THE MUSHROOM OF CIVILIZATIONS 191

THE HUMAN MUSHROOM 191
GLOBAL CIVILIZATION: THE END OF THE MUSHROOM? 192
BEEHIVE-EARTH 193

18. THE IMPORTANCE OF BEING IN SPACE 194

ENVIRONMENTAL PROTECTION WILL NEVER COMPLETELY WORK 194
PROPOSAL FOR A TRI-PLANET HOMELAND FOR HUMANITY 195

19. THE EFFECT OF GENETIC ENGINEERING, MUTATIONS AND MEDICAL ADVANCES ON CIVILIZATIONS 197

GENETIC ENGINEERING, MUTATIONS AND MEDICINE 197

MANKIND AND CIVILIZATIONS NOW	197
IMPLICATIONS OF EXTENDING MANKIND'S LIFETIME	202
A LARGER OLDER POPULATION IS A POTENTIAL HANDICAP	202
REQUIRED: A YOUTHFUL, OLDER POPULATION	203
STRUCTURE OF A CIVILIZATION FOR A LONG LIVED MANKIND	203
FEATURES OF A CIVILIZATION WITH A LONG LIVED POPULATION	205

POSTSCRIPT – IMPLICATIONS OF A HISTORY WITH PATTERNS — 208

RELATION TO THE PHILOSOPHY OF HISTORY	208
TYPES OF PATTERNS	208
THE END OF "THE END OF HISTORY"	209
HOW WOULD A PATTERN ARISE?	210
ARE WE THE PAWNS OF MINDLESS GENETICS?	210

APPENDIX A. QUALITATIVE THEORY OF CIVILIZATIONS — 211

DOW THEORY	211
A QUALITATIVE THEORY OF CIVILIZATIONS	212

APPENDIX B. RECONSTRUCTING PREHISTORIC AND UNKNOWN CIVILIZATIONS — 226

RECONSTRUCTING FORGOTTEN CIVILIZATIONS	226
PREHISTORIC CIVILIZATIONS	228
A PREHISTORIC, UNRECOGNIZED EGYPTIAN CIVILIZATION?	231
A PREHISTORIC UNRECOGNIZED CHINESE CIVILIZATION?	233
HINTS OF AN EARLY CHINESE CIVILIZATION	233
CHINESE HISTORY FROM 3000 BC TO 2205BC	234
CHINESE HISTORY FROM 2205 BC TO 768 BC	235

A YELLOW RIVER CIVILIZATION	236
A NEW VIEW OF CHINESE AND EGYPTIAN CIVILIZATIONS?	239
THE EFFECT ON THE CUMULATIVE PROGRESS	239

APPENDIX C. RECONSTRUCTING MAYAN CIVILIZATION — 241

THEORY COMPARED TO MAYAN HISTORY	241
MAYAN CIVILIZATION WORLD WAR	243

APPENDIX D. COMPARISON TO TOYNBEE — 245

CONCEPTS DEVELOPED BY TOYNBEE AND OTHERS	245
NEW CONCEPTS DEVELOPED IN THE QUANTITATIVE THEORY OF CIVILIZATIONS	246

REFERENCES — 248

INDEX — 249

LIST OF FIGURES

Figure 1. Toynbee's family tree of human civilizations. A view of the family tree of human civilizations showing his three generations of civilizations (not drawn on a time scale), and the higher religions generated through their interactions and evolution. 15

Figure 2. Arnold Toynbee's general view of the life cycle of a civilization. The timing of events for a specific civilization is variable. So the above diagram is not meant to describe each civilization's evolution in precise detail. It describes the observed general pattern of civilizations. 19

Figure 3. A diagram illustrating the growth pattern of a civilization. The societal level of a civilization is the combination of social institutions and arrangements that "make the society work." This combination includes political mechanisms, technology, and cultural/ethical features—all the parts of the civilization that are vital for its growth and success as a society. This concept is implicit in the work of Toynbee. 21

Figure 4. The transition from a creative minority to a dominant minority. During a civilization's period of growth a creative minority plays a leadership role making successful responses to challenges with the assent of the internal proletariat. After the breakdown, the former creative minority becomes the dominant minority and rules through coercion and force. 27

Figure 5. The evolution of a civilization's players as time progresses. Initially the creative minority and internal proletariat have a unity of ideas and goals. After a period of time the creative minority becomes static and unable to develop successful solutions to challenges. It then becomes a dominant minority that rules by coercion and force. In parallel with these developments an external proletariat ("the barbarians") from beyond the frontiers of the civilization penetrates the civilization peacefully at first as workers, soldiers or visitors. The external proletariat develops a familiarity with the civilization and progresses from awe to perhaps mild contempt. Eventually the external proletariat attacks to acquire the riches of the civilization, and the internal proletariat, recognizing their superior "barbarian drive", adopts aspects of their ideas and customs even to the extent of emulating them. 30

Figure 6. The locations of the six first generation civilizations. The relative closeness of the Sumeric, Minoan and Egyptaic civilizations and the civilizations they parented may have led to the origin of most of the world's higher religions: Christianity, Judaism, Islam, Hinduism, Buddhism and Zoroastrianism through cultural cross-fertilization. 32

Figure 7. Some major events in the last 100,000 years. 34

Figure 8. Rough diagram of the last 100,000 years of temperature (Greenland). The relative change in temperature in degrees Centigrade is depicted along the right side of the graph. The zero point line is at the average temperature in the past 10,000 years. As shown, Ice Age temperatures dipped as much as 20° C below this average temperature. Note also the relative lack of major temperature fluctuations in the last 10,000 years. Recent civilizations have enjoyed a warmer, more stable climate. 40

Figure 9. The typical pattern of the routs and rallies of a civilization. 51

Figure 10. Values of d, a and the ratio of successive peaks. 52

Figure 11. The S societal level curve for various values of d. 56

Figure 12. The standard societal level S curve for a civilization. 58

Figure 13. A four and a half beat pattern for a civilization. 59

Figure 14. Comparison of Hellenic civilization with the general theory of civilization. The plotted societal level is $S_{Hellenic}(t)$. 61
Figure 15. Comparison of Egyptaic civilization (2555 BC to 1660 BC) with general theory of civilization. The plotted societal level is $S_{Egyptaic}(t)$. 62
Figure 16. Comparison of Sinic civilization with general theory of civilization. The plotted societal level is $S_{Sinic}(t)$. 63
Figure 17. Graph of societal level for an arrested civilization with d = 5. 68
Figure 18. The societal level S and the historical events of the successive Egyptaic civilization. 75
Figure 19. Early Japanese civilization and Far Eastern (Japan) civilization. 79
Figure 20. The regions of successive civilizations considered. 82
Figure 21. The pattern of Sinic, New Sinic, and Far Eastern civilizations. 86
Figure 22. The pattern of Hellenic, Western and Technic civilizations. 91
Figure 23. The pattern of Syraic, JudaeoPalestinic, and Arab Islamic civilizations. 93
Figure 24. The pattern of Syraic, Iranic, and Iranian Islamic civilizations. 98
Figure 25. The pattern of Indic, Early Hindic, and Hindu civilizations. 101
Figure 26. Hellenic, Byzantine, and Orthodox Christian (main body) civilizations. 104
Figure 27. Pattern of Hellenic, Byzantine, and Orthodox Christian (Russian) civilization. 106
Figure 28. A New Family Tree of Human civilizations based on the theory. 110
Figure 29. General pattern of a civilization's routs and rallies a la Toynbee. 115
Figure 30. The theory applied to the Roman Catholic Church showing the theory is based on the long-term social nature of mankind. 121
Figure 31. A comparison of the phases of contemporary civilizations. 124
Figure 32. The effect of the Theran volcanic eruption on Minoan civilization. The dates are based on a widely accepted date of 1645 BC for the eruption. 134
Figure 33. Effect of technology on western civilizations: 565 BC to 2439 AD. 142
Figure 34. Expanded view of the recent impact of technology on the West. 143
Figure 35. Gothic barbarian culture and Hellenic civilization. 148
Figure 36. Interacting Hellenic and Egyptaic civilizations with g = 0. 154
Figure 37. Close-up of interacting Hellenic & Egyptaic civilizations with g = 0. 155
Figure 38. Interacting Hellenic & Egyptaic civilizations with g = 0.2. The interacting Hellenic and Egyptaic civilizations have the same S level after 246 AD. 156
Figure 39. Close up of Hellenic - Egyptaic interaction with g=0.2. Egyptaic civilization had a flat petrified S curve. It begins "oscillating" due to the interaction with Hellenic civilization. 157
Figure 40. Possible time periods of extraterrestrial civilizations. 161
Figure 41. Possible values of a for extraterrestrial civilizations. 162
Figure 42. S for extraterrestrial civilizations with an 800 year period. 163
Figure 43. S for extraterrestrial civilizations with an 8,000 year period. 164
Figure 44. S for extraterrestrial civilizations with a 20,000 year period. 165
Figure 45. Effect of an extraterrestrial civilization with an 800 year period on Western Technic civilization. 169
Figure 46. Close view of the effect of an extraterrestrial civilization with an 800 year period on Western Technic civilization. 170
Figure 47. The effect of an extraterrestrial civilization with an 8,000 year period on Western Technic civilization. 171

Figure 48. A close view of the effect of an extraterrestrial civilization with an 8,000 year period on Western Technic civilization. 172

Figure 49. The time required by earth civilization to reach the level of various extraterrestrial civilizations in our theory. 173

Figure 50. Man progresses through a series of civilizations that are born and die. 178

Figure 51. The progress of civilizations showing the progress of mankind without American civilizations or technical contributions. 181

Figure 52. The progress of civilizations including American civilizations but without taking account of the effects of modern technology. 183

Figure 53. The progress of all known, non-abortive civilizations including the effects of technology. ... 186

Figure 54. T = 9500 supercivilization compared to actual progress. 189

Figure 55. Close-up comparison of Progress and supercivilization curve. 190

Figure 56. The spreading mushroom ring of civilizations. The expansion of the Western and Far Eastern civilizations is shown to illustrate the mushroom effect. 192

Figure 57. A table showing how the life expectancy of the populations of the less developed and more developed countries has changed over the past two hundred years. 198

Figure 58. The trend of life expectancy over the past two hundred years. 199

Figure 59. The measured average maximum age of the population in Sweden over a 130 year period. .. 200

Figure 60. Projections of the average maximum age of people in advanced countries. 201

Figure 61. A comparison of societal levels of a civilization with a long-lived population with the standard civilization of three and a half beats. 204

Figure 62. A fifty year picture of the Dow Jones Industrial Average. 212

Figure 63. The typical pattern of evolution of a civilization. 220

Figure 64. Societal Level curve of Nile River civilization. 231

Figure 65. The Nile River and Egyptaic civilizations 3691 BC – 1000 BC. 232

Figure 66. Societal Level curve of Yellow River civilization. 237

Figure 67. The civilizations of China including a prehistoric civilization and recent technological effects. 238

Figure 68. The cumulative progress of civilizations modified to include the Nile River and Yellow River civilizations (together with recent technological effects.) 240

EXHIBITS

Exhibit 1. The White House, Washington DC in more placid times circa 1900. 3
Exhibit 2. Ceiling of the famed Alabaster Mosque of Mohammed Ali in Cairo, Egypt. 5
Exhibit 3. Courtyard of the Alabaster Mosque of Mohammed Ali in Cairo, Egypt. 6
Exhibit 4. A Muslim guide in an Upper Egypt temple. 7
Exhibit 5. Mohammed Ali, an Albanian Muslim who became the ruler of Egypt (1805-48). He attempted to introduce Western armament and military discipline in the Egyptian army. He was also active in promoting education and cultural development. 10
Exhibit 6. Western Civilization Percentage of World Population. 11
Exhibit 7. Seventh Century BC scene in Ashurbanipal's palace showing him slaying a lion. 17
Exhibit 8. The Tower of London where members of the creative minority occasionally met their doom. 23
Exhibit 9. Scene from the Odyssey in a First Century AD Roman house. 26
Exhibit 10. Paleolithic cave drawing of bison from 10,000 to 15,000 ago. 35
Exhibit 11. Paleolithic cave drawing of herd of bison from 10,000 to 15,000 ago. 36
Exhibit 12. The tolling bells of civilization. 49
Exhibit 13. Eskimos enjoying the summer in Greenland. Their summer tent is called a toupik. 69
Exhibit 14. Passageway to the burial chamber of a New Kingdom Pharaoh in the Valley of the Kings in Egypt. 71
Exhibit 15. Burial chamber of a New Kingdom Pharaoh in the Valley of the Kings in Egypt. A question that has apparently not been addressed: How did the workers who created the magnificent wall paintings in tombs and pyramids obtain light with which to see? Torches would have left smudges on the walls and ceilings – not to mention the effect of fumes in these poorly ventilated chambers. One possible answer is a series of mirrors that reflected light down into the chambers and thence onto the wall or ceiling being painted. 72
Exhibit 16. Osaka, Japan street scene in 1890. 77
Exhibit 17. A footbridge in the Empress' Palace (nineteenth century) Beijing, China. 83
Exhibit 18. The Imperial Ancestral Temple – 19th Century Beijing, China. 84
Exhibit 19. Cologne Cathedral. Perhaps the finest example of Gothic architecture. 87
Exhibit 20. Bed chamber of Catherine de Medicis at the palace of Fontainebleau, France. 89
Exhibit 21. Fourth Century AD Sasanian drinking bowl showing a king hunting stags. 96
Exhibit 22. View of the Taj Mahal, India. 99
Exhibit 23. View of the Vatican and St. Peter's Cathedral in 1900. 119
Exhibit 24. Nineteenth Century sailing-steamer ship. 137
Exhibit 25. Nineteenth century railroad train. 138
Exhibit 26. Three planets home for humanity. 196
Exhibit 27. The Narmer Palette. J.E. Quibell discovered the Palette while excavating royal residences of early Egyptian kings at Hierakonpolis in Upper Egypt in 1898. Narmer's name appears in the serekh sign at the top. 229
Exhibit 28. The pattern of Mayan civilization. 242

PREFACE

*If you can look into the seeds of time, and say which grains will grow,
and which will not, speak then to me*
Banquo
Macbeth - Shakespeare

Some years ago Isaac Asimov wrote a series of Science Fiction books called the Foundation Series. In those books a mathematician Hari Selden developed a theory of history and formed a group of individuals called the Second Foundation who applied Selden's theory to manipulate the Galactic Empire and the following interregnum.

This book presents a realistic mathematical theory of history that we call the Theory of Civilization. The Theory of Civilization explains the rhythms of history seen in earthly civilizations over the past six thousand years. It also makes predictions about the future.

It has very different conclusions when compared to the outline of the Selden theory in Asimov's books. In fact the Galactic Empire setting for the Foundation books is not possible from the viewpoint of this theory because it is inconsistent with the long term social nature of mankind.

Returning to today's realities, we see a world that is facing several continuing crises involving civilizations: an ongoing conflict between Western civilization and certain parts of Islamic civilization; and a probable approaching crisis point in Japanese civilization in roughly 2002. The Theory of Civilization provides an understanding of these events. It may even provide some long-term guidance as to how to proceed into the future, and on the future prospects of contemporary civilizations.

Mankind has survived through twenty-six plus civilizations since emerging from prehistoric times according to Arnold Toynbee. (We suggest the existence of fifteen additional civilizations based on the analysis of the Theory of Civilization developed later in this book giving a total of at least forty-one civilizations.) Today Mankind appears to be in the process of developing a world civilization based on Western technology. Standing in the way are national self-interest; continuing conflicts between parts of Islamic civilization and Western civilization; and socio-economic conflicts between poor Third World countries and affluent Western and Far Eastern countries.

The purpose of this book is to present a *quantitative* theory of human civilizations that is based on intrinsic social features of humanity rather than on the seemingly random events of history such as barbarian invasions, natural catastrophes, or the appearance and actions of great men. Although these factors certainly influenced the evolution of individual civilizations, we will see that the overall evolution of each civilization is more dependent on the intrinsic social properties of its population. A growing, healthy civilization can overcome challenges. A disintegrating civilization is easily overwhelmed.

We will see that each civilization goes through a growth phase followed by a disintegration phase. The cycles of events, and the time frames of its phases, are governed by the long-term social behavior of humanity. Our Theory of Civilization describes the time evolution of civilizations in some detail and can predict aspects of the future of civilizations.

We begin by suggesting that human civilizations arose due to the combination of 1) a human mutation 40,000 years ago that created risk-taking, creative individuals; and 2) a favorable change of climate 10,000 years ago that provided the stable (and warm) climactic conditions needed for the development of long-term human societies and cities. It is possible that the leadership group of a civilization which Toynbee calls the "creative minority" may consist, to some degree, of individuals carrying this genetic mutation. Toynbee did not suggest an origin, or a distinguishing feature, of the creative minority.

When we apply our theory it suggests that Western civilization is in a process of decline that began in 1914 (when the West effectively ruled the world) and will last until roughly 2048 when an upswing is projected. Continuing major technologic progress seems to have greatly softened the decline that Western civilization has been experiencing since 1914.

The Theory of Civilization also suggests that Japanese Far Eastern civilization (which had been growing for roughly the last one hundred and thirty four years) is about to enter a state of decline in approximately 2002. Japanese economic problems and emerging social problems such as a rapidly aging population seem to support this prediction.

Other contemporary civilizations are apparently in a growth phase. This includes the Chinese, Indian and Islamic civilizations, which are projected to continue growing until roughly 2084.

We have tried to look at the seeds of time and see which will grow. Needless to say the prediction of human events is a risky proposition so this author (and hopefully the reader) realizes that "the future is subject to change without notice." *All predictions made in this theory can only be interpreted as plus or minus a generation (thirty-four years) or so, and are subject to changes induced by major events (environmental, invasions, and so on) originating from outside the civilization in question.*

The observations, upon which this *quantitative* Theory of Civilization is based, are due in large part to the pioneering work of Arnold Toynbee to which the reader is strongly recommended. Toynbee developed an organized view of historical events based on the concept of civilizations.

Appendix A contains a *qualitative* "Dow Theory of Civilizations" based on the observations and conclusions of generations of historians. Just as the original Dow Theory provides a qualitative understanding of general aspects of the New York Stock Market, the observations (theorems) in Appendix A provide a qualitative understanding of general aspects of the growth and evolution of civilizations.

From this qualitative base we developed a *mathematical* theory of the evolution of civilizations. We then made a detailed comparison of this theory with all reasonably documented civilizations. There appears to be good agreement between the predictions of the theory and actual historical events in all cases. We have gone to great lengths to show the close correspondence between theoretical predictions and actual historical events with numerous detailed figures.

After developing a successful Theory of Civilization we consider the interaction of two civilizations, the effect of major natural events on a civilization (such as the Theran volcano that effectively ended Minoan civilization), the interaction of civilizations and barbarians, the effect of technology on civilization, and the effect of a vastly increased human life span on a civilization. All these studies are mathematically based and not just qualitative observations.

Along the way we found that the shape of historical events, when viewed from the perspective of the Theory of Civilization, enabled us to identify thirteen new civilizations in historic times and two new prehistoric civilizations in China and Egypt.

In order to show that our Theory of Civilization derives from the social nature of mankind we apply the theory to the only large, long-lived human organization that is not a civilization: the Roman Catholic Church. Events in Church history closely match theoretical predictions over the past 1500 years. The "ups and downs" of Church history seem to be based on the long-term social nature of the men and women that comprise it.

The Roman Catholic Church is projected to have a breakdown in approximately 2004. (A breakdown is usually a major event that causes a civilization or organization to enter a significant period of decline which Toynbee calls a rout.) Recent events suggest the Church is entering a crisis stage that might constitute a breakdown.

In the opinion of this author extraterrestrial civilizations will eventually be found. Therefore we extend our theory to describe extraterrestrial civilizations, and then study the impact of advanced, and very advanced, extraterrestrial civilizations on earthly civilizations. It appears that it would take three hundred to five hundred years for mankind to reach the social level of an extraterrestrial civilization. Technical and scientific advances to the level of the extraterrestrial civilization will, of course, be faster. Savages can quickly learn to drive cars.

We point out that the cutting edge of civilizations is always at the periphery (frontier) on "new land." Witness the Americas. Civilization is like an expanding mushroom ring. Now, when the earth is close to being fully exploited, mankind has no choice but to expand into space or face ultimate decline and disintegration. This argument is the primary reason for going into space. Expand or decline.

Medical advances and genetic engineering also constitute a new frontier. They offer the prospect of a vastly increased human lifetime. A major change in life span could have a profound effect on human civilizations. We show that a significantly increased life span, *and work life*, would enable mankind to reach a much higher level of civilization while also increasing the danger that these civilizations could become static (arrested) if the older elements in the population retard creativity or sap the resources of the civilization for growth.

Using our mathematical theory of past and contemporary civilizations we develop a mathematical definition of Progress as the sum of the societal levels of the earth's civilizations at each point in time. Surprisingly we find that Progress has been advancing at approximately a linear growth rate for the past five thousand years.

This book contains mathematical equations that define a theory of civilizations. The equations, and the discussions associated with them, have been purposefully kept at a level understandable by a second year (American) collegiate physics, chemistry or mathematics major in the hope that it would thus be understandable to a wider audience.

The sixty-eight provocative figures are for the rest of us. They illustrate the theory in a qualitative manner and show the match of the theory with history is surprising detailed.

ACKNOWLEDGMENT

I am grateful to my wife Margaret for reading the manuscript and providing great support and encouragement for this effort. My thanks to Mr. John Glasscock for technical assistance in bringing this book to press.

1. The Importance of Understanding Civilizations

Westernization gained the upper hand before any Islamic universal state was in sight, and its various member states—Persia, Iraq, Saudi Arabia, Egypt, Syria, Lebanon, and the rest—are making the best of a rather bad job as 'poor relations' in the Western comity of nations.
A. Toynbee

This is a momentous occasion in world history. For the first time, all anti-Islamic forces are united against Islam.
Sufi Mohammad, October, 2002
Moslem Cleric, Pakistan

Western Civilization vs. Islamic Civilization

With the demise of the Communist World in the early 1990's Western civilization led by the United States has achieved practical dominance on Earth. All countries have committed to a goal of a Western standard of living and have accepted Western technology. The ideas and life styles of the West have been spread around the world through television, the Internet and other forms of communications and travel.

A graphic instance of the spread of Western culture occurred during a telephone call to a friend in Accra, Ghana. After a bit of conversation he said, "I will have to end the call now. Oprah is about to start on the telly. You're familiar with the Oprah show aren't you?"

The people of other contemporary cultures and civilizations have accepted bits and pieces of the trappings of Western civilization little realizing that the trappings are a trap. A slow process of Westernization is taking place that eventually will eventually lead to a worldwide civilization in perhaps four hundred to eight hundred years.

In the mean time we have a motley array of cultures that are partly westernized in externals and that are desirous of sharing in the good life of western societies. The main points of difference are in religious, and cultural, values and mores.

Western civilization today is materialistic—focused on personal happiness and well being. While religion is an important part of Western civilization it does not have a central role in the life of the society compared to its role at an earlier stage of Western civilization, or compared to religion's role in other civilizations such as Islamic civilization. (See Sorokin's book for more details on the types and phases of societies. It is listed in the References section.)

Islamic civilization places faith and religious values above materialistic pursuits. Islam provides a total solution to the organization of society with a code of civil and criminal law, Sharia, and a standard of conduct that governs all parts of a Muslim's life. Islamic civilization today has the religious mindset of Europe during the Middle Ages.

Growth of Islam

Islamic civilization enjoyed a rapid period of expansion from its beginning in the seventh century until about the fifteenth century when European countries started to reverse the tide of Muslim expansion through superior military and marine technology. Since then, Western civilization has taken a leadership position in world politics and in technical progress. So much so, that a large part of Muslim society is hundreds of years "behind" in modern technology and the societal adaptations that modern technology has necessitated.

The Current Situation

The frustration of the modern-medieval Muslim majority with their backwardness, poverty and social ills—accentuated by seeing the high standard of living in Western civilization on television and in newspapers—has created resentment and hatred. This hatred is enhanced by the presence of Israel on land that most Muslims view as the sacred heartland of Islamic civilization. Israel's military dominance further increases the sense of frustration and impotence.

Muslim governments cannot win a conventional war with Israel and Muslim governments are unable to successfully confront an overwhelmingly strong United States. Therefore, Islamic civilization has responded with the only viable military approach at its disposal—a form of guerrilla warfare that is called terrorism mostly because it tends to attack civilians and also because it takes place on an international stage.

Terrorism is an admission of failure and weakness in the face of a powerful adversary. The *techniques* of terrorism (bombs, suicide attacks and so on) were used against the Nazi's in World War II, against the Japanese by the Chinese and Filipinos in World War II, and in countless guerrilla wars in Asia, Africa, South America and Europe since then. The new dimension of terrorism is its use – not against dictatorships – but against peaceful non-combatants in free, open democratic countries. The net result of this new form of terrorism will be to harden the surviving victims and lead their governments to strike back at the heartland of the terrorists as the United States has done in Afghanistan.

The United States and Western civilization is now engaged in a small Vietnam-style war on a global scale at the time of this writing (Spring, 2002). This war is still in the early stages of development. Its beginnings can be seen in the Iraqi Gulf War, the bombings in the years since, the Somali and Yemeni incidents, and the attack on American cities on September 11, 2001—a day that will live in history as the beginning of a global war between parts of Western civilization and parts of Islamic civilization.

Exhibit 1. The White House, Washington DC in more placid times circa 1900.

The Life Cycle of Civilizations

Western political leaders have gone to great lengths to describe the reaction to the World Trade Center (New York) tragedy as specifically against the terrorist perpetrators and not against the Islamic people in general. Elements in the Islamic masses, on the other hand, have given worldwide applause and approval to the attack on the World Trade Center. Most Islamic religious leaders have either kept a discreet silence or praised the war against the infidels. Conservative Muslim governments have condemned terrorism but most of them are unable or unwilling to take concrete action against terrorists.

A particularly interesting aspect of the terrorist organization al Qaeda is its leadership They come predominantly from the affluent Saudi Arabian community.

While many Muslims do not want a war or confrontation with the United States, or the West in general, the predominant belief of the vast majority of Muslims is that a conflict with the West exists. Most Muslims do not believe the denials of Western leaders.

The attack on the World Trade Center by Muslim terrorists may have the same significance for Western civilization that the Gothic invasion of Rome itself in the prime of the Empire (the First Century AD) had for the future of Rome. They may be a premonition of things to come – not necessarily soon but perhaps in a few centuries. The Goths returned three centuries later and remained as permanent conquerors.

Important Current Factors

There are several factors that will play a role in the near term evolution of the conflict between Islam and the West. These include the use of the oil weapon, the large immigration of Muslims to Western countries, and the developments in the Israeli-Palestinian conflict.

The Oil Weapon

Perhaps the most important card Islamic civilization has is the massive dependence of the West (and Far East) on oil from Islamic countries.

As this book is being completed (Spring, 2002) Iraq has declared an oil embargo to punish the western supporters of Israel. In addition Iran has announced its willingness to join in a general oil embargo.

The al Qaeda leader, Osama bin Laden, viewed the attack of his organization on the World Trade Center as an attack on the *economy* of the West and particularly, the greatest economic center of the West, Wall Street. His stated goal in broadcast interviews was to create economic problems in the West. To some extent he succeeded since the attack has had a demonstrable effect on the weakened American economy.

Exhibit 2. Ceiling of the famed Alabaster Mosque of Mohammed Ali in Cairo, Egypt.

The Life Cycle of Civilizations

Exhibit 3. Courtyard of the Alabaster Mosque of Mohammed Ali in Cairo, Egypt.

The oil embargo of Iraq, and possibly others, is another attempt to attack the Western economies. A sharp increase in the price of oil, or even the anticipation of a possible increase, can significantly dampen the recovery of the Western and Far Eastern economies currently in progress.

Over the long term the West must free itself from a dependence on Muslim oil. Muslim oil revenues are the fuel for the development of weapons of mass destruction by Iran and Iraq. In the future they will supply the revenues of an expansionist Islam.

The best hope of the West is to find an alternative energy source that would substantially eliminate the need for oil. As the silk trade looted the Roman Empire of its gold and reduced its economy, the trade in oil is looting the West of its prosperity and freedom of action. The rise and fall of oil prices has a significantly greater effect on the American and world economy than the raising and lowering of interest rates by central banks.

The Life Cycle of Civilizations

Muslim Immigration to the West

In the heyday of the Roman Empire barbarians migrated into the territory of the Empire in search of a better life. They took jobs as workmen, tradesmen and soldiers. They sometimes returned to their tribes for visits or to again take up life beyond the Empire's frontier.

This passage of barbarians back and forth across the frontiers, together with border contact and warfare, enabled the barbarians to learn Roman technology and methods of warfare. The barbarians also changed their view of the Romans from one of awe to one of familiarity and, eventually, of contempt. They saw the riches of the Empire and the Empire's growing weakness. The combination was an invitation to invasion and conquest for booty and land. After a few hundred years the barbarians conquered the Western Roman Empire and nearly conquered the Eastern Roman Empire.

Exhibit 4. A Muslim guide in an Upper Egypt temple.

The Life Cycle of Civilizations

Today there is an ongoing wave of immigration to the United States and Europe from Muslim countries. Large-scale immigration has been taking place for ten to fifteen years. Aspects of this immigration are encouraged and financed by Muslim countries. Saudi Arabia, for instance, provides Muslim community centers and mosques in the United States. It appears that the events are following a similar course to that of the barbarians and the Romans. The United States was an unthinkably remote place for most Muslims twenty years ago. Today everybody has a friend or relative amongst the seven million Muslims in the United States.

Twenty years ago Muslim terrorism in the United States was unthinkable – not only for Americans but also for Muslims. Today, many Muslim youths dream of going to America. They dream of becoming "holy martyrs" like the World Trade Center terrorists. America has become familiar to the Muslim masses through the immigration gateway. Similar considerations apply to Europe, which has also experienced a vast Muslim immigration. The wave of terrorist attacks in France may be a hint of the future.

In fairness it should be said that most Muslim immigrants are good people in search of a better life. Many are highly educated professionals (among whom I count my late Ph.D. advisor Mirza Abdul Baqi Beg). However it is important to understand the overall effect of the mass migration of Muslims to Western countries from the viewpoint of interacting civilizations.

The open question is not whether Islam will make inroads into the West today but whether it will enter as a conqueror a few hundred years from now.

The Israeli-Palestinian Conflict

The West is committed to the existence of Israel. The Israelis will not abandon their country under any circumstances. Leaders of a number of Muslim countries have recently embraced a Saudi Arabian peace plan based on the recognition of Israel's right to exist in exchange for a return to the pre-1967 borders. Presumably a Palestinian state would then rise on the West Bank and in the Gaza Strip.

The main issue that started the recent round of warfare was the Palestinian and Arab fear that Israeli religious groups will attempt to rebuild the Temple of Solomon on the Temple Mount in Jerusalem. Mohammed is believed to have ascended into Heaven from the Temple Mount. Thus the site is one of the three holiest places in Islam. The Temple Mount is also the site of one of Islam's greatest mosques. Muslims are worried that the mosque might be affected (violated?) by the building of a new Jewish Temple.

The net result of the warfare resulting from this confrontation has been the dismantling of the Palestinian State and the destruction of Palestinian authority on the West Bank and the Gaza Strip. Ironically, the new situation of the Palestinians will make it easier for Israel to begin building the Temple. Mr. Arafat and the Palestinian State might have been able to develop a negotiating position that might have protected the Dome of the Rock mosque. Now the only party that potentially stands in the way of the rebuilding of the Temple is the people of the other Islamic nations: primarily Saudi Arabia, Egypt, Syria, Iraq, Libya and Iran. Their only viable threat is a major war with Israel, which none of them appear anxious to enter. Consequently, a careful Israeli construction effort that is sensitive to Muslim sensibilities will probably succeed without a war.

In the longer term the construction of a new Jewish Temple will become a major rallying point for Muslim hatred.

Possible Futures for Islam and the West

Most Islamic religious leaders see a conflict between the West and Islam. They regard it as a war between civilizations. They remember the dominance of the Muslim world over the West before 1500 when the Mediterranean was a Muslim lake. They remember the rise of the West to world dominance in the following centuries up to the present.

They seek the resurgence of Islam and the religious conquest of all non-Muslims.

What does the future hold for the relations of Islamic civilization and Western civilization? As we shall see in later chapters it appears that Islamic civilization had a new startup after World War II due to the withdrawal of the colonial powers combined with a massive growth in oil revenues. The freed Middle Eastern Islamic nations have been able to develop Western-style technological capabilities. Recently they have been able to advance in weapons of mass destruction (nuclear proliferation and biological weapons) and missile delivery systems.

The peoples of these nations have come to life again through mass communications (TV and the Internet) and trade and travel. According to the theory of civilizations that will be developed in the following chapters we expect the upsurge in Islamic civilization to continue to 2084 when it reaches a turning point, a breakdown of growth, and enters a time of troubles and decline.

While our theory cannot predict the precise events that will cause this turnaround, the theory does suggest it will be due to internal social reasons within the populace of Islamic civilization. The most likely cause is an international conflict within the nations of Islam – possibly over religious issues or perhaps because a nation such as Iran assumes such a dominant position that other Islamic nations will feel compelled to unite against it in an all-Islamic war.

Exhibit 5. Mohammed Ali, an Albanian Muslim who became the ruler of Egypt (1805-48). He attempted to introduce Western armament and military discipline in the Egyptian army. He was also active in promoting education and cultural development.

Western civilization, on the other hand, has been in a state of societal decline, perhaps masked by technological advances, since the outbreak of World

The Life Cycle of Civilizations

War I in 1914. This decline has been marked by worldwide conflicts, the loss of control over much of the earth (by the ending of colonial empires), and internal social changes that have weakened the social fabric of many Western nations. The population of the West which was around *one-third* of mankind in 1900 has declined to roughly 17% of mankind in 2000 (according to United Nations statistics).

The percentage is expected to decline to about 13% (roughly *one-tenth* of mankind) of world population by 2030. This decline, which is reflected in our theory of Western civilization presented later, has been largely masked by the technological boom that has enabled the West to maintain overall military and economic superiority. Western superiority is primarily based on technological innovations. Their importance for the West will increase as the population of the West becomes an increasingly smaller part of world population.

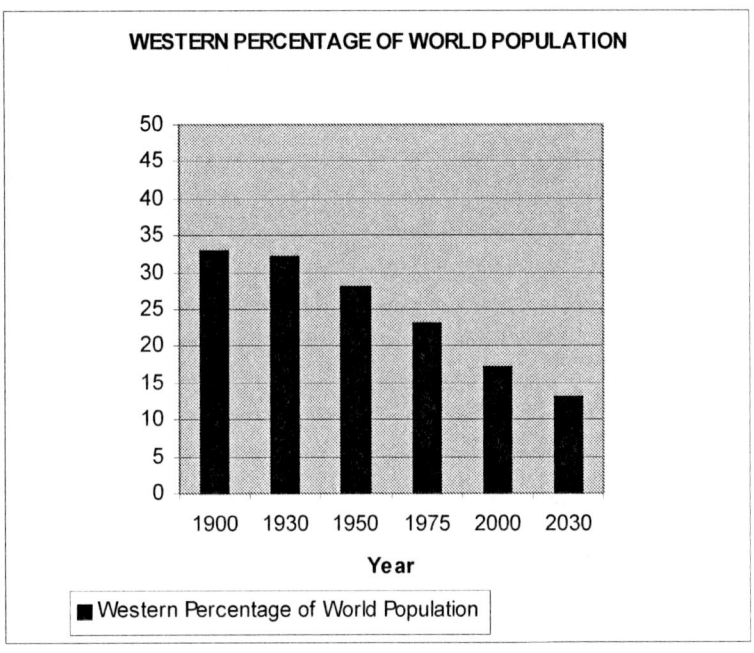

Exhibit 6. Western Civilization Percentage of World Population.

The decline of Western civilization is projected to end around 2048 when a period of societal growth is predicted. Based on the projected beginning of growth of Western civilization later in this century combined with a projected decline in Islamic civilization and Far Eastern Chinese civilization it appears that Western civilization will continue to prosper well into the twenty-second century.

The Life Cycle of Civilizations

China Resurgent

China (Far Eastern civilization) appears to have entered into a new phase around 1900. Symptoms of this renewal are the Boxer Rebellion against foreign domination, the development of a Western-style democratic government (of President Sun Yat Sen), and large scale industrialization and technological development since 1950 in particular.

Today China has a massive economy, booming exports, a growing entrepreneurial sector, and an impressive research and development sector. China stands on the threshold of space with plans for manned space flights and a Chinese space station in the near future. According to the theory, to be presented later, China should be in a phase of maximal growth. This prediction appears to be confirmed by an economic growth rate in excess of 9% in the 1990's.

The Chinese people are being encouraged in schools and the media to be brave and courageous. The Chinese people are united in their pursuit of a great and prosperous China.

The application of our theory of civilization to Chinese Far Eastern civilization suggests the tremendous growth that has occurred since 1950 will end roughly around 2084. After 2084 Far Eastern civilization (like Islamic civilization) will experience a decline. Again the reasons will be social in nature and based on the internal dynamics of Chinese society. The most probable cause will be a breakup of the unity of the Chinese people. When China has reached a high standard of living, and large numbers of the population are college educated, there is a strong likelihood that a widespread desire for a political change to a Western-style democracy will lead to internal civil strife. The stirrings of this desire for democracy can be seen in the Tien An Men Square uprising in Beijing. China will then enter a time of troubles that will last for four centuries.

The Need for a Deeper Understanding of Civilizations

The nature of, and the relations between, civilizations is obviously of great importance in understanding current world conflicts and projecting the future of mankind. The following chapters describe a view of human civilizations that is more or less based on the ideas of Arnold Toynbee. (References to other important work by Sorokin, Coulborn, Kroeber and others can be found in *The Boundaries of Civilizations in Space and Time* listed in our References section.)

This book develops a *quantitative* theory of civilizations that can help us understand how we reached the point in history at which we now find ourselves. With it we can perhaps see a bit into the future realizing that "We know what we are but know not what we may be."

2. Toynbee's Theory of Civilizations

The fundamental similarity in the purposes of all civilizations is not to be forgotten.
A. Toynbee

Societal Units

Mankind is organized into social groups. No one will dispute the role of the family as a primary social group. Humanity also is organized into larger social groups: clans, tribes, and nations. There are also religious groupings to which large parts of mankind belong: Buddhism, Christianity, Hinduism and Islam.

Arnold Toynbee developed the history of larger groupings of mankind that he called *civilizations* in a massive twelve-volume work entitled *A Study of History*. The concept of a civilization is somewhat vague and subject to dispute. If we can group branches of humanity into civilizations it must mean, at the very least, that these units have many more social interconnections within themselves compared to their connections to exterior groups.

The premier example of a civilization from this point of view is Egyptaic civilization, which was concentrated along the Nile with minimal connections, relatively speaking, with other societies due to the deserts and mountains on either side of the Nile valley.

Some historians would deny the existence of civilizations; other historians have different views on what constitutes a civilization. Toynbee's theory of civilizations has a large measure of acceptance and a substantial amount of scholarship behind it. It also provides the empirical data upon which our quantitative theory of civilizations is based. Thus we will start with a careful look at Toynbee's theory of civilizations in this chapter.

What is a Civilization?

Man has had many societies but only a few civilizations. Arnold Toynbee identifies twenty-six civilizations. Other scholars identify more or less a similar number of civilizations. (We suggest the existence of up to fifteen additional civilizations based on the theory developed later in this book giving a possible total of forty-one civilizations.) In comparison there are many thousands of human societies.

What is a civilization? For that matter what is a society? The definitions of a society and a civilization are a bit fuzzy and subject to dispute. Practically speaking, a society is a large group of individuals who have a set of shared beliefs or culture and who participate in a social organization with mores, and standards of conduct and social intercourse. Although we could quibble over refinements of this definition, and suggest additional details that might be added to the definition, it is clear that we can recognize societies when we encounter them. And that will suffice for our purposes.

The definition of a civilization is a somewhat more difficult matter. There are significant disagreements over the definition of a civilization. It seems the most accurate characterization of a civilization is a large society (in population and/or geographical extent) that has an enveloping culture that is extensive and growing (or was growing in the past) in significant ways. The hallmark of civilizations appears to be the potential for growth. Societies, on the other hand, may be growing or static. Societies tend to be smaller in scope geographically and in population.

The growth of a civilization to which we refer is not geographical growth or population growth. It is the growth in the spirit, ideas, mechanisms, or social institutions of a civilization. This type of growth is hard to characterize and hard to measure.

Often growth is a response to a challenge to the culture. For example, Hellenic civilization faced a challenge when the population of Greece outstripped the ability of the land to adequately feed it. It responded by developing its maritime capability so that it could use trade to support food purchases from nearby countries. In addition it sent settlers to colonies created in other parts of the Mediterranean.

The development of maritime trade and a group of colonies constituted a successful response to the challenge of overpopulation. It added a new dimension to Hellenic civilization leading to significant growth. The new window of the Hellenes on the world enabled them to develop a wider world-view. The many cultures that they encountered in countries such as Egypt enriched Hellenic civilization enormously.

The concept of the growth of a civilization, and related concepts, provided a basis for our theory of civilizations. Although Toynbee recognized only twenty-six civilizations, he, and a number of other historians and sociologists, have been able to show the existence of significant patterns and regularities in the nature and in the development of civilizations.

The Life Cycle of Civilizations

Genealogy of Human Civilizations

In his treatise Toynbee described the interrelationships of civilizations—their parentage in earlier civilizations and their interrelationships. Toynbee developed a genealogy of civilizations with six first generation ancestors, and three generations of civilizations.

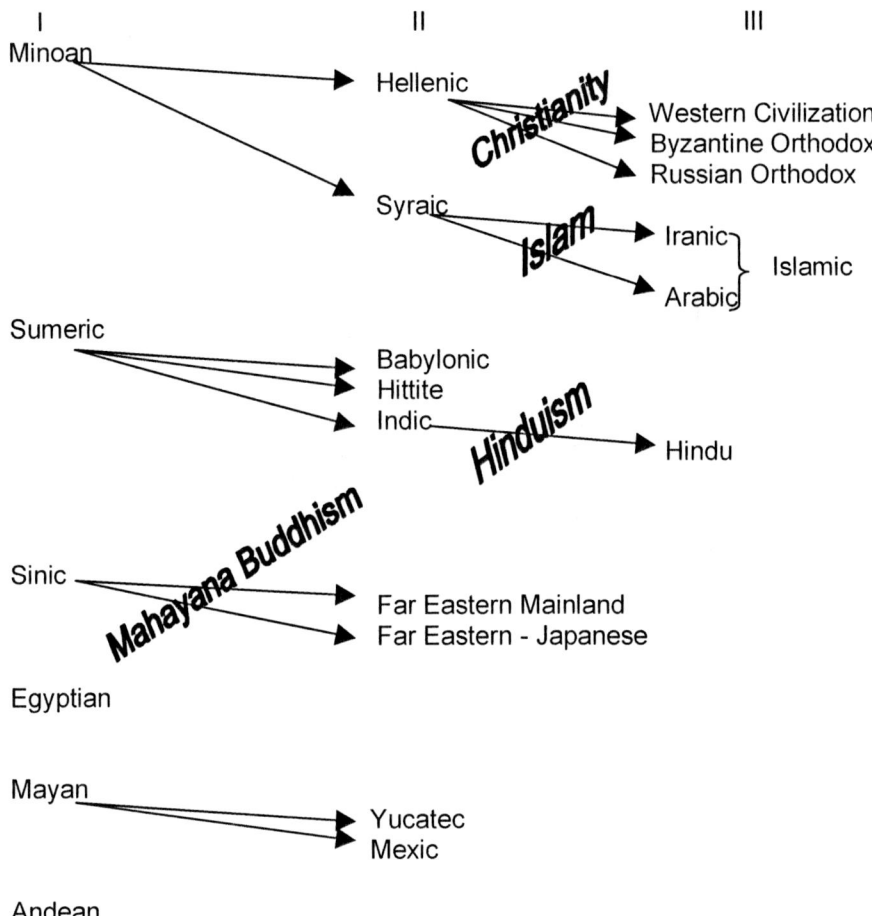

Figure 1. Toynbee's family tree of human civilizations. A view of the family tree of human civilizations showing his three generations of civilizations (not drawn on a time scale), and the higher religions generated through their interactions and evolution.

Western civilization is a third generation civilization in his view. Figure 1 displays the Toynbee family tree of civilizations. Our Theory of Civilization suggests that there are many more (overlooked) civilizations. It also suggests that there are at least four generations of civilizations.

The first civilizations developed in response to the challenge of taming a difficult natural environment. Four civilizations: the Egyptaic, Sumeric, Indic and Sinic civilizations developed in jungle-like river valleys. The Mayan developed in dense jungle; the Andean developed in mountainous terrain; and the Minoan developed in the Greek isles. These primary civilizations gave birth to other civilizations over the course of time. The history of this progression of civilizations is described in detail in *A Study of History* to which the interested reader is referred.

Civilizations were also the birthplaces of the higher religions. Toynbee showed how the birth of the higher religions was intricately related to the disintegration of civilizations. Christianity, Islam, Hinduism and Buddhism each developed as a civilization disintegrated.

Toynbee's Theory of Civilizations

Numerous authors have sought to discover patterns or laws of history similar to those of the physical sciences. Arnold Toynbee developed a particularly interesting theory of History based on the concept of civilizations.

Toynbee assumed that the twenty-six civilizations that he identified could be studied on the same footing despite their differing locations and times. In a sense they are members of the same "species" of organisms. From this small sample of "organisms" he abstracted features and patterns, and developed a theory of civilizations. While there are points in his theory with which one could disagree, and despite some apparent internal inconsistencies, Toynbee's theory appears to accurately portray the major features of human civilizations.

Primary Patterns of Civilization

In Toynbee's theory of civilizations each civilization follows a similar general pattern of evolution. In a particular civilization the general pattern may be modified in small ways, or in large ways, by chance events. Consequently a given civilization may deviate significantly from the general pattern of development. Deviations of this sort are often seen when social or economic theories are compared to actual situations.

In Toynbee's view a civilization arises in response to a challenge. In the case of the earliest civilizations that had no predecessors (Egyptaic, Minoan, Sinic, Sumeric, Mayan and Andean) the challenge was the physical environment. For example, the Egyptians had to make the Nile river valley habitable by

The Life Cycle of Civilizations

transforming it from a dense jungle/swamp to cultivated land. In the case of later civilizations the challenge was social—usually the disintegration of the preceding civilization.

Some examples of social challenges that led to new civilizations are: the emergence of Hittite civilization from the disintegration of the Sumeric civilization; the emergence of the Syraic civilization from the disintegration of the Minoan civilization; the emergence of the Babylonian civilization from the disintegration of the Sumeric civilization; the emergence of the Far Eastern (Main Body) civilization from the disintegration of the Sinic civilization; and the emergence of the Hindu civilization from the disintegration of the Indic civilization.

Exhibit 7. Seventh Century BC scene in Ashurbanipal's palace showing him slaying a lion.

After a new civilization is born from a successful response to a challenge(s) the civilization enters a period of growth. This period of growth in the social fabric of the civilization eventually reaches a point where a major challenge is presented to the civilization that the civilization is unable to successfully handle. This point is called the *breakdown* point of the civilization. The civilization then proceeds to slowly disintegrate. Along the path of disintegration a civilization often encounters new challenges during a *"time of troubles"* that leads it to establish a *universal state* (normally an "empire") to underpin the security of the civilization.

Eventually the civilization crumbles—often due to an attack from outside barbarians (Toynbee calls them "the *external proletariat*") and internal dissent from the people ("the *internal proletariat*"). If a higher religion appears before this point it normally survives the barbarian onslaught and continues on into the successor civilization that eventually develops.

Life Cycle of a Civilization

The life cycle of a civilization parallels the life cycle of an organism: birth, growth, decline and death. This parallel has led some philosophers and historians such as Herbert Spencer and Oswald Spengler to characterize human societies and civilizations as social organisms. While there is some truth in this view it is also true that this analogy breaks down in a number of ways. We see societies fragmenting during the course of their evolution; we see societies uniting with other societies; we see societies changing in their parts under the influence of other societies. They are not organisms in the usual sense because of their fluidity and their ability to join, divide and change.

Nevertheless the analogy has some merit since it provides a readily comprehended framework for discussing the features and evolution of societies and civilizations.

The three major phases of a civilization can be described as growth, breakdown and disintegration. Figure 2 summarizes the general features of the life cycle of a civilization. There are two general types of civilizations: the first civilizations that emerged from prehistory such as the Egyptaic, Sumeric and Sinic civilizations, and the secondary civilizations that emerged from the ruins of previous civilizations. Remarkably, the life cycles of both types of civilizations are similar. A civilization emerges and then proceeds to grow until a point of breakdown is reached. At this point the civilization enters a disintegration phase. First, a time of troubles develops with attendant difficulties. Then a "universal state" such as the Roman Empire is created which provides temporary relief but the process of disintegration continues.

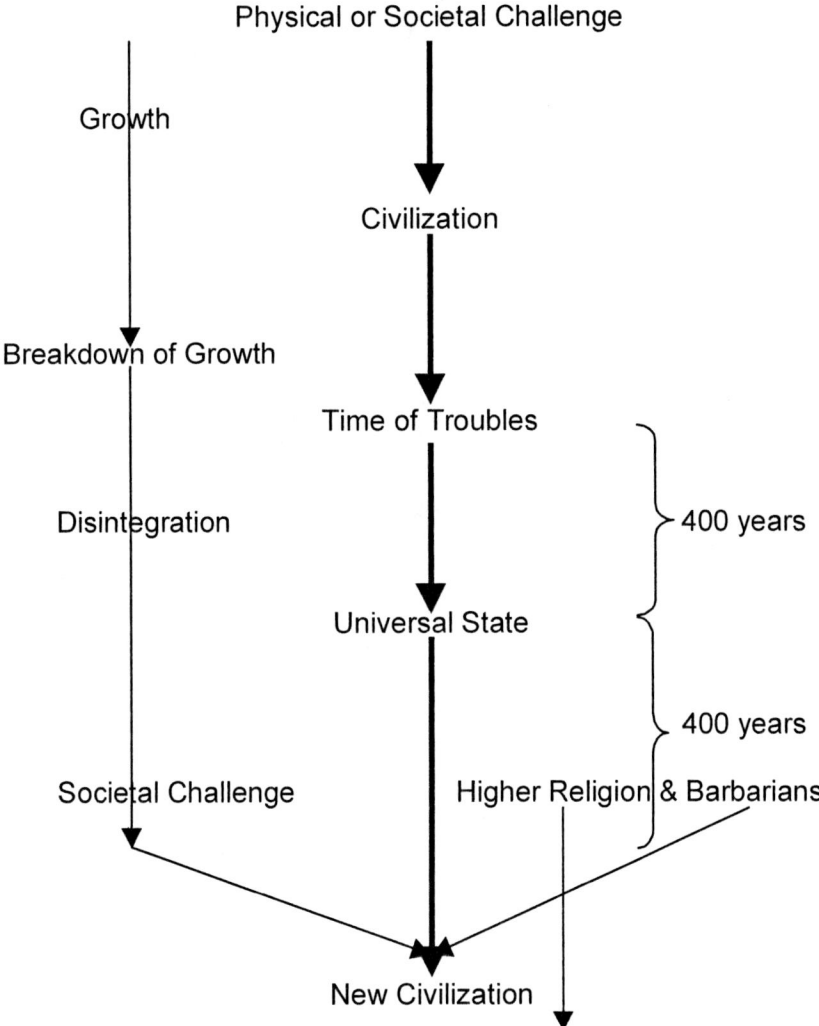

Figure 2. Arnold Toynbee's general view of the life cycle of a civilization. The timing of events for a specific civilization is variable. So the above diagram is not meant to describe each civilization's evolution in precise detail. It describes the observed general pattern of civilizations.

The process of disintegration normally takes about eight centuries. A higher religion may develop during this phase. Most civilizations have had their demise helped by obliging barbarians. After a fallow period a new civilization emerges from the ruins of the dead civilization. Figure 2 shows the general life cycle of a civilization.

Growth of a Civilization

The overall process of birth, growth and decline can be diagrammed in several ways to show the general features of the life cycle of a civilization. Figure 3 shows the growth cycle of a civilization. Toynbee is somewhat vague in his definition of growth and "what grows." Also he does not define the concept of breakdown. Instead he illustrates these concepts with numerous historical examples.

It appears that Toynbee views the growth of a civilization primarily in terms of its social institutions, its moral and cultural values and the social mechanisms that enable it to function successfully as a society. He sees these external manifestations of civilizations as having inner analogues within the psyches of the population of the civilization. The outer manifestations grow in parallel with their inner analogues.

Eventually the focus of the growth of the civilization shifts from external growth to the internal growth of the individual. He calls this shift of focus *etherialization*. In Toynbee's view the most important aspect of growth and progress is etherialization: the inner growth of the individual.

In this view science and technology are secondary. Perhaps Toynbee's view is correct when we consider that a steam boiler was known in Roman times as a curiosity and the wheel was used by the Aztecs on children's toys but not on carts or wagons for work and transportation. A civilization must have the social insight to be able to use technology for technology to have an effect. The mere existence of technical knowledge is not enough.

In the last hundred years there has been a change in Western civilization that has elevated the importance of technology to a new level in terms of its impact on civilization. Advanced countries in Western civilization such as France, Germany, the United Kingdom, and the United States have created organized social institutions for the development and application of technology.

In prior history science and technology were primarily the results of the efforts of private individuals or groups, or of the transient efforts of individual rulers. Organized, large scale research and development on a continuing basis seems to have started in the nineteenth century in large German chemical companies and in British companies that were leading players in the Industrial Revolution.

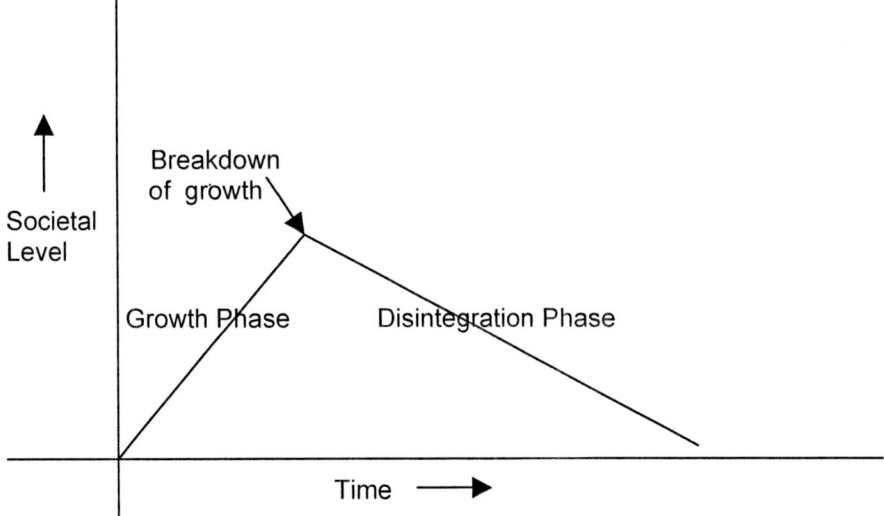

Figure 3. A diagram illustrating the growth pattern of a civilization. The societal level of a civilization is the combination of social institutions and arrangements that "make the society work." This combination includes political mechanisms, technology, and cultural/ethical features—all the parts of the civilization that are vital for its growth and success as a society. This concept is implicit in the work of Toynbee.

World War I, and especially World War II, led to the development of governmental institutions for the development and application of technology.

Since World War II the Cold War and industrial competition between companies and nations have promoted large-scale technological research and development. Japan, for example, has developed a national research and development program that has placed it in the front rank of industrial countries.

The development of new social/governmental institutions for the promotion of technological progress represents an entirely new facet of civilization. Perhaps the most analogous development in prior civilizations was the development of maritime commerce by Hellenic civilization. Maritime commerce not only enriched the Greeks and enabled them to support a much larger population it also broadened their horizons dramatically giving them a wider and deeper understanding of the world and brought them into contact with the civilizations of the Middle East and the culture of Egypt.

The Life Cycle of Civilizations

Technology appears to be playing a similar role in Western civilization by broadening and deepening our understanding of the earth and of the universe. Technology is also leading Western civilization to the other planets and eventually to the stars.

Considering the central role technology has assumed in Western civilizations, and by adoption in other civilizations, it seems Toynbee's definition of growth must now include technological progress.

The Players in the Evolution of a Civilization

Toynbee identifies four groups of players in the drama of the life of a civilization: the creative minority, the dominant minority, the internal proletariat, and the external proletariat. Each plays a distinctive role. Together they create and destroy a civilization.

Creative minority

The creative minority is a small group of individuals that is part of the genesis of a civilization and that develops solutions to challenges presented to the civilization. It leads through the success of its solutions. The populace, the internal proletariat, follows the lead of the creative minority. It imitates them—a process called *mimesis*. The creative minority in civilizations up to the present Western civilization has consisted of political, religious and military leaders.

The role of the creative minority is to develop new social, political and economic solutions, and to develop new techniques of warfare (primarily the organization of troops, logistics and battle strategy). The creative minority develops new institutions and mechanisms to meet the needs/challenges that the civilization faces.

In current Western civilization the creative minority has been expanded to include technologists and scientists. To some extent this change is also evident in other contemporary civilizations. Since science and technology can "progress" or advance to new technologies and scientific theories Western civilization has become imbued with the notion of Progress. The idea that Western civilization is progressing is supported by the improved living conditions, educational level and health of the middle classes and the working classes in western countries.

The combination of a technologically supportive political/social creative minority and modern advancing technology introduces a new component in the analysis of civilizations that may dramatically change the life cycle of civilizations. Modern civilization may not follow the pattern of development of past civilizations. If anything, a progressing technological civilization may have a substantially longer lifetime than the average lifetime of previous civilizations (which was around one thousand years).

Exhibit 8. The Tower of London where members of the creative minority occasionally met their doom.

A technological civilization should also be more able to meet internal and external challenges than an old style civilization. This advantage requires the active support of the political/social part of the creative minority as well as the support of the people (the internal proletariat).

The tremendous technological advantage of Western civilization in the past two hundred years may account for the "failure" of Western civilization to create a universal western state (an empire). Simply put, in recent centuries no combination of "barbarians" could challenge Western civilization to the point where an empire would be the required response. Universal states (empires) often develop to provide a surrounding security cushion for the heartland of a civilization.

Dominant Minority

The breakdown of a civilization, in Toynbee's view, is accompanied by the transition of the creative minority of the civilization to a dominant minority. A creative minority leads the people by example and by successfully meeting the periodic challenges that face a civilization. The leaders and the people are united and in agreement.

When a breakdown in a civilization occurs due to a civilization's failure to successfully respond to a major challenge the creative minority changes to a dominant minority. A dominant minority does not lead through the willing support of an admiring people. A dominant minority rules by custom, force and social intimidation. A simple example of this type of transition often appears in the case of a country that loses a war. Before the war, and during the war, while the country is winning, the leaders are praised and willingly followed. After the war, if the leaders are still in power, they lead a disgruntled country by coercion. The unity of the country is destroyed.

Internal Proletariat

The internal proletariat of a civilization is the people of the civilization—the workers, the soldiers, the middle class, the merchants—in short, all the individuals that follow. While a civilization is growing they are united with the creative minority in their thinking and follow the creative minority's lead in a process called *mimesis*—imitation of the creative minority's example.

After the growth of a civilization breaks down they do not willingly follow the lead of the dominant minority. The civilization's loss of unity helps promote the disintegration of the civilization.

As the civilization disintegrates the internal proletariat becomes open to outside influences ("the barbarians") and often develops a higher religion—partly to replace the vacuum created by its withdrawal of belief in the dominant minority's ideas and leadership.

External Proletariat

The external proletariat is the mass of people outside a civilization who penetrate the civilization and influence its historical development. They are often called "the barbarians". The external proletariat often originates at, or beyond, the fringes, the frontier, or borders of a civilization. In the earlier phases of the civilization they may be at war with the civilization's frontier soldiers. Later they become mercenaries, workers and allies of the civilization. Later still, they migrate into the central regions of the civilization and may even assume leadership roles in the civilization. Lastly, through familiarity with the civilization and its weaknesses they decide to conquer the civilization and often perform the finishing touches on the civilization's disintegration. A perfect example of this process is the decline of the Roman Empire and the Hellenic civilization that it embodied.

Breakdown of Growth

The growth of a civilization is stimulated by the challenges and opportunities that it encounters. First, a challenge is presented to a civilization. The civilization responds by changing or creating a new institution or mechanism to handle the challenge. An example of a challenge and solution is the challenge of over-population faced by Hellenic civilization. The initial temporary responses such as family limitation and infanticide were unacceptable. The Greeks then responded by developing a maritime commerce with trade and colonies that enabled them to obtain foreign food and to send excess population to colonies. This successful response led to the Athenian golden age.

Civilizations face many challenges. First, the great challenge that leads to the beginning of the civilization such as the clearing and domestication of the Nile River valley that led to Egyptaic civilization. After the great initial challenge(s) a civilization faces a continuing series of significant challenges that cause it to grow and evolve. If the civilization is to grow it must overcome each significant challenge with a successful response. Challenges can be internal such as population growth in Greece or the conflict between classes in Rome. Challenges can be external such as barbarian attacks or changes in climate that affect food production producing famines.

A breakdown in a civilization is a failure of the civilization to successfully handle a significant challenge or set of challenges. Up to the point of breakdown the civilization was successfully growing by meeting challenges through the change and evolution of its social institutions and social mechanisms.

The failure of the creative minority to respond successfully to a challenge(s) leads to a breakdown in the unity of the civilization's players. The internal proletariat of the society reacts to the failure of the creative minority by withdrawing its acceptance of the ideas and actions of the creative minority. It no longer strives to imitate the creative minority. The creative minority is in turn led to change its role to that of a dominant minority. Having lost the voluntary support of the internal proletariat the dominant minority tries to maintain its leadership position through coercion and force—thus further alienating the internal proletariat.

The Life Cycle of Civilizations

Force leads to insensitivity and the dominant minority tends to preserve the customs and practices of the civilization when it was growing successfully. The resulting rigidity and inflexibility prevents further growth and, as more challenges appear, and are not successfully handled, the civilization disintegrates.

The breakdown of a civilization is a subtle event that normally happens before a civilization's people, or its historians, are aware of it. Like the stock market, a peak is only known in retrospect after a significant decline. Civilizations, like stock markets, have their peaks and valleys, and trends that are only ascertained afterwards.

Exhibit 9. Scene from the Odyssey in a First Century AD Roman house.

Toynbee provides a remarkable example of a breakdown showing how difficult it is to assess the breakdown point. Toynbee starts with Edward Gibbon's classic *The History of the Decline and Fall of the Roman Empire* in which Gibbon identifies the Age of the Antonines (with emperors Marcus Aurelius and others around 200 AD) as the height of the Roman Empire.

Then Toynbee goes on to point out that Hellenic civilization actually had its breakdown in 431 BC with the outbreak of the Peloponnesian War. The challenges that were presented to Hellenic Society at that time were the outbreak of war between the Greek city-states and the outbreak of class warfare between the classes within Greek city-states. These challenges, and the failure to successfully respond, were evidenced by the devastation of the Melians by the Athenians after the Athenians conquered them, and by the vicious fighting between the factions on Corcyra.

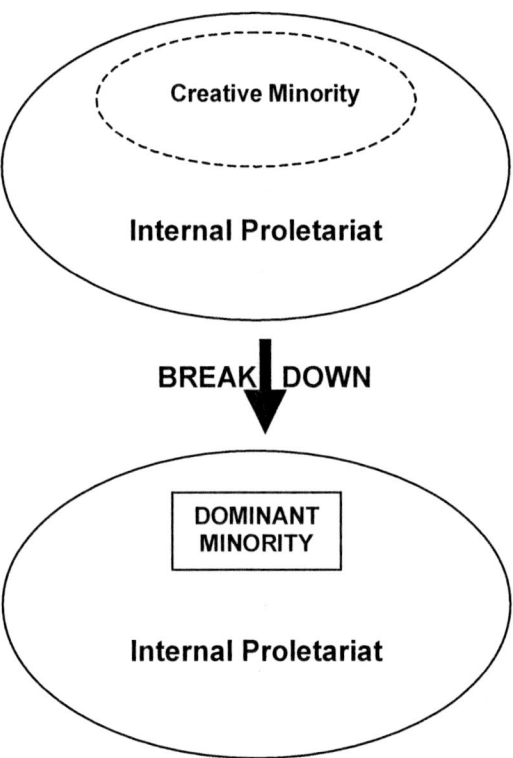

Figure 4. The transition from a creative minority to a dominant minority. During a civilization's period of growth a creative minority plays a leadership role making successful responses to challenges with the assent of the internal proletariat. After the breakdown, the former creative minority becomes the dominant minority and rules through coercion and force.

Toynbee's breakdown point is six hundred years earlier than Gibbon's breakdown point. A period that Gibbon viewed as the flowering of Hellenic civilization, Toynbee viewed as part of the disintegration phase. Toynbee's advantage over Gibbon is that he looked at Hellenic civilization with a viewpoint developed from an analysis of all human civilizations. His more general theoretical perspective enabled him to "see" the pattern of Hellenic civilization more clearly and to discern its phases with more understanding.

Disintegration of a Civilization

The disintegration of a civilization begins with the civilization's breakdown. The creative minority becomes the dominant minority that presides over the disintegration of the civilization. The initial phase of the disintegration of a civilization is often a time of troubles when wars and other social disturbances break out.

Perhaps the most striking example of a civilization that entered a time of troubles after a breakdown is Ancient Egypt. After more than a century of the greatest monument building in the history of mankind—the building of the pyramids—Egypt entered a time of troubles that lasted for approximately four centuries reputedly (Egyptian legend) because of a single act of a pharaoh.

According to the legend, during the pyramid building phase the reigning pharaoh was told by the gods to close the temples of Egypt and make the people of Egypt labor on the pyramids as a punishment for transgressions against the gods. For a hundred years all temples doors were kept shut and the people were denied the solace of religion and the pleasantness of worshipping in the temples.

After a hundred years a new pharaoh succeeded to the throne and feeling sorry for the people he opened the doors of the temples to the people allowing them to worship and offer sacrifices again. The gods became angry at this act and gave Egypt a time of troubles that lasted for four hundred years.

This story graphically illustrates a breakdown in Egyptaic civilization due to the action of the ruler, the pharaoh, and a time of troubles that ensued as a result.

After the time of troubles a central government/universal state was formed—a reunified Egypt.

In the general case a time of troubles normally leads to the creation of a universal state whose strength masks the disintegration of the civilization and may partly undo some aspects of the disintegration process. Eventually due to external and internal factors the civilization completes the process of disintegration and ends. After an interregnum another civilization emerges out of its ashes.

The Life Cycle of Civilizations

The phases and players in the disintegration process of a civilization are described next. Detailed examples of the disintegration phase can be found in Toynbee's *A Study of History* to which the reader is referred.

The Time of Troubles

A time of troubles marks the beginning of the disintegration of a civilization. Times of trouble can take a number of forms: wars between the nations that constitute the civilization, wars with barbarians or nations of other civilizations, wars between the classes and/or political parties of a civilization's society, and economic or natural disasters. For example, the Hellenic civilization's time of troubles was marked by the Peloponnesian War and its aftermath as well as fierce struggles between parties within Greek city-states.

A Universal State

A time of troubles often ends with the formation of a universal state or empire perhaps with greatly expanded borders. A familiar example of a universal state is the Roman Empire—the universal state of Hellenic civilization. Although the formation of a universal state often appears to represent an improvement in the civilization's condition it actually represents a stage in the process of disintegration. Expansion can be a sign of decay just as it is for a corpse.

A civilization that expands in order to have a "buffer zone" as Rome did to keep back the barbarians beyond the Danube signals the decline of its belief in its strength. Contrast Rome building boundaries with the Spartans whose city had no walls because of the Spartan belief, "Our soldiers are our walls." Or the Japanese saying,[1] "People are the walls; people are the castle." A civilization with a vigorous, united populace does not fear barbarians.

The Triumph of Barbarism and Religion

Gibbon describes the later stages of the Roman Empire in his monumental work *The History of the Decline and Fall of the Roman Empire*. Gibbon summarizes his book with the well-known statement: "I have described the triumph of Barbarism and Religion."

Toynbee disagreed with Gibbon for several reasons. First, as stated earlier Toynbee believed that the breakdown of Hellenic civilization occurred much earlier and that Gibbon began his story at a point six hundred years into the period of disintegration. More importantly, Toynbee believed "the triumphant Church and Barbarians were really children of the Hellenic household who had been morally alienated from the dominant minority."

---

[1] See for example Buhei's comment in the movie *Samurai Banners* directed by Inagaki Hiroshi (Toho Company Ltd and Mifune Productions, 1969).

The Life Cycle of Civilizations

Toynbee's comments show the intricacy of the final stages of the disintegration of a civilization. On the one hand the internal proletariat is alienated from the dominant minority and culturally adrift following one current or another from sources within and without the civilization. Religions, philosophies and cults appear and disappear as the internal proletariat seeks to find a mooring in the absence of moral and spiritual leadership from the dominant minority.

EVOLUTION OF A CIVILIZATION'S PLAYERS

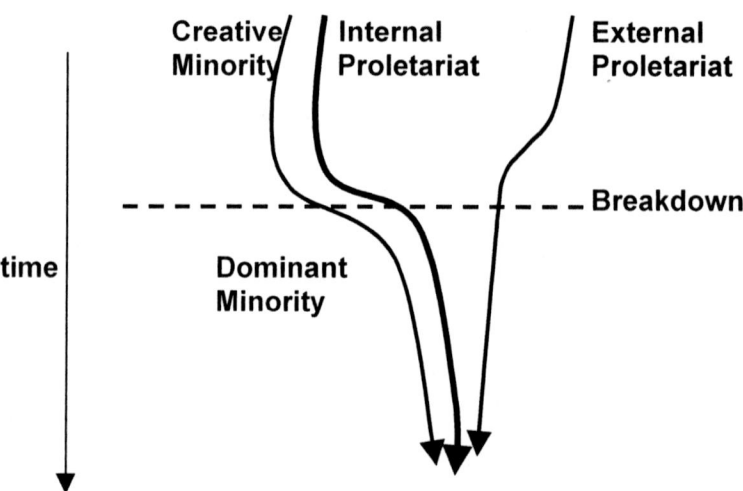

Figure 5. The evolution of a civilization's players as time progresses. Initially the creative minority and internal proletariat have a unity of ideas and goals. After a period of time the creative minority becomes static and unable to develop successful solutions to challenges. It then becomes a dominant minority that rules by coercion and force. In parallel with these developments an external proletariat ("the barbarians") from beyond the frontiers of the civilization penetrates the civilization peacefully at first as workers, soldiers or visitors. The external proletariat develops a familiarity with the civilization and progresses from awe to perhaps mild contempt. Eventually the external proletariat attacks to acquire the riches of the civilization, and the internal proletariat, recognizing their superior "barbarian drive", adopts aspects of their ideas and customs even to the extent of emulating them.

The Life Cycle of Civilizations

On the other hand the civilization is often under pressure from an external proletariat both physically and culturally. The external proletariat often has an advance guard of immigrants within the civilization who learn the nature of the civilization's skills (war making, agricultural, industrial and political) and, after time, may assume leadership roles in the civilization. The internal proletariat may come to admire the physical strength, athletic abilities and personal qualities of the new members of society. It mentally moves closer to the thinking of the external proletariat. The external proletariat in turn moves closer to the thinking of the internal proletariat as it learns of the civilization (see Figure 5). In some cases the dominant minority tries to imitate the style of the now semi-civilized barbarians within their society.

The semi-civilized barbarians remember their origins, and may visit their homeland and spread tales of the wealth of the civilization and the ease with which they may be overcome. Together with the external proletariat outside the borders of the civilization they form a battering ram to bring down the last vestiges of the disintegrating civilization.

The barbarians only participate in the final stages of the civilization's disintegration. Before the breakdown of the civilization the barbarians are largely irrelevant in the face of the overwhelming strength of the civilization.

The development of a religion, which may occur in the latter stages of the disintegration of a civilization, also is not the cause of the breakdown of the civilization. It is part of the latter stages of the disintegration when the internal proletariat sensing the moral bankruptcy of the civilization develops a religion to fill the void. Usually a number of religions appear and one of them becomes the universal choice because of the broad appeal of its doctrines and the superiority of its proselytizers. The higher religions have all appeared in the disintegration of second generation civilizations in Toynbee's view.

After a civilization disintegrates a period of turbulence, an interregnum, ensues which normally lasts for several hundred years until a new civilization emerges.

The Civilizations of Man

Six civilizations constitute the first generation of the civilizations of mankind. These civilizations appeared at different locations and at different times. Following Toynbee we treat these civilizations on the same basis despite their differing chronology. The Egyptaic civilization was the first civilization appearing before 4,000 BC and the Andean civilization the most recent of the first generation civilizations appearing around 0 AD.

The second and third generation civilizations emerge from predecessor civilizations and, as a result, are somewhat different from first generation civilizations. As Toynbee observes civilizations grow best on new turf. The first

The Life Cycle of Civilizations

generation civilizations grew more quickly and more luxuriantly then secondary civilizations that arose on the sites of earlier civilizations.

Although it would be interesting to study the individual civilizations in detail there are many fine books that discuss their features. The interested reader is referred to books by Toynbee, Spengler, Melko, Sorokin, and Braudel among others.

THE FIRST GENERATION OF CIVILIZATIONS

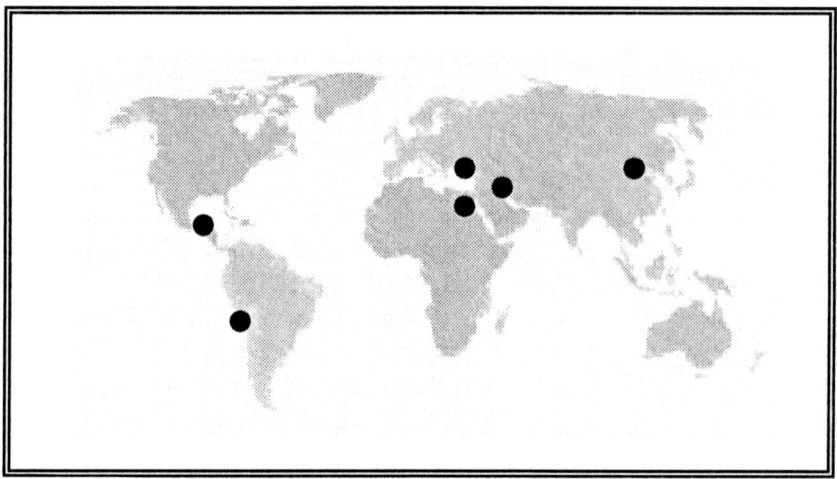

Figure 6. The locations of the six first generation civilizations. The relative closeness of the Sumeric, Minoan and Egyptaic civilizations and the civilizations they parented may have led to the origin of most of the world's higher religions: Christianity, Judaism, Islam, Hinduism, Buddhism and Zoroastrianism through cultural cross-fertilization.

3. The Emergence of Civilizations

> *Mankind is once more on the move.*
> *General Smuts*

Why Did Civilizations Emerge?

Toynbee asked what was the "permanent and fundamental point of difference between permanent societies and civilizations." He failed to find an answer to this question. He, and others, also asked why did it take so long for civilizations to emerge, and why did civilizations emerge when they did? Modern man has existed for at least one hundred thousand years. Yet civilizations only appeared about six thousand years ago. Why was there such a long delay? When civilizations did emerge what was the cause of their sudden emergence at approximately the same time at several widely separated locations?

Historians have also not explained the origin of the creative minority (Why weren't they present in Stone Age societies? Or were they present?), and why some individuals are part of the creative minority and others wind up in the internal proletariat.

An answer to all of these questions may be emerging in current research. It appears the answer is partly genetic and partly environmental. Approximately forty thousand years ago a genetic mutation occurred in man that fostered bold, adventurous personal traits. These traits seem to be similar to the traits found in the creative minority of civilizations. The differentiation between the creative minority and the internal proletariat (the followers) may well lie partly in this genetic difference.

The creation of a leadership group is not enough to generate a civilization. Environmental conditions must provide for the possibility for life beyond the mere struggle to survive. The last hundred thousand years have seen wide environmental changes and fluctuations that dwarf the current worries over global warming.

The last major ice age ended about ten thousand years ago. Then the climate became more stable and much warmer. The combination of a new genetic disposition towards boldness and novelty and a more favorable environment may have led to the first generation of civilizations six thousand years ago.

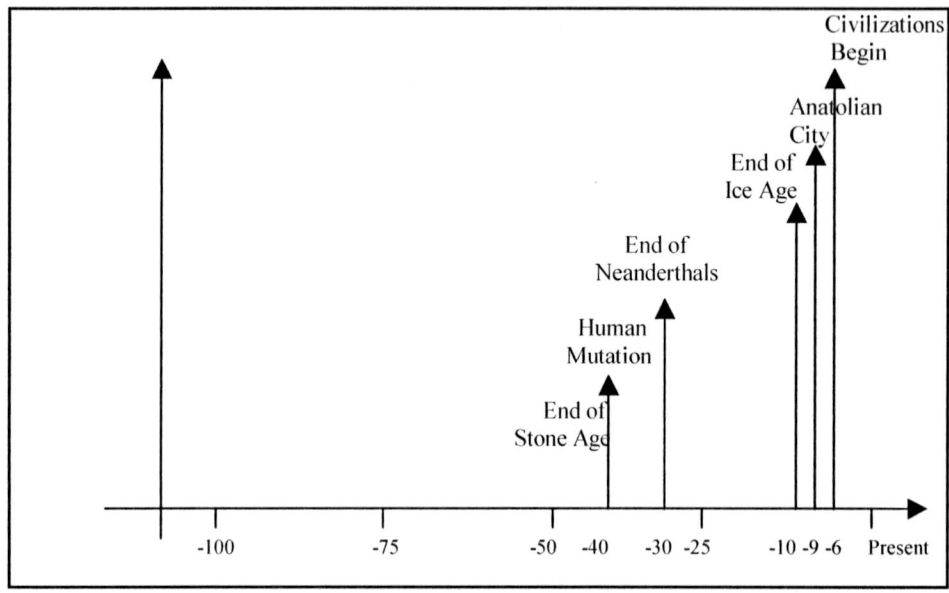

Figure 7. Some major events in the last 100,000 years.

Indeed the first stirrings of civilizations can be seen in a city on the Anatolian plateau about 9,000 years ago shortly after the end of the last major Ice Age. An ice age represents a major environmental negative for the development of civilizations. Even as small a difference as the difference between the climates of Maine and Massachusetts (adjoining states in the USA) had a notable effect on the cultural levels of these states in the opinion of Toynbee. Massachusetts had a lively intellectual life while Maine languished due to its slightly more severe climate.

From 150,000 BC to 40,000 BC – Static Social Groups

Anatomically modern humans with a brain and a capacity for speech and language existed one hundred and fifty thousand years ago. These humans congregated in hunter/gatherer social groups that ranged from hunting bands to clans and small tribes. They made four basic tools in a manner that changed little in this hundred thousand year period. The types of tools were the same in all regions.

There is archaeological evidence that they understood symbols and there is clear evidence of artistic work in cave drawings and personal adornments. The quality of the artistry suggests an artistic development with a history of perhaps tens of thousands of years.

Modern man coexisted with the Neandertals for tens of thousands of years. In the Middle East there is evidence that they coexisted together from about 90,000 BC until 30,000 BC approximately.

Overall human cultural and social development was slow at best and the level of the Neandertals and humans in tool making and artistic endeavors was comparable. They used similar techniques. They drew with similar artistry. Their jewelry and personal adornment appeared similar.

From 40,000 BC to 8,000 BC – A Creative Burst

Around 40,000 years ago human culture started a period of explosive cultural growth called the Upper Paleolithic Explosion. The Upper Paleolithic Explosion saw major progress in tools, habitations, personal adornment, burials, and art together with evidence of advances in language and social organization.

Exhibit 10. Paleolithic cave drawing of bison from 10,000 to 15,000 ago.

The cause of this growth has been attributed to a major change in humans such as a "rewired brain" or some other mutation in human intelligence. Recently a genetic change has been found to have occurred about that time that might be the source for the dramatically new developments in humanity in that period.

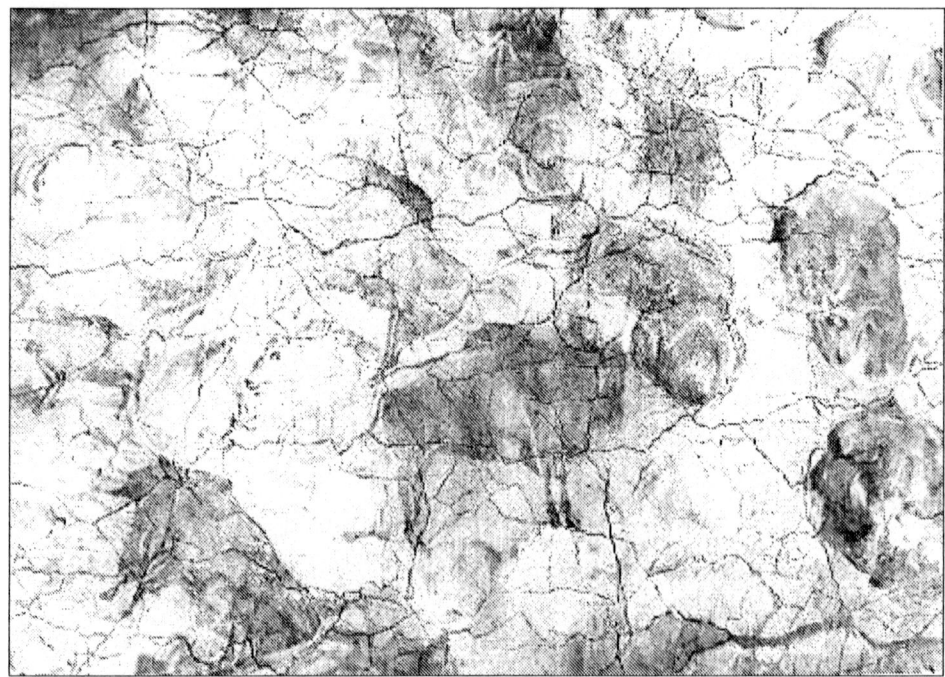

Exhibit 11. Paleolithic cave drawing of herd of bison from 10,000 to 15,000 ago.

Some of the developments that occurred in the thirty three thousand year period beginning 40,000 years ago are:

- Major progress in tools, habitations, personal adornment, burials, and art together with evidence of advances in language and social organization.

- A dramatic increase in tools and skills of man relative to the contemporary Neandertals (although Neandertal skills did improve during this period as well).

- The elimination of the Neandertals by 30,000 BC.

- The development of "blade technology" about 40,000 years ago with standardization and a much greater variety of tools. Also new materials were used for tools such as ivory and bone.

- An explosion of artistic efforts in the period 40,000 BC to 30,000 BC.

- A major worldwide domestication of plants 9,000 BC to 8,000 BC.

- Around 8,500 BC Middle Eastern populations started to soar.

- Around 8,000 BC sheep and goats were domesticated.

- Around 8,500 BC true farming villages started appearing Middle East.

- Around 7,000 BC a city emerged on the Anatolian Plateau that may have been the first city.

- Around 7,000 BC pigs and cattle were domesticated.

A Gene Mutation in 40,000 BC

Recently, new evidence[2,3] has emerged that a genetic mutation occurred in man around 40,000 years ago. The discoverers of this genetic mutation (Ding et al) suggested it might be the cause of the Upper Paleolithic Explosion. They postulated that the mutation might have occurred about 50,000 years ago and then diffused sufficiently throughout the human population over the following ten thousand years to spark the Explosion. Thus it is reasonable to attribute the Upper Paleolithic Explosion in human culture to the effects of this mutation. While Man's intellectual and artistic abilities existed before the genetic mutation, the genetic mutation may have stimulated Man to utilize them more, and in a better and bolder way.

Today the mutated gene is the second most prevalent form of the DRD4 gene—a gene that codes for a type of dopamine receptor found on brain cells. This gene is known to affect personality traits. The mutation is believed to be a rare mutational event that became widespread due to Darwinian positive

---

[2] Yuan-Chun Ding, Han-Chang Chi, Deborah L. Grady, Atsuyuki Morishima, Judith R. Kidd, Kenneth K. Kidd, Pamela Flodman, M. Anne Spence, Sabrina Schuck, James M. Swanson, Ya-Ping Zhang, and Robert K. Moyzis, Proceedings of the National Academy of Sciences **99**, 309-314 (2002).

[3] Joan Arehart-Treichel, Psychiatric News, **37**, 20 (2002).

selection. Individuals with this mutated gene have leadership skills and daring that might give them advantages in survival and in the selection of mates. Such individuals would also have advantages in leading a tribal group in successful hunts of game such as mastodons, and also in warfare.

Mankind coexisted with Neandertals in close proximity from approximately at least ninety thousand years ago until forty thousand years ago when individuals carrying this gene became fairly prevalent. The aggressiveness and leadership skills of individuals carrying this gene might have given the human population an edge producing a leadership that led to the extermination of the Neandertals in the succeeding ten thousand years. By approximately 30,000 BC there were no more Neandertals. The Neandertals, despite their size, may have been sheep (gentle giants) led to the slaughter.

The mutated gene enhances boldness, leadership role taking, novelty seeking, and "nerviness" as well as novelty seeking. The discoverers of the mutation (Ding et al) have conjectured that individuals carrying this mutation might have provided the intrepid leadership that led man in the trek out of Africa.

Today one-third of modern people of all races has this gene variant. It is ironic that this gene is related to attention deficit/hyperactivity disorder (ADHD). It is even more ironic that children with ADHD are treated as patients in need of medical treatment (such as drugs) and special education when in fact they may actually be part of the natural leadership of mankind. Restless energy is often a strength in adults and a source of superior performance. Yet we penalize it in children—often because teachers prefer docile students, and also because there is a profession devoted to finding problems in children for their own financial benefit. How can Mankind advance when human predators prey on children?

Did the Creative Minority Emerged Genetically?

Toynbee developed a theory of civilizations based on the growth of a civilization due to the efforts of a creative minority. He did not attribute any special quality to the individuals that constituted the creative minority. They simply existed and were responsible for the creative successful responses to challenges to a civilization.

The discovery of the DRD4 gene mutation that enhances boldness and novelty seeking suggests that the creative minority of a civilization may consist to a significant degree of individuals carrying the DRD4 mutation. If this were the case we would have an explanation for the long period in the history of Man before the appearance of civilizations:

- 150,000 BC   - Anatomically modern Man exists
- 4,000 BC   - The first civilizations begin

Civilizations began as soon as it was genetically and environmentally favorable. Although the DRD4 genetic mutation provided the creative minority needed for the leadership of a civilization, the harshness of the environment during the Ice Age prevented the development of civilizations until after the Ice Age ended ten thousand years ago.

The first city appeared about one thousand years after the end of the Ice Age. The first civilizations started to appear about four thousand years after the end of the Ice Age. Various plants and animals were domesticated in this four thousand year period, and human populations grew. Then around 4,000 BC civilizations began to emerge:

> Egyptaic civilization began before 4,000 BC
> Sumeric civilization began before 3,500 BC
> Minoan civilization began before 3,000 BC
> Peruvian pyramids built around 3,000 BC

Climatic Conditions Delayed the Emergence of Civilizations

The severity and major temperature fluctuations of the Ice Age climate that lasted from 100,000 BC to 8000 BC would have been sufficient to explain the failure of Mankind to develop civilizations. Difficult climatic conditions make the food supply uncertain, and insufficient to sustain significant populations.

Perhaps the best example of the effects of an Ice Age on a culture is Eskimo culture. The Eskimos successfully adapted to a severe cold climate around the Arctic Circle. They developed specialized tools for hunting such as harpoons and spears as well as other technology such as kayaks and dog sledges for survival.

However the harshness of the Arctic climate and the dominance of the Eskimo by the yearly cycle of the Arctic totally absorbed the Eskimo's energy with the result that their culture was unable to grow beyond meeting the daily needs of life. As a result they have been called an *arrested civilization*—a civilization that reached a certain point in development and then froze.

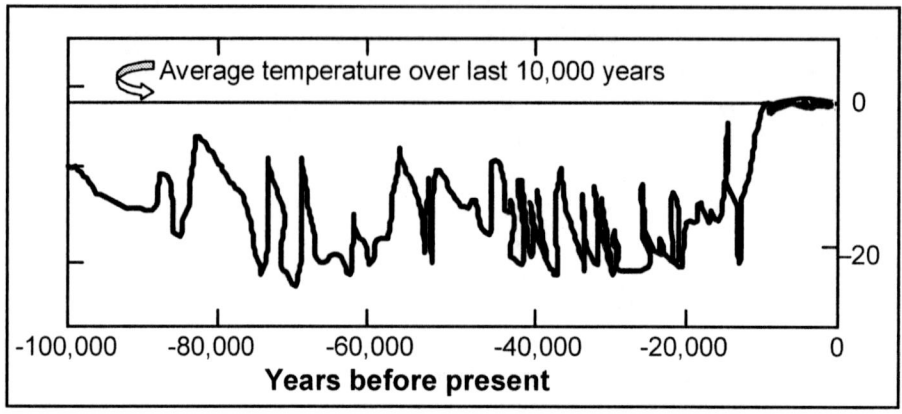

Figure 8. Rough diagram of the last 100,000 years of temperature (Greenland).[4] The relative change in temperature in degrees Centigrade is depicted along the right side of the graph. The zero point line is at the average temperature in the past 10,000 years. As shown, Ice Age temperatures dipped as much as 20° C below this average temperature. Note also the relative lack of major temperature fluctuations in the last 10,000 years. Recent civilizations have enjoyed a warmer, more stable climate.

It is an interesting question to consider whether Ice Age cultures existed which were similarly successful in adapting to their environment but were unable to grow further due to the harshness of the environment. Should these cultures be characterized as "arrested civilizations"? If so, then Mankind may have a prehistory containing arrested civilizations that will remain unknown except for a few bones and stone tools.

The Nature of a Theory of Civilizations

Having developed a plausible scenario for the development of a creative minority and the emergence of civilizations we now turn to the task of developing a theory of civilizations. In this effort we are aided by the ground breaking work of historians and students of civilization—particularly in the last eighty years.

---

[4] See for example A. Ganopolski and S. Rahmstort, Physical Review Letters **88**, 038501 (2002).

The development of a theory of civilizations is a difficult and problematic task. Unlike scientific theories where a precise statement of a theory is possible a theory of civilizations is by its nature not precise and not capable of detailed scientific verification. The definition of a civilization and the unambiguous historical identification of a civilization are themselves fuzzy concepts.

Mankind has had only about twenty-six to thirty civilizations in most historians' estimations—a very small sample from which to abstract regularities and patterns that could serve as the basis of a theory of civilizations. Add to this problem the chance occurrences of Nature and history, and the difficulty of finding regularities and patterns is substantially increased. For example, the death of a Mongol Khan on one occasion caused a Mongol army in the process of conquering Europe to withdraw saving Europe from Mongol devastation. The death of another Mongol Khan similarly led to the withdrawal of a Mongol army advancing on Palestine and Egypt. The history of Western civilization and the Middle East would have been substantially different if these two khans had lived a bit longer. There are many such chance occurrences of events that have had a major impact on the course of history and civilizations.

Furthermore, if a theory of civilizations were developed, its application to civilizations would have to be broadly interpreted because of the wide range of deviations that can be expected in any theory of human behavior.

The first step in the development of a theory—especially a biological or social theory— is to develop a descriptive theory of the actual phenomena. A descriptive theory attempts to provide a simple accurate overall description of the phenomena without seeking to base the theory on more fundamental concepts. Appendix A provides a descriptive theory in the form of statements about the form and development of civilizations. These statements provide something like a Dow theory for civilization that is analogous to the Dow Theory of the New York stock market.

The second step in the development of a theory is to make it quantitative. A quantitative theory has two advantages: it depicts the phenomena in a compact way that language cannot do, and it provides an unambiguous specification of the theory. Words are more subject to the misinterpretation and ambiguity than equations.

The development of a quantitative theory of civilizations starts in the next chapter from Toynbee's deep observation that the disintegration of civilizations has a "three and a half beat" pattern in most cases.

4. The General Theory of Civilization

Mankind is surely more complicated than lifeless matter. It is therefore not reasonable to expect that we should understand mankind by using techniques simpler than those required for physics.
Lewis F. Richardson

The Approach

The Foundation series of Science Fiction novels by Isaac Asimov portray a galactic civilization with a decidedly Toynbee-esque structure and historical development. It shows phases of growth and disintegration similar to the Toynbee life cycle of a civilization with a transition period between the original civilization and the emergence of a successor civilization.

A social scientist/mathematician, Hari Selden, appears in these novels. Selden develops a detailed theory of societal dynamics that enables him to predict in detail the evolution of civilization and to calculate the effect of events on its evolution. Armed with this knowledge a group of scientists attempt to manage the course of history in order to minimize the destruction associated with the disintegration of the galactic civilization.

With this story as a backdrop we will try to make a beginning at a mathematical theory of civilizations. The thought process behind this effort will be based on the form of economic theory, and on the thought processes, behind Lewis F. Richardson's theory of arms races and wars.[5]

The non-mathematically inclined reader is advised to read the text, enjoy the figures and ignore the equations. The implications of the theory are understandable without mathematics. Courage!

We will try to develop a quantitative theory of the development, decline, and interplay of civilizations. Needless to say, it is difficult to develop a mathematical theory that describes sociological phenomena and has predictive

---

[5] Richardson, L. F., *Arms and Insecurity* (Quadrangle Books, Chicago, IL, 1960)

power. So our theory will fall far short of the detailed sociometric theory of Hari Selden in Asimov's Science Fiction novels. History has so many chance events and complications that we can only hope to develop an overall theory of civilizations at this stage.

The theory will not have detailed predictive power because we do not have a sound mathematical way to assess the impact of events on a civilization. What numerical value can we give to an invasion of barbarians relative to the numerical value of a series of crop failures? How can we develop a mathematical theory when we cannot quantify the events that occur in the history of a civilization? How can we predict the effect of an event on the future of a civilization if we cannot assign a numerical value to the event? Mr. Spock's calculation of the probability of success of an action in Star Trek episodes is far beyond our capabilities now or in the foreseeable future.

The issues we face in developing a quantitative theory of civilizations are similar to the issues economists have faced when they developed theories of the financial markets. If a war starts what is the effect on the Dow Jones average? If a large company fails how will the market react? We can form rough estimates but there is no detailed theory that numerically predicts the effect of events on the markets. Instead we have quantitative theories for special, simpler financial situations such as the Black-Scholes Model for evaluating options pricing. And we have the qualitative Dow Theory to "understand" the movements of the Dow Jones average. But we do not have a mathematical theory of the financial markets with detailed predictive power.

So we cannot expect too much from a theory of an infinitely more complex entity such as a civilization—although it is surprising how accurately our theory correlates with historical events.

Our approach is based on simplicity: we will not postulate entities and features unless necessary. This principle is often called Ockham's Razor after the gentleman who first formulated it. Going one step further we will attempt to keep the mathematical apparatus as uncomplicated as possible.

We will attempt to develop a theory that describes the life cycle of a civilization under various conditions knowing that no civilization will conform to the ideal and yet realizing that our theory will embody the general characteristics of the dynamics of civilizations.

Our development will be based on the outstanding work of Toynbee and others in developing a qualitative knowledge of civilizations based on an extraordinary amount of historical data (Appendix A). We will call the description that historians have developed the "experimental" data. A reading of historians such as Toynbee's works reveals a great deal of detail about the structure and dynamics of civilizations. Our goal is to provide a simple dynamical theory of civilizations based on this experimental data.

The situation is reminiscent of the development of the theory of electromagnetism in the nineteenth century. In the early nineteenth century Faraday and others developed a mass of experimental data on electromagnetic phenomena which Maxwell developed into the dynamical theory of Electromagnetism—Electrodynamics—after the passage of a number of years.

We will develop a mathematical theory of civilizations based on variables that describe a civilization. As Richardson points out, "A rule of the theoretical game is that a nation is represented by a single variable". A rule of our game will be to represent a civilization by a single variable (actually two variables).

Historians have noted that civilizations have certain common patterns. Toynbee has pointed out that most civilizations display a "three and a half beat" pattern of ups and downs: rout, rally, rout, rally, rout, rally, rout. The fact that civilizations show a common pattern despite vastly different circumstances suggests that the cause of the pattern may be internal to the civilizations and may reflect a fundamental, inherent trait of human societies of that type.

If we consider the case of the Roman Empire, we see that the Rome of 100 BC would have easily repulsed the barbarians that successfully overcame Rome in the fourth century. As Toynbee points out it was "the 'loss of nerve' ... which was at the heart of the Hellenic breakdown." In those latter days of Rome philosophers talked of "cosmic senescence" as the source of declines in society, agriculture, population, the weather, and other aspects of their civilization. We see here the situation of the pessimist ("the wine bottle is half empty") versus the optimist ("nonsense, the wine bottle is half full"). If the spirit of the people is strong then adversities can be overcome. If the spirit of the people is weak then feeble efforts result in consequent failures.

As stated above we will use simple variables to represent the state of a civilization. The primary variables are S, which represents the "societal level" of a civilization, and C, which represents the amount of change a civilization is currently undergoing. At any point in time a civilization has a certain level S and is changing by the amount C.

Defining the *societal level* of a civilization is a difficult issue. We will start with a preliminary definition that will undoubtedly require refinement:

S = Societal Level = the strength of a civilization in terms of political and social institutions, social cohesion, ability to innovate to solve social problems, capacity for technological innovation, flexibility in finding solutions, enterprise in meeting challenges. The societal level is a measure of the inner development and inner strength (the psyche) of the people of a civilization. Historical events, social conditions and material conditions reflect the societal level in the sense that they are the symptoms that measure its state just as a doctor measures the health of a patient by the patient's symptoms. Historical events are the symptoms of the "health" (societal level) of a civilization.

C = Change = the rate of change of the societal level with time. Mathematically, C is the time derivative of S.

$$C = dS/dt \qquad (1)$$

The definition of the societal level of a civilization is necessarily imprecise. The societal level S is a measure of the "health" or strength of a civilization. It can also be viewed as a measure of the "sentiment" of the civilization's members about the future. In a sense Rome fell because the sentiment of the Roman Empire turned negative – people had very negative expectations about the future. The phrase "cosmic senescence" summarized that view – the universe, and Rome, was winding down. As Rome expected to fail, it did, and the barbarians easily overcame a dispirited populace. Societal level can be viewed as a civilization's equivalent to "consumer sentiment" in economics. Consumer sentiment indicates the consumer's view of the future and thus the consumer's likelihood to spend. Societal level indicates the populace's view of the future and the health of its civilization.

When we think of civilizations we often think of the forces at play in the civilization: internal social forces and forces due to external threats such as barbarians or environmental changes. It is natural to think of forces moving a civilization in one direction or another. Based on this thought we will construct a simple mechanical model of civilizations using Newton's force law:

$$F = mA \qquad (2)$$

where F is the force on the civilization, m is the "mass" of the civilization, and A is the acceleration of the civilization (its growth rate socially).

As we will see, a three and a half beat pattern arises naturally in this Newtonian picture. The ups and downs of a civilization are analogous (mathematically as well as poetically) to the swings of a pendulum or the tolling of a bell.

We will develop our theory of civilizations with the standard pattern seen in many civilizations. Then we will consider more complex situations such as the interactions of civilizations, and the effect of environmental events and barbarians.

Static Societies

By definition a civilization is a dynamic form of society. For most of Mankind's existence societies have been static. From the perspective of the theory that we are trying to construct we will say the force on these "almost-civilizations" is zero; the change is zero, and the societal level is constant:

$$S = \text{constant} \qquad (3)$$

The Standard Pattern of Civilizations

Civilizations are dynamic. They grow and change. External and internal forces mold them.

It is reasonable to assume that the societal level of a civilization is the cumulative effect of the changes that have taken place since its inception. The changes may be positive or negative. Therefore we will define the societal level S by

$$S = \int_0^t dt'\, C(t') \qquad (4)$$

where $C(t')$ is the change in societal level taking place at time t'. The integral begins at $t' = 0$ which is assumed to be the time of the origin of the civilization or, put differently, the time at which a society starts growing thus transforming itself into a nascent civilization.

As a civilization evolves its pattern of change ebbs and rises in response to challenges both internal and external. We will model the pattern of change in a civilization using Newton's force law together with the simplest forces that can produce the observed pattern of growth and disintegration in a civilization.

We will assume the change C is directly related to the forces on a civilization just as the swings of a pendulum are directly related to the forces on the pendulum. Consequently we will assume the acceleration is:

$$A = C'' \qquad (5)$$

where the symbol $'$ indicates a time derivative (a derivative with respect to time) and C'' represents the second derivative with respect to time:

$$C'' = d^2C/dt^2$$

(Equation (5) is analogous to the statement that the acceleration is the second time derivative of the position—a well-known fact of Mechanics.)

Since many civilizations in different regions and different environments have been observed to have a "three and a half beat" pattern it appears reasonable to assume that this pattern is somehow inherent in a civilization and not the result of external forces. Toynbee suggests this point when he writes of the 'Laws of Nature'. Consequently we will assume that civilizations have internal forces affecting societal change as well as external forces. Thus we will separate the total force into an internal force F_{int} and an external force F_{ext}.

$$F = F_{int} + F_{ext} \qquad (6)$$

We will specify the internal force using simple everyday thinking. When we think of change in society or in individuals we notice that there is often a resistance to change. Resistance to change takes two forms: a resistance to the increasing rate of change and a resistance to the total change. We often hear "the accelerating pace of change is leaving me further behind" or "things are moving too quickly for me" and "one more change and I will explode. I am at my limit." These types of comments are not only for the individual but also appear at the level of societies. We remember Iran, which exploded under forced rapid modernization by the last Shah.

The "social resistance" to the *total* amount of change we express mathematically as sC where C is the amount of change and s is a proportionality constant. We use the symbol s since it is the first letter of 'sated' reflecting the thought: "The civilization is sated by the amount of the change." A civilization will tend to change up to a certain point building up to a "peak" and then turn around in reaction. The forced, rapid modernization of Iran that led to the Fundamentalist reaction is an example of this phenomenon.

In principle, the constant s depends on the civilization. It may be smaller or larger depending on the capacity of the civilization for change. Remarkably we will see that the resistance to change is the same for all human civilizations reflecting a long-term property of human nature.

The resistance to the increase of the rate of change we express mathematically as rC' where r is a constant embodying the civilizations resistance to an *increase* in the rate of change. The constant r depends on the civilization and reflects a civilization's resistance to an increase in the rate of change. This type of resistance is familiar in Western civilization. It is reflected by statements like, "The continually increasing pace of change is getting to be too much for me."

The Life Cycle of Civilizations

Combining the resistance terms we express these socio-psychological concepts with the expression for the internal force:

$$F_{int} = F_0 = -rC' - sC \qquad (7)$$

The minus signs are necessary to express the negativity of the force—the resistance tends to limit the amount of change. We introduce the variable named F_0 (which in this case is the same as F_{int}) above for later use in this chapter.

A Dynamical Law of Civilizations

If we ignore external forces for the moment Newton's law (equation (2)) gives us the differential equation:

$$mC'' + rC' + sC = 0 \qquad (8)$$

The constant m represents the "mass" of the civilization. Crudely speaking, the mass of the civilization is a factor in the momentum of a civilization. If a civilization is moving, then the larger m is, the greater the momentum to persist in that direction of motion. Thus m represents the "inertia" or staying power of a civilization. A civilization with a large mass requires a greater force to change its motion or progress in time than a civilization with a small mass.

The Tolling Bells of Civilizations

Equation (8) is a well-known equation in Physics: the equation for the damped harmonic oscillator. It describes the cyclic motion of pendulums and bells. Here it describes a cyclicity in civilizations.

The appearance of this equation as a description of the changes in civilizations evokes images of the ebb and flow of civilizations that have appeared in literature for thousands of years. As Matthew Arnold wrote in *Dover Beach*,

> Begin and cease, and then again begin,
> With tremulous cadence slow
> …
> Sophocles long ago heard it on the Aegean, and it brought
> Into his mind the turbid ebb and flow,
> Of human misery; …

and Shelley wrote in *The World's Great Age*:

> The world's great age begins anew,
> The golden years return,
> The earth doth like a snake renew
> …
> A brighter Hellas rears its mountains
> …
> Another Athens shall arise,
> And to remoter time
> Bequeath, like sunset to the skies,
> The splendor of its prime;

There is a certain satisfaction in seeing the literary descriptions of history realized in our theory of civilizations.

The damped harmonic oscillator of civilization (equation (8)) moves like the clapper in a bell: back and forth with diminishing amplitude until it comes to rest. The clapper comes to rest due to friction. The effect of friction is represented in the damped harmonic oscillator by the damping term rC'. In our theory it represents societal friction. The sC term "causes" the periodicity in the oscillations of the civilization.

Exhibit 12. The tolling bells of civilization.

Solutions for Civilizations

The solution to the damped harmonic oscillator equation is well known in Physics (see page 95 of Joos' book listed in the References section):

$$C = c_1 e^{-at} \sin(bt - c_2) \qquad (9)$$

where a, b, c_1, and c_2 are constants, and t is the time since the beginning of the civilization. The constants a and b are related to the constants r and s appearing in the damped harmonic oscillator equation:

The Life Cycle of Civilizations

$$a = r/(2m) \qquad (10)$$

$$b = \sqrt{s/m - r^2/(4m^2)} \qquad (11)$$

We make the reasonable assumption that the change C is zero at the beginning of a civilization. The predecessor society can be assumed to be static with zero growth. Then equation (9) becomes

$$C(t) = c_1 e^{-at} \sin(bt) \qquad (12)$$

Using equations (4) and (12) we can determine the societal level:

$$S(t, r) = c_1 [b - e^{-at}(a \sin(bt) + b \cos(bt))]/(a^2 + b^2) \qquad (13)$$

Notice the change and societal level are both zero at the beginning of the civilization according to equations (12) and (13). At the end of a civilization's disintegration the change approaches zero and the societal level S is approximately a constant value representing the culminating societal level of the civilization:

$$S(t, r) \rightarrow c_1 b/(a^2 + b^2) \qquad (14)$$

as t becomes large. Although a civilization may disintegrate, parts of its social structure and culture will survive. So we do not expect the societal level to return to zero normally. (It could return to zero in the event of a catastrophe as we indicate in the case of the Theran volcanic eruption that ended Minoan civilization. We consider this case later.) Normally there is a social and cultural accumulation during the lifetime of the civilization.

Determination of Parameters of Theory From History

We will now take equation (13) and determine the constants appearing in it from the observed general pattern of the growth and disintegration of civilizations. Since we do not have a method to measure the societal level on an absolute scale we will set c_1 equal to 1 throughout the remainder of the book.

The observed three and a half beat pattern leads to a graphical pattern shown in Figure 9. The time interval up to the breakdown point we will call the Startup phase. The interval of time between the breakdown of a civilization (the point at which growth stops) and the beginning of the universal state (at the end of the time of troubles) is approximately 400 years.

The Life Cycle of Civilizations

Since the curve in Figure 9 oscillates in a uniform manner we wish to determine the time period of the oscillation. The period of an oscillation, which we denote T, is defined to be the time interval between successive peaks. An examination of Figure 9 shows that a rout-rally-rout episode takes 400 years. This time period of 400 years thus corresponds to 1.5 times the period of the oscillation T. A rout and rally cycle takes T years to happen. For the oscillations specified by equation (13) the period is specified by

$$bT = 2\pi \qquad (15)$$

or

$$T = 2\pi/b \qquad (16)$$

since the angle in the sine and cosine functions in equation (13) changes by 2π radians in the time it takes for one rout and rally (one period).

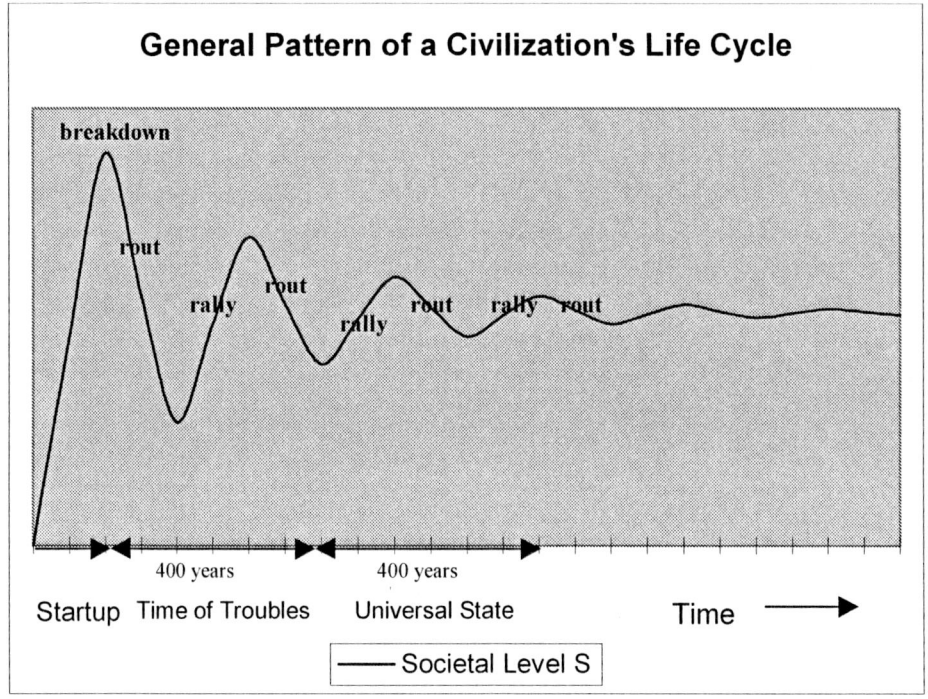

Figure 9. The typical pattern of the routs and rallies of a civilization.

The Life Cycle of Civilizations

If $1.5T = 400$ years then $T = 267$ approximately. Then $b = 0.0235$ if we measure time in years. The constant b fixes the period of oscillation and thus the time intervals of routs and rallies.

The determination of the parameter a is more problematic. It is directly related to the decline in S associated with the disintegration of a civilization. The ratio of successive maximums (the successive peaks in a plot of S versus time) in the disintegration phase is (see Joos)

$$e^{aT} = e^{rT/(2m)} = e^d \qquad (17)$$

The quantity

$$d = aT = rT/(2m) \qquad (18)$$

can be solved for a to yield

$$a = d/T \qquad (19)$$

The appropriate value of d for a civilization can only be approximately determined through a study of the *shape* of the disintegration curves of civilizations for various choices of d.

The number of significant peaks in the plot of S versus time is determined by the value of a. We will look at plots of S for various values of a and try to find the value of a that corresponds to a three and a half beat pattern.

The following table shows values of a for various choices of d. It also shows the ratio of succeeding peaks (a measure of the rate of decline) for each value of d.

d	.5	.6	.7	.75	.8	1.	2	5
a	0.00187	0.00225	0.00262	0.00281	0.003	0.00375	0.00749	0.01873
Ratio of peaks	1.649	1.822	2.014	2.117	2.226	2.718	7.389	148.413

Figure 10. Values of d, a and the ratio of successive peaks.

We will plot S for these representative values of d and look for an S plot that displays the three and a half beat pattern. The following pages show the curve of S for various values of d.

The Life Cycle of Civilizations

S for d = .5

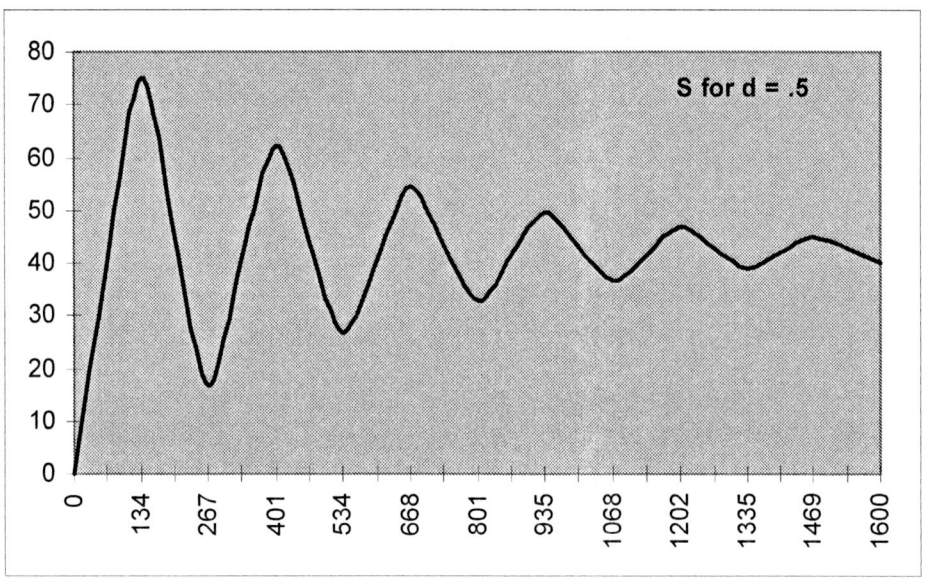

S for d = .6

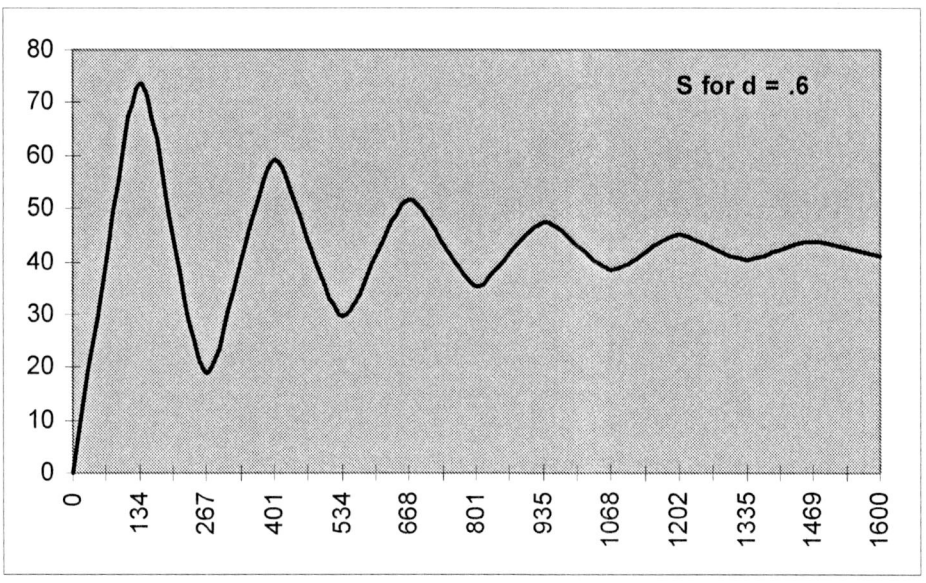

The Life Cycle of Civilizations

S for d = .7

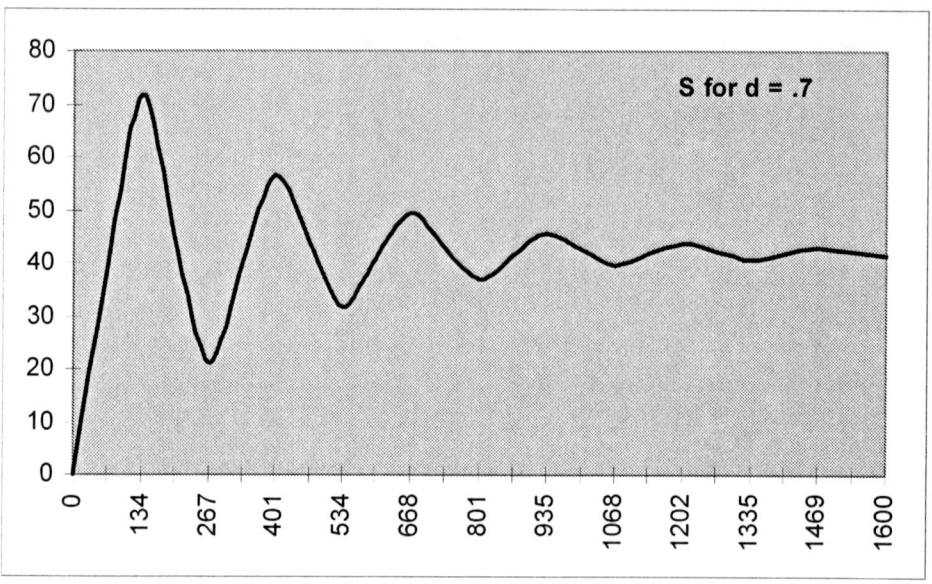

S for d = .75

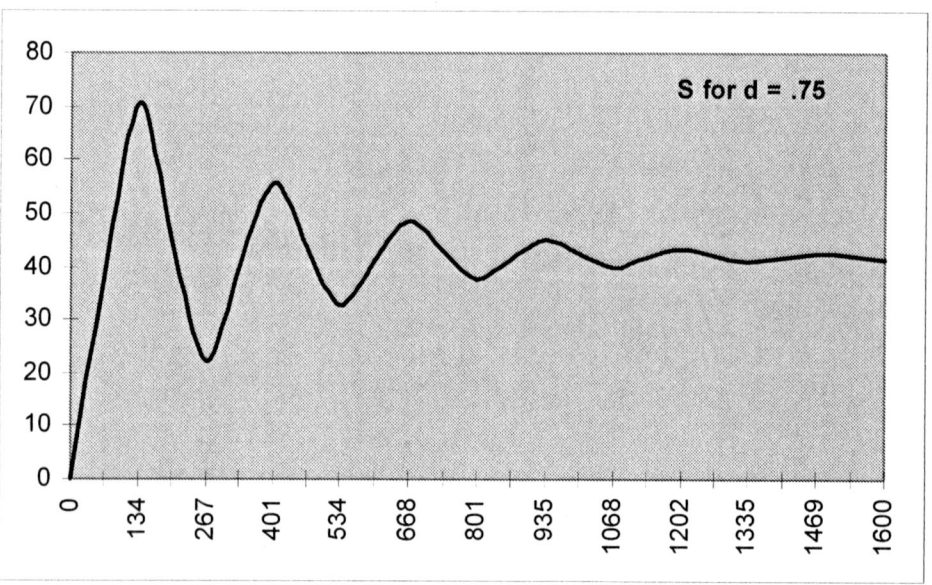

The Life Cycle of Civilizations

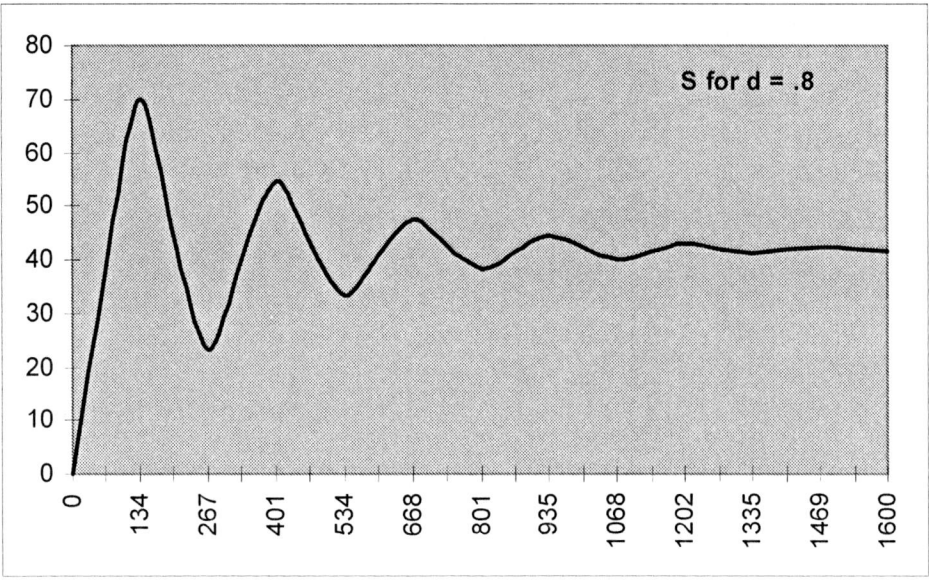

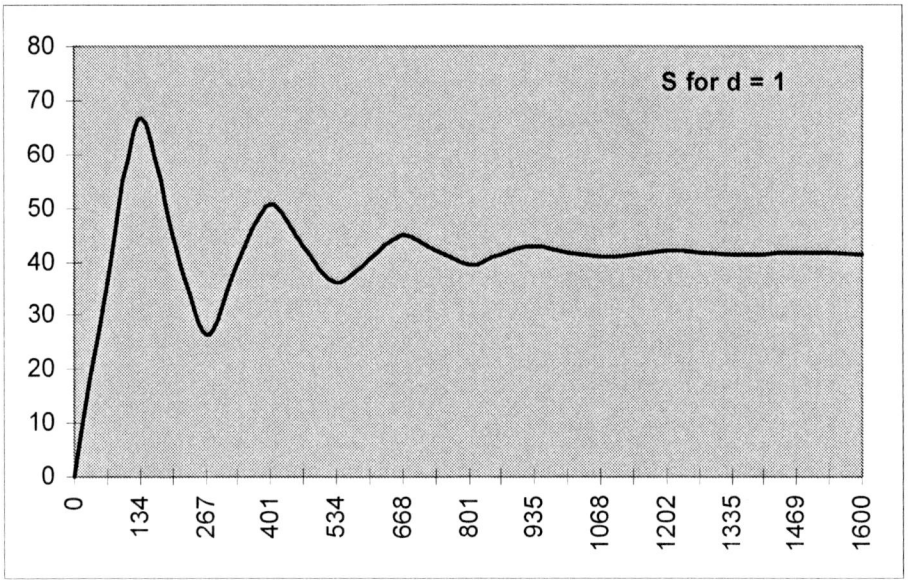

The Life Cycle of Civilizations

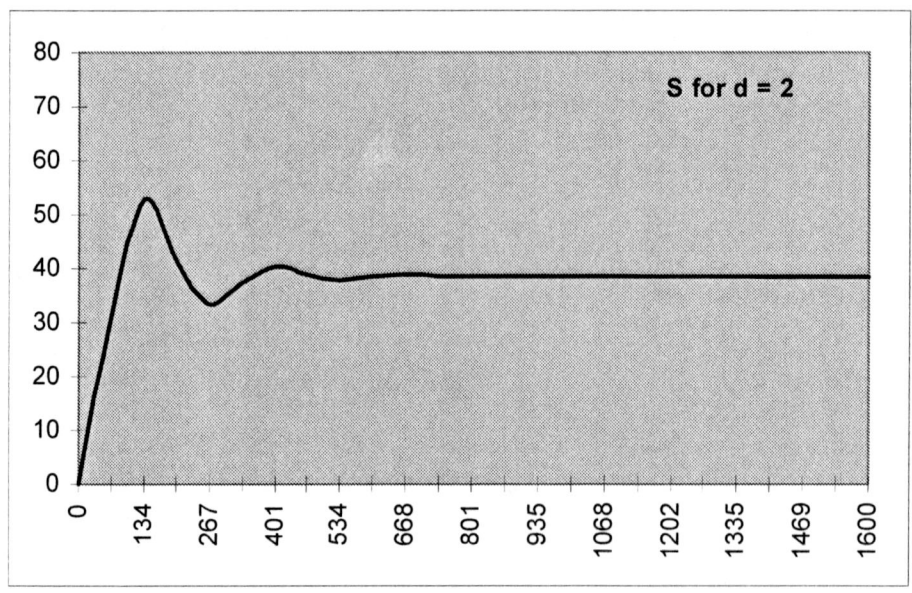

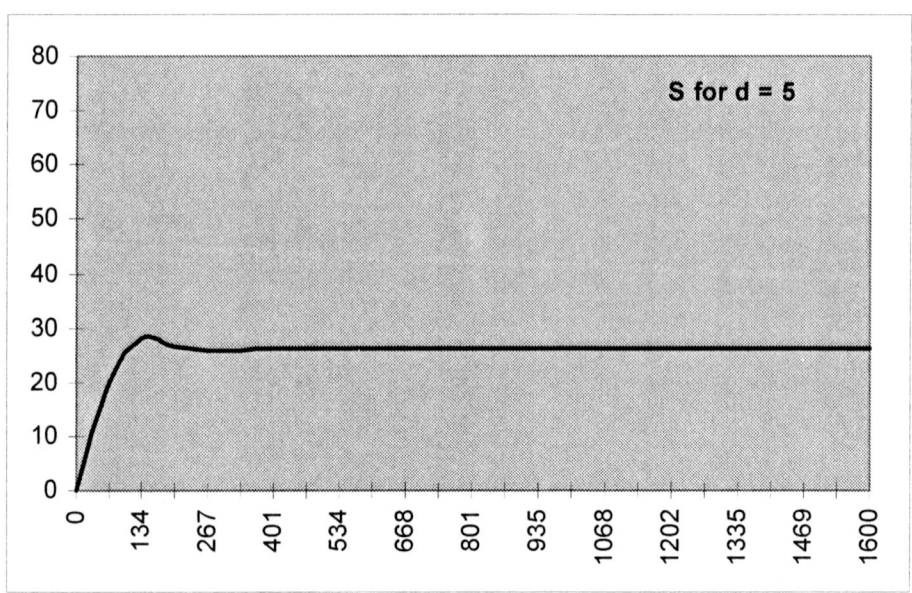

Figure 11. The S societal level curve for various values of d.

It appears that the value of d = 0.75 is a good choice for generating a three and a half beat curve although the d = .7 and d = .8 choices cannot be ruled out. We will take d to be approximately 0.75 in value. As a result the ratio of successive maximums is

$$e^{.75} = 2.117$$

The maximum (peak) of the societal level S declines by roughly a factor of two in each period T of 267 years in the disintegration phase of a civilization. The peak succeeding the previous peak is about half (a factor of .472) as large as the previous peak.

The ratio .472 is remarkably close to the natural logarithm of the well-known asymptotic ratio of Fibonnacci number 1.618: .481 = ln(1.618). If we choose .481 as the ratio of successive peaks then d = 0.731. Fibonnacci numbers play an important role in theories of cyclic movements in the commodities and stock markets. Elliott wave theory is based in part on Fibonnacci numbers. Thus the closeness of values may reflect a deeper, fundamental statistical theory of societies upon which our theory of civilization is ultimately based. We will continue to use d = .75 since it is easy to remember and differs only by about 3% from the Fibonnacci equivalent—an amount that does not significantly affect our comparisons of theory with historical events.

For d = .75 the value of a is

$$a = .00281$$

Since a is about a factor of ten smaller than b the expression for S becomes approximately (with time measured in years):

$$S(t) = [1 - e^{-.00281t}(.12\sin(.0235t) + \cos(.0235t))]/.0235 \quad (20)$$

and the damped harmonic oscillator equation (8) becomes

$$C'' + C'/178 + C/1811 = 0 \quad (21)$$

if time is measured in years. We will call equation (20) with a = .00281 and b = .0235 the *standard curve for S*. A plot of the standard curve for S appears in the next figure.

The Life Cycle of Civilizations

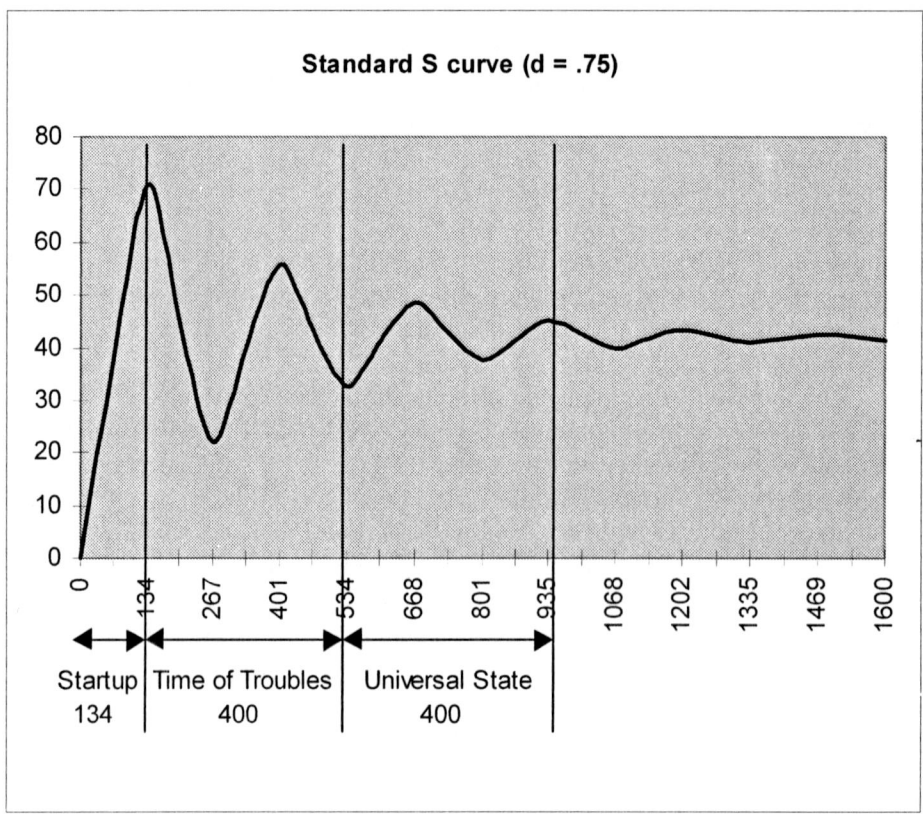

Figure 12. The standard societal level S curve for a civilization.

Toynbee points out that four and a half beat civilizations and other beat pattern civilizations are possible. These civilizations would have other values for d and thus a. For example a four and a half beat pattern appears if d = .6.

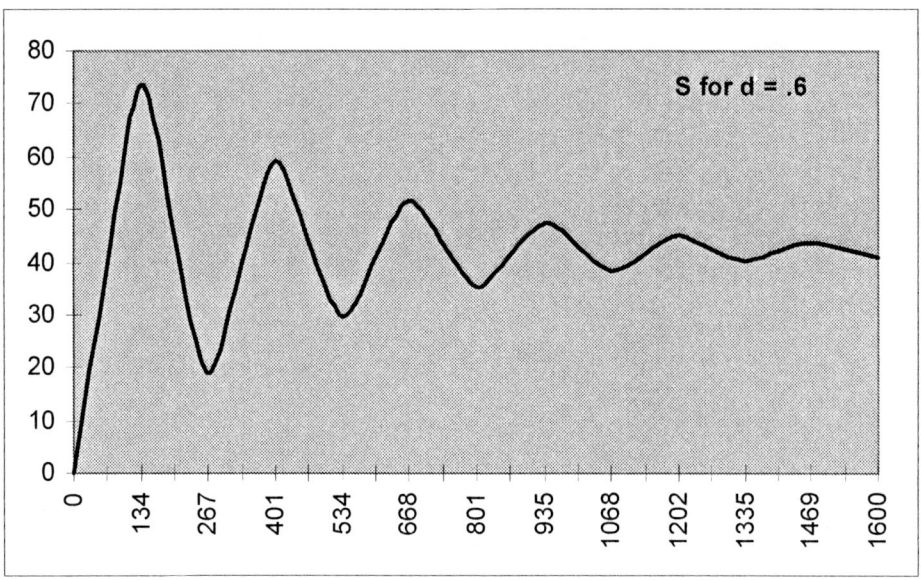

Figure 13. A four and a half beat pattern for a civilization.

Comparison of Theory with Civilizations

The three and a half beat pattern together with the observed periodicity of the societal level of four hundred years pin down the theory for the life cycle of a civilization. Since there is currently no apparent way to experimentally determine the precise numerical value of the societal level of a civilization, the absolute values of the societal levels are not relevant—the *relative* values of societal levels are of interest. They can be compared to historical events to test the theory. Thus we can set the constant c_1, which sets the overall size of the S curve, to one in equation (13).

We will now compare the standard solution given by equation (20) of the basic dynamics of our theory to various civilizations to see if the peaks and valleys of the solutions match the routs and rallies of these civilizations. Historical events are the symptoms of routs and rallies just as chills and fevers are the symptoms of a cold.

If we find that historical events match the peaks and valleys of our S curves then we will have verified the mathematical theory of civilizations. A mathematical theory of civilizations has many implications for the nature of civilizations and, in fact, suggests a new view of the long-term social nature of mankind. We will discuss these issues after comparing the general theory of civilizations with past events in civilizations.

The Life Cycle of Civilizations

The following pages compare equation (20) with the events of the Hellenic, Egyptaic (prior to the Hyksos conquest) and Sinic civilizations. In each case we use the date of the breakdown point to set the time scale. For example, in the case of Hellenic civilization, we assume the Hellenic breakdown at 431 BC corresponds to the breakdown point in the year 133.5 embodied in equation (20). The beginning year of Hellenic civilization (the beginning of the startup phase) is then 564.5 BC.

Mathematically we set the S curves for each civilization in terms of the standard S curve using the breakdown points (minus 133.5 years) to specify the time offset needed for each civilization:

$$S_{Hellenic}(t) = S(t + 564.5)$$
$$S_{Egyptaic}(t) = S(t + 2557.5) \qquad (22)$$
$$S_{Sinic}(t) = S(t + 767.5)$$

with $S(t)$ being the standard curve for S given in equation (20). BC years are treated uniformly as negative numbers throughout.

Thus

$$S_{Hellenic}(-564.5) = 0$$

corresponds to the beginning of Hellenic civilization in 564.5 BC. (*Please note that the theory must use precise numbers since it is mathematical. The interpretation of these numbers is always "plus or minus a generation (roughly thirty years)".*

And

$$S_{Hellenic}(-31)$$

is the societal level at the beginning of the Roman Empire in 31 BC.

The Life Cycle of Civilizations

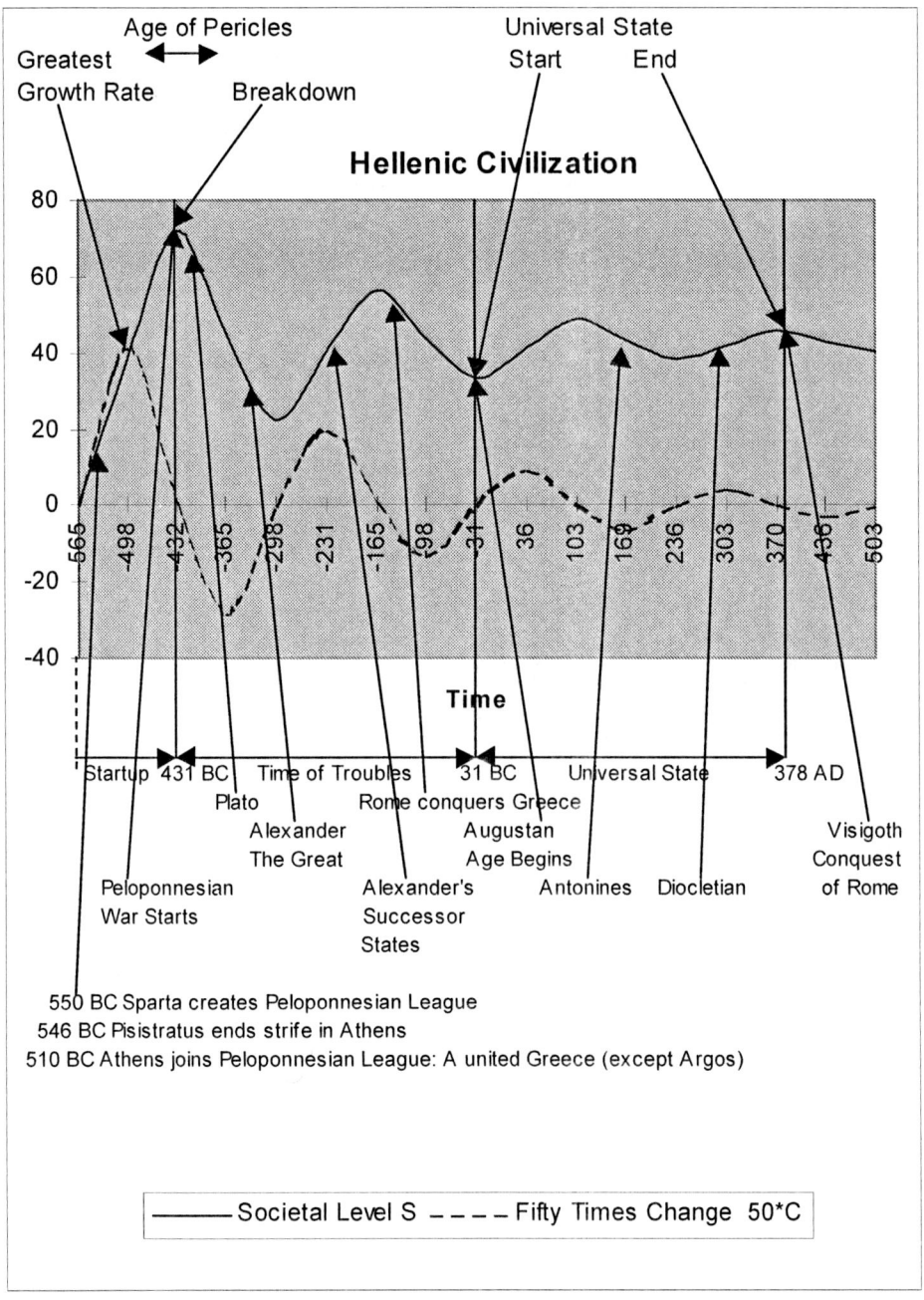

Figure 14. Comparison of Hellenic civilization with the general theory of civilization. The plotted societal level is $S_{Hellenic}(t)$.

61

The Life Cycle of Civilizations

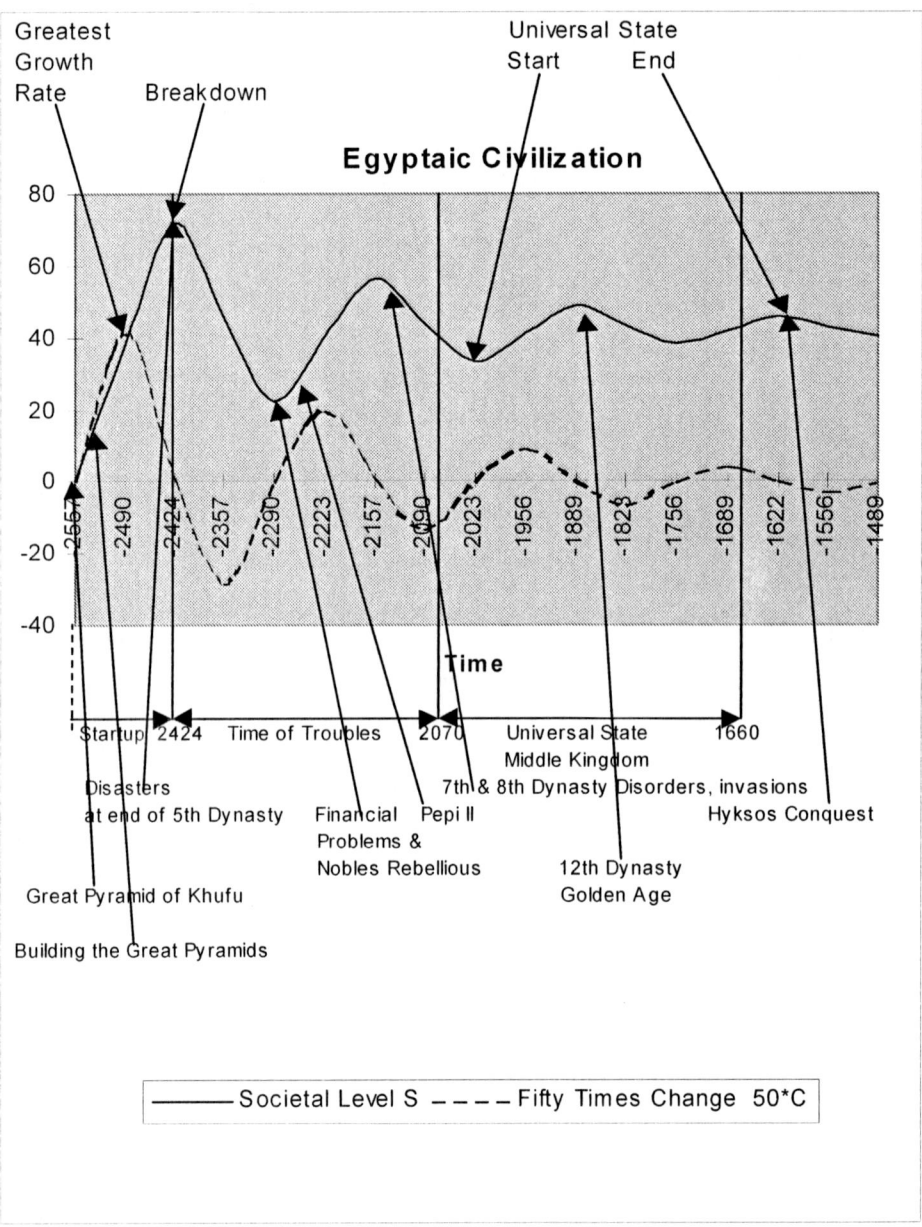

Figure 15. Comparison of Egyptaic civilization (2555 BC to 1660 BC) with general theory of civilization. The plotted societal level is $S_{Egyptaic}(t)$.

The Life Cycle of Civilizations

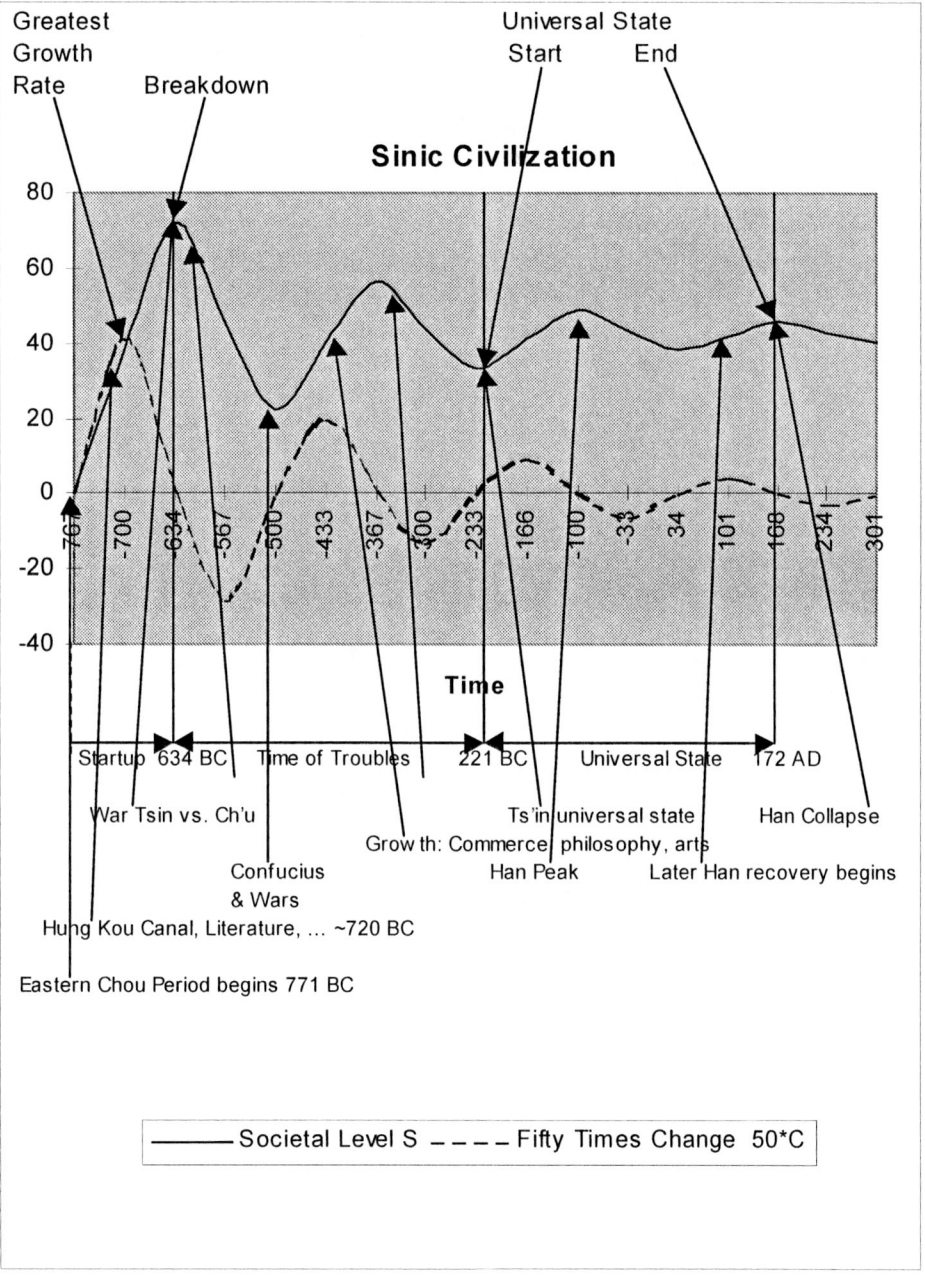

Figure 16. Comparison of Sinic civilization with general theory of civilization. The plotted societal level is $S_{Sinic}(t)$.

The Life Cycle of Civilizations

Comments on the Successful Match with History

The preceding three comparisons of our theory with Hellenic, Egyptaic and Sinic civilizations show that the periodicity in the theory (which reflects the three and a half beat pattern) corresponds to the pattern of events seen in the well documented histories of these civilizations.

The figures plot S versus time measured in years as a solid line. They also plot fifty times the change C (so C will be visible on the scale of S) as a dashed line. Significant times and events are indicated on the plots.

When analyzing the plotted events on the graphs we must remember that events in human history are subject to chance and the vagaries of time so we should not expect exact agreement. However it is clear that a significant correlation exists between the ups and downs of S and historical events.

The three civilizations examined were all first generation civilizations. We will consider other civilizations from the point of view of this theoretical approach in the following chapters. The remainder of this section will develop points related to the preceding figures.

The Initial Growth Spurt of Civilizations – the Startup Phase

An interesting point of these examples is the 133.5 year Startup time period before the breakdown of the civilization. This time period is a period of rapid societal growth in a civilization: the first growth spurt that carries it to the heights. Note the middle of this period corresponds to the maximum in the growth rate C.

Remarkably we find the Age of the Great Pyramids in the Startup period in Egyptian history. In Sinic civilization we find the first great canal, the Hung Kou (big ditch) Canal and great developments in literature and the arts in the Startup period. In Hellenic civilization we find major developments including the unification of almost all of Greece in the Peloponnesian League, the development of the Athenian economy (cash crops and international commerce), and the end to Athenian civil strife by Pisistratus—all in the Startup period. Thus our theory accounts for the almost miraculous "hundred year" growth spurts seen at the takeoff points of civilizations. In particular it provides a "reason" why the pyramid age (the age when the three great pyramids were built) lasted about a hundred years. We attribute the limited time frame to the pattern of development of civilizations based on human nature.

We will call this phase of initial rapid growth of civilizations the Startup phase in the following chapters.

We note in passing that Toynbee states that he cannot see a pattern in the growth phase of a civilization (unlike the disintegration phase in which he discerns the three and a half beat pattern). We suggest the shortness of the growth phase is the source of his difficulty. Toynbee thought the growth phase lasted for centuries when in actuality it is only 134 years. The years prior to a Startup phase contain the random movements of a prior society with little or no net growth, and thus no discernible structure.

The Value of S

The value of S in itself is not meaningful at the present time. The relative values of S at different times are significant in the sense that they indicate the relative societal levels at those times.

Some may object that the absolute value of S should be made meaningful. Unfortunately we do not know how to quantify the components of the societal level. A similar situation exists in other social science areas such as economics.[6]

Why a 267 Year Period?

The 267 year period which seems to be a general feature of civilizations is remarkable for several reasons. First, if it is universal for all civilizations it must be an inherent feature of civilizations and not the result of external events. Secondly, if it is an inherent feature of all civilizations it must reflect an inherent long-term feature of the social makeup of mankind.

It appears that this long-term social feature of mankind may be based on the observation that it takes about four generations to accomplish a significant social change. In a cyclic situation it would take four generations to go from the top to the bottom of a cycle (a rout) and another four generations to reach the top again (a rally). If the average generation is 33.375 years (a not unreasonable value) then the eight generations could total to 267 years which is roughly the average observed time T from peak to peak used in our theory.

Relation of the End of a Civilization to its Beginning

When we examine the preceding figures we see that the societal level at the end of a civilization's life cycle is approximately equal to the societal level at the time of maximal growth. If a is much smaller than b as it is in our case then by equation (14)

$$S(t, r) \rightarrow c_1/b \qquad (23)$$

---

[6] See for example Copeland, T. and Weston, J. F., *Financial Theory and Corporate Policy* (Addison-Wesley, Reading, MA, 1979) or Brealey, R. and Myers, S., *Principles of Corporate Finance* (McGraw-Hill, New York, 1981).

as t gets very large. At the first maximum of C where $C' = 0$ we find that S has about the same value:

$$S(t, r) \approx c_1/b \qquad (24)$$

if a is much less than b. Thus the societal level at the period of maximal growth is approximately the same as at the end of the civilization. The difference is that the civilization is rapidly growing at the point of maximal growth while it is essentially static at the end of the civilization's disintegration. Thus *the theory implies that the cumulative growth of a civilization is a function of the beginnings of the civilization as Spengler, among others, has suggested.* "Our beginnings know our ends."

If we look at a civilization at the end of its disintegration there is a net gain. The people of the civilization have their accumulated culture and world-view. Yet the civilization is in disarray as it was near its beginning while it was still developing societally.

Additional Comments

The breakdown of a civilization takes place at the peak of its societal level when it begins a rout that is followed by a number of rally and rout cycles. Eventually the cycles of rallies and routs dissipates as the civilization reaches the final stages of disintegration.

5. Arrested Civilizations

Arrested Civilizations

In some cases the (usually physical) severity of an environment may absorb all the energies of a growing civilization causing its growth to end—thus producing a static society. This type of civilization is called an *arrested* civilization. Some examples of arrested civilizations are the Eskimo, the Nomads, and the Polynesian civilizations.

Arrested civilizations can be accommodated in our theory of civilizations if the constant r (see equations (7) and (8)) specifying the resistance to an increasing rate of change becomes large. The resistance r in this case reflects in large part the effect of the environment in retarding change.

The resistance r is related to the parameter d through equation (18). If we set d to a large value we can obtain a curve for the societal level with the features expected of an arrested civilization: an initial growth spurt to adapt to a harsh environment followed by a period of no growth – a petrified state of civilization. We therefore set the parameter d to a representative value of 5 and obtain the following curve for S as a function of time.

From Fig. 17 we note that the arrested civilization goes through a period of growth to adapt to the environment. After adaptation is achieved the civilization finds the continuing demands imposed by the adaptation prevents it from further growth. The civilization then enters a static condition that we call petrified. The achievement of a successful adaptation may lead to a temporary high as the figure shows followed by a retreat to a lower petrified level.

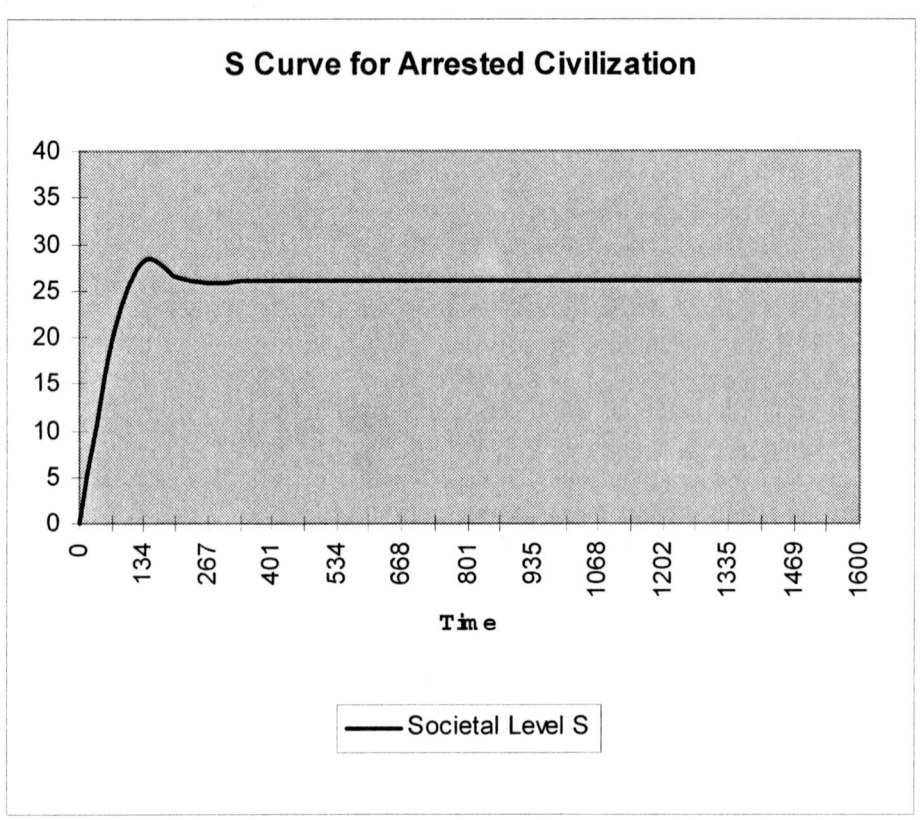

Figure 17. Graph of societal level for an arrested civilization with d = 5.

The Life Cycle of Civilizations

Exhibit 13. Eskimos enjoying the summer in Greenland. Their summer tent is called a toupik.

6. Successive Civilizations

Successive Isolated Civilizations

We have successfully applied our theory to civilizations lasting about a thousand years: the Hellenic, Egyptaic and Sinic civilizations. All of these civilizations were followed by successor civilizations in the same geographic area that included the descendants of the populations of these civilizations.

Can we establish a longer term theory that encompasses both civilizations and their successors? Toynbee calls civilizations having a predecessor-successor relationship *affiliated civilizations*.

As a first step in this direction we will look at Egyptaic civilization. Egyptaic civilization can be viewed can be viewed as either two phases of one civilization or as two separate but almost identical civilizations culturally with a different dynamical evolution. The Egyptaic civilization that we considered in a preceding chapter concluded with the Hyksos conquest of Egypt around 1600 BC. After a short time the Egyptians successfully expelled the Hyksos and formed the New Kingdom, which lasted for approximately 300 years.

This second phase of Egyptian civilization was culturally very similar to the latter parts of the first phase of Egyptian civilization before the Hyksos Conquest. However the second phase was static—Toynbee called it *petrified*—there was no societal growth to speak of. It had the static features that we have ascribed to an arrested civilization in the preceding chapter. Perhaps it looked to the past. A wall graffiti on an old temple dating back to the age of the pyramids by an Egyptian of this phase states in effect, "They sure knew how to build things back then!"

Perhaps the threat of foreign invasions, and the many invasions that did take place, absorbed all the resources of the second phase of Egyptaic civilization. In any case we have two phases of Egyptian civilization in which the first phase had $d = .75$, and the second phase had a much larger value for d, perhaps $d = 5$, reflecting a petrified civilization.

The Life Cycle of Civilizations

Exhibit 14. Passageway to the burial chamber of a New Kingdom Pharaoh in the Valley of the Kings in Egypt.

The change from a three and a half beat civilization to a petrified civilization was one of the effects of the Hyksos conquest. Another effect was the appearance of a new Egyptian universal state after the expulsion of the Hyksos. The Hyksos conquest had a major effect on subsequent Egyptian civilization.

The Life Cycle of Civilizations

Exhibit 15. Burial chamber of a New Kingdom Pharaoh in the Valley of the Kings in Egypt. A question that has apparently not been addressed: How did the workers who created the magnificent wall paintings in tombs and pyramids obtain light with which to see? Torches would have left smudges on the walls and ceilings – not to mention the effect of fumes in these poorly ventilated chambers. One possible answer is a series of mirrors that reflected light down into the chambers and thence onto the wall or ceiling being painted.

Returning to our mechanistic theory of civilization (equations (2) and (6)) we can use an external force F_{ext} to simulate the hammer blow to Egyptaic civilization delivered by the Hyksos. We do not know the exact mathematical form of this force. But it appears reasonable to approximate this force with a Dirac delta-function. A Dirac delta-function can be viewed as a hammer blow of infinite strength at precisely one moment of time. It corresponds to our intuitive idea of a hammer blow. One advantage of a Dirac delta-function force is that it leads to tractable mathematical results.

The Life Cycle of Civilizations

Dirac Delta-Function Hammer Blow to a Civilization

A Dirac delta-function is a somewhat bizarre function that is widely used in quantum Physics. This function has the value zero everywhere except at one point where it has an infinite value:

$$\delta(x - y) = 0 \quad \text{if } x \neq y$$
$$\delta(x - y) = \infty \quad \text{if } x = y \tag{25}$$

where the symbol ∞ represents infinite.

Step Function

It will also be useful to use another function called the *step function*. The step function normally is symbolized by the Greek letter theta and has the value zero when its argument (the quantity in parentheses) is less than or equal to zero. It has the value one if its argument is positive. This function is defined by

$$\theta(x - y) = 0 \quad \text{if } x \leq y$$
$$\theta(x - y) = 1 \quad \text{if } x > y \tag{26}$$

The Force of the Hyksos Conquest

We will assume that the Hyksos hammer blow to Egyptaic civilization can be represented by the external force terms:

$$F_{ext} = f\,\delta(t + 1580) - 5.67rC'\theta(t + 1580) \tag{27}$$

where f is a constant and the additional term represents the change in the resistance after the Hyksos expulsion in 1580.

The first term in equation (27) represents the hammer blow delivered by the Hyksos. This term starts the civilization oscillating again just as pushing a bell clapper starts a bell tolling. The additional step function term increases the resistance after the Hyksos expulsion to the equivalent of d = 5. (Note BC years are treated as negative numbers. Thus 2000 BC is –2000.) Increasing the resistance is equivalent to lowering a bell into a tub of oil after starting the bell clapper ringing. The clapper and the civilization's oscillations come to a stop rather more quickly due to the increased friction.

The resulting differential equation for the change C is:

The Life Cycle of Civilizations

$$mC'' + rC' + sC = f\,\delta(t + 1580) - 5.67rC'\theta(t + 1580) \quad (28)$$

Equation (28) is an inhomogeneous differential equation with a solution that leads to the following expression for the total societal level S_{Egypt}:

$$S_{Egypt} = S(t + 2557.5, r) + g\,\theta(t + 1580)\,S(t + 1580, 6.67r) \quad (29)$$

where r is specified by d = .75 and where

$$g = f/mb \quad (30)$$

The value of the constant f (and thus g) is difficult to specify based on rational grounds. However based on the case of Egyptaic civilization, and the other cases studied later, it seemed reasonable to choose

$$g = 1/5 \quad (31)$$

This value of g makes the peak following the hammer blow roughly the same height as the peak immediately preceding the hammer blow. As Toynbee observes a brutal conquest often causes a civilization to respond by recovering to its previous height (with a universal state) and prolonging its existence.

The graph of equation (29) with g = .2 is displayed in the next figure together with the events associated with the peaks and valleys of the curve. There appears to be a reasonably close agreement between the curve and historic events occurring over a 2600 year period.

The Life Cycle of Civilizations

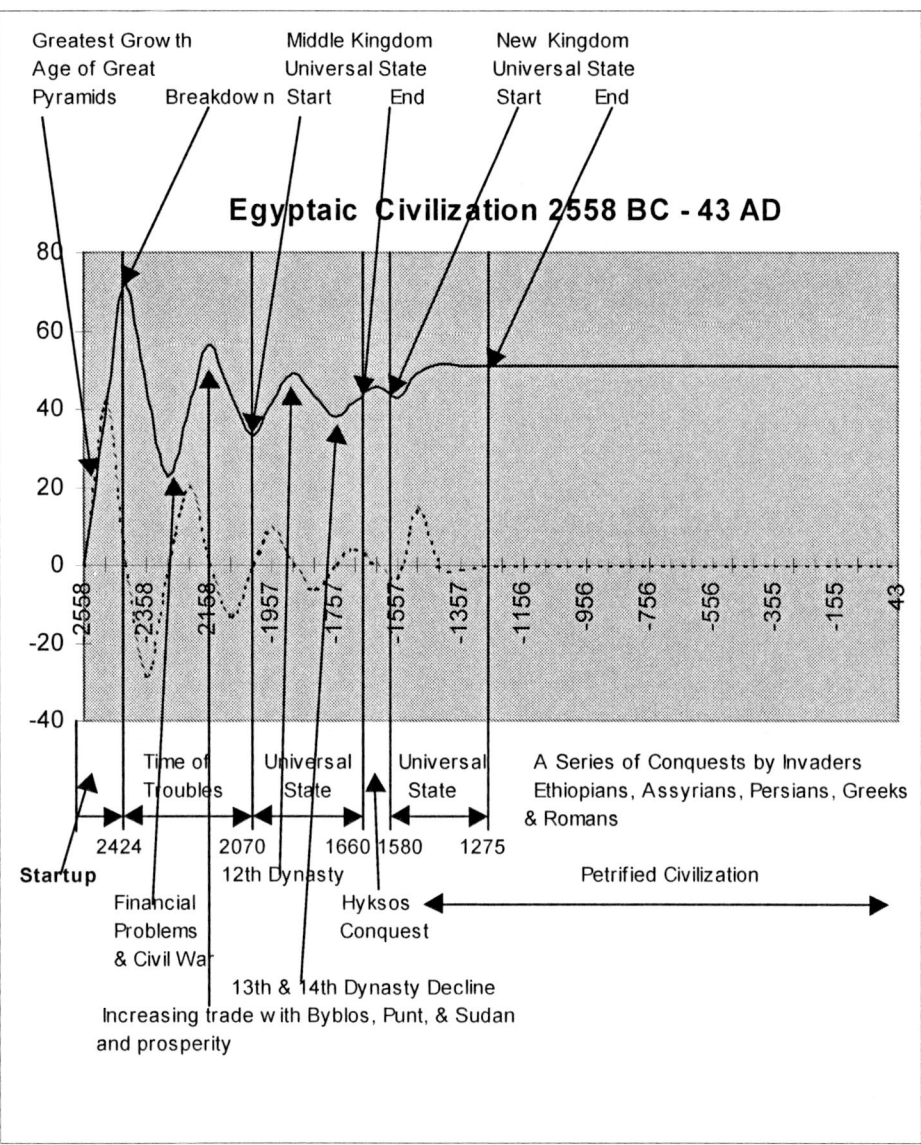

Figure 18. The societal level S and the historical events of the successive Egyptaic civilization.

Fig. 18 shows the changes of S_{Egypt} with time and reveals the effects of the Hyksos conquest. The reaction that expelled the Hyksos produced a revived but petrified universal state. The petrified condition of the revived Egyptaic civilization is shown by the lack of change in the societal level after the creation of the New Kingdom. The period after the New Kingdom is marked with a series of conquests by foreign states that had little impact on Egyptian society as a whole although they did represent changes at the top of the governmental hierarchy. In this period of Egyptian society the recipient of the tribute (taxes) was not a significant factor in the societal level of a petrified static society.

Japanese Civilizations

We will next look at the civilizations of Japan. Japan, like Egypt, developed a unique and distinctive civilization. A Far Eastern civilization began in Japan at some point after 500 AD. As we shall see it appears that it was preceded by an earlier civilization that does not seem to have been noted by Toynbee or others.

Although Japan is separated from the Asiatic mainland it has a long history of exchanges with Korea and China. The Japanese people migrated to Japan from the Asiatic mainland primarily in the period from 250 BC to 250 AD. Consequently Japanese culture has been influenced by other cultures and civilizations to a much greater degree than Egyptian culture.

In our examination of Japanese history there appears to be three Startup phases: one at approximately 58 BC, one at approximately 1048 AD and one at 1868 AD. The first startup took place when a sufficiently large group of Japanese migrants assembled and began the rapid development of the first Japanese civilization. The second startup occurred in 1048 AD when the Minamoto clan joined forces with the Fujiwara clan causing a major reorganization of Japanese society. The third startup occurred in 1868 when the American Navy opened Japan with a shocking display of modern technology. This display caused a profound change in Japan that was signaled by the Meiji Restoration.

In one generation Japan leaped from a "medieval culture" to an industrialized nation able to defeat a European power (Russia) and from a largely illiterate nation to a nation with a 100% literacy rate. Because of these three startups we will introduce two "hammer blow" Dirac delta function forces to simulate the second and third startups.

Since none of these Japanese civilizations were petrified we will take r to have the value corresponding to d = .75 for the entire history of Japan. As a result the total force on Japanese civilizations is:

$$F_{Japan} = F_0 + f_1 \delta(t - 1048) + f_2 \delta(t - 1868) \quad (32)$$

where f_1 and f_2 are constants, and F_0 is given by equation (7).

The Life Cycle of Civilizations

Exhibit 16. Osaka, Japan street scene in 1890.

The total force specified in equation (32) results in an inhomogeneous differential equation using Newton's force law. The solution leads to the following expression for the total societal level S_{Japan}:

$$S_{Japan} = S(t + 58) + g_1 \theta(t - 1048)S(t - 1048) + \\ + g_2 \theta(t - 1868)S(t - 1868) \qquad (33)$$

where $S(t)$ is specified by equation (20) and where

The Life Cycle of Civilizations

$$g_1 = f_1/mb \qquad (34)$$
$$g_2 = f_2/mb \qquad (35)$$

The value of the constants f_1 and f_2 (and thus g_1 and g_2) are difficult to specify based on rational grounds. Following the choice in the case of Egyptaic civilization we will set

$$g_1 = g_2 = 1/5 \qquad (36)$$

These values of g_1 and g_2 makes the peak following a hammer blow roughly the same height as the peak immediately preceding the hammer blow.

The graph of equation (33) is plotted in the next figure. The startup at 1048 was caused by an internal event and the pattern generated by it begins with a time of troubles followed by a universal state. The startup in 1868 was caused by an external force—the opening of Japan by the American Navy. The ensuing pattern begins with a universal state, the Meiji Restoration as did the Egyptaic civilization after the Hyksos conquest.

The ups and downs of S_{Japan} correlate well with important events in Japanese history. In particular the events in the early period up to 1048 seem to correlate well with S_{Japan}. The appearance of the "good emperor" Nintoku at a peak and the "bad emperors" Yuryaku and Buretsu at a low point are noteworthy. Another peak corresponds to the renowned Prince Shotoku. The pattern we see in early Japanese history suggests Japan had a civilization of the standard pattern in that period. We will call this civilization the Early Japanese civilization.

The events of the Far Eastern civilization (Japanese branch) also show a strong correlation with the curve of S_{Japan}.

The projected ending of the 1868 startup in 2002 seems to correlate with the difficulties that Japan has experienced since the late 1980's. Perhaps Japan will have an economic or political event of great significance somewhere around 2002. Recent Japanese problems may be indicating a coming crisis that could constitute a breakdown. Japan is projected to enter a growth phase again in 2136.

The Life Cycle of Civilizations

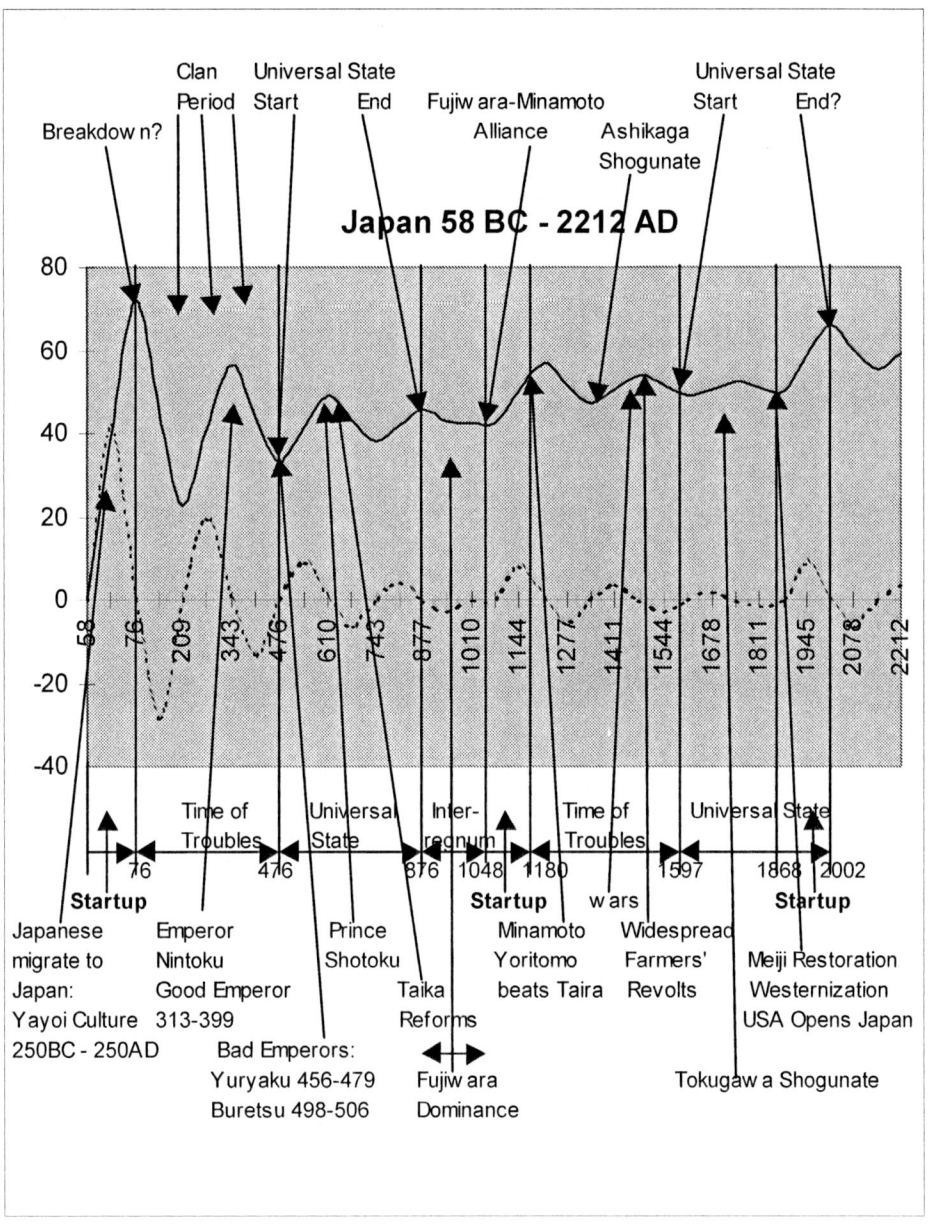

Figure 19. Early Japanese civilization and Far Eastern (Japan) civilization.

7. The Continuity of Civilizations

Continuity of Consecutive Civilizations

The continuity that we have observed between successive civilizations in Egypt and Japan raises the question whether civilizations consecutively occupying the same "turf" may have a continuity beyond the standard S curve that we have found for individual civilizations. In most cases the people of successive civilizations are the same people on the same land. This fact argues for continuity between successive civilizations. The continuity will, of course, be affected by external events such as invasions, major natural events, and conquests by "barbarians."

We will see that we can develop a societal curve for the entire recorded history of large regions with a significantly large permanent population such as China, India, the Middle East, Japan and Europe (including North America). There is a remarkable correlation between historical events, and the peaks and valleys of S for all known civilizations (together with their successor civilizations) if we make the following choices of parameters:

1. The period T of the cycle is 267 years.

2. Set $d = .75$ for all civilizations except petrified civilizations where $d = 5$.

3. Set g for all successor civilizations to 0.2.

4. Set the initial startup times based on the historical events of the civilizations realizing that the events producing a startup are often external and unpredictable. The initial startup at the beginning of a civilization is set by the breakdown: the startup is 133.5 years before the breakdown. The breakdown is followed by a time of troubles.

5. Subsequent startups in a civilization or its successor civilization are set by historical events. If a foreign conquest takes place the startup is at the point where the conqueror is expelled. In this case the civilization normally reacts by creating a universal state followed by a time of troubles. If the startup is the result of internal events in a civilization then the startup is followed by a breakdown (133.5 years later), a time of troubles, and then a universal state.

The cases of continuity of initial and successor civilizations located in the same geographical region that we will consider in this chapter are:

- Sinic and Far Eastern (China)
- Hellenic and Western
- Hellenic and Orthodox Christian (main body)
- Hellenic and Orthodox Christian (Russian branch)
- Syriac and Arab Islamic
- Syriac and Iranian Islamic
- Indic and Hindu

We note that we have examined the civilizations in Egypt and Japan in the preceding chapter. Thus we will have examined almost all civilizations outside of the Americas after viewing the cases in this chapter. In chapter 16 we will apply our theory to the following civilizations:

- Mayan – standard S curve with an initial startup in 223 BC, and continuing to 2447 AD based on a continuing culture with a Western overlay which has been there until the present.
- Andean – standard S curve with a startup in 912 AD and continuing to 2447 AD based on a continuing culture with a Western overlay that has been there until the present.
- Minoan – standard S curve with a startup in 2424 BC and a cutoff to zero in 757 BC.
- Sumeric-Babylonian - standard S curve with a startup in 2824 BC and a cutoff to zero in 156 BC.
- Hittite - standard S curve with a startup in 1556 BC and a cutoff to zero in 1088 BC.

in order to compute the progress of mankind as measured by the cumulative impact of civilizations.

The Life Cycle of Civilizations

Figure 20 indicates the regions where the six cases that we will examine in this chapter are located. These cases represent the major civilizations of mankind and are located throughout the Eurasian land mass and Africa.

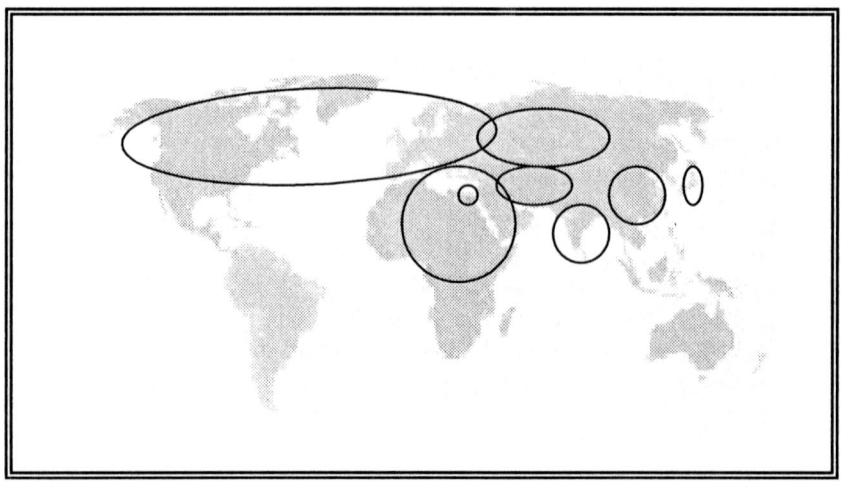

Figure 20. The regions of successive civilizations considered.

Sinic and Far Eastern (China) Civilizations

China, and some surrounding territory, were the seat of the Sinic civilization and its successor, the mainland Far Eastern civilization.

Sinic civilization had its startup in 768 BC based on a breakdown date of 634 BC advocated by Toynbee and others. This civilization includes Eastern Chou, Ch'in, Han and Later Han Dynasties. It lasted until approximately 172 AD.

Around 172 AD, the Later Han Dynasty started to collapse due to conflicts in the court and among the nobility and military. The resulting social chaos generated an internal startup that peaked (breakdown point) with the short-lived reunification of the empire by the Tsin (265-317). Since the source of the collapse was internal the period following was a time of troubles and then a universal state.

The period from 172 AD to 878 AD contains a startup, a time of troubles and a universal state. This pattern of historical events suggest that we classify this period as a civilization. We will call this civilization New Sinic civilization. It contains the Sui and T'ang Dynasties.

The Life Cycle of Civilizations

In 878 the universal state of the T'ang was essentially ended. China plunged into a short period of anarchy and chaos lasting about eighty years. This period of internal chaos generated another startup that we place at 878 with an ensuing time of troubles lasting until 1280. The societal peak of this period was the Sung dynasty with a peak around 1078 when K'ai-feng the capitol city was rebuilt. Other major cities (with populations over 1,000,000) were built during this period including Soochow, Huchow, Hangchow and Canton. The period from 878 to 1853 is identified as Far Eastern civilization (main body) by Toynbee.

A third startup in 1368 was generated by the preceding Mongol conquest. As in the case of Egypt and the Hyksos the reaction to the foreign conquest was the creation of a universal state with civilization reverting to a static state of petrifaction.

Exhibit 17. A footbridge in the Empress' Palace (nineteenth century) Beijing, China.

The Life Cycle of Civilizations

Exhibit 18. The Imperial Ancestral Temple – 19th Century Beijing, China.

The following figure shows the curve of societal level S (and fifty times the change C) based on the three startups. The force used to generate C and S is:

$$F_{China} = F_0 - 5.67rC'\theta(t - 1368) + f_1 \delta(t - 172) + f_2 \delta(t - 878) + \\ + f_3 \delta(t - 1368) \quad (37)$$

where f_1, f_2 and f_3 are constants, and F_0 is given by equation (7).

The total force specified in equation (37) results in an inhomogeneous differential equation using Newton's force law. The solution leads to the following expression for the total societal level S_{China}:

$$S_{China} = S(t + 768, r) + g_1 \theta(t - 172)S(t - 172, r) + \\ + g_2 \theta(t - 878)S(t - 878, r) + \\ + g_3 \theta(t - 1368) S(t - 1368, 6.67r) \quad (38)$$

where $S(t, r)$ is specified by equation (13), r is specified by $d = .75$ and where

$$g_1 = f_1/mb \quad (39)$$

$$g_2 = f_2/mb \quad (40)$$

$$g_3 = f_3/mb \quad (41)$$

The value of the constants: f_1, f_2 and f_3 (and thus g_1, g_2 and g_3) are specified as previously. Following the choice in the cases of the Egyptaic and Japanese civilizations we will set

$$g_1 = g_2 = g_3 = 1/5 \quad (42)$$

The plot of S_{China} in the following figure shows a close correlation between the shape of the curve and significant events in Chinese history.

The Life Cycle of Civilizations

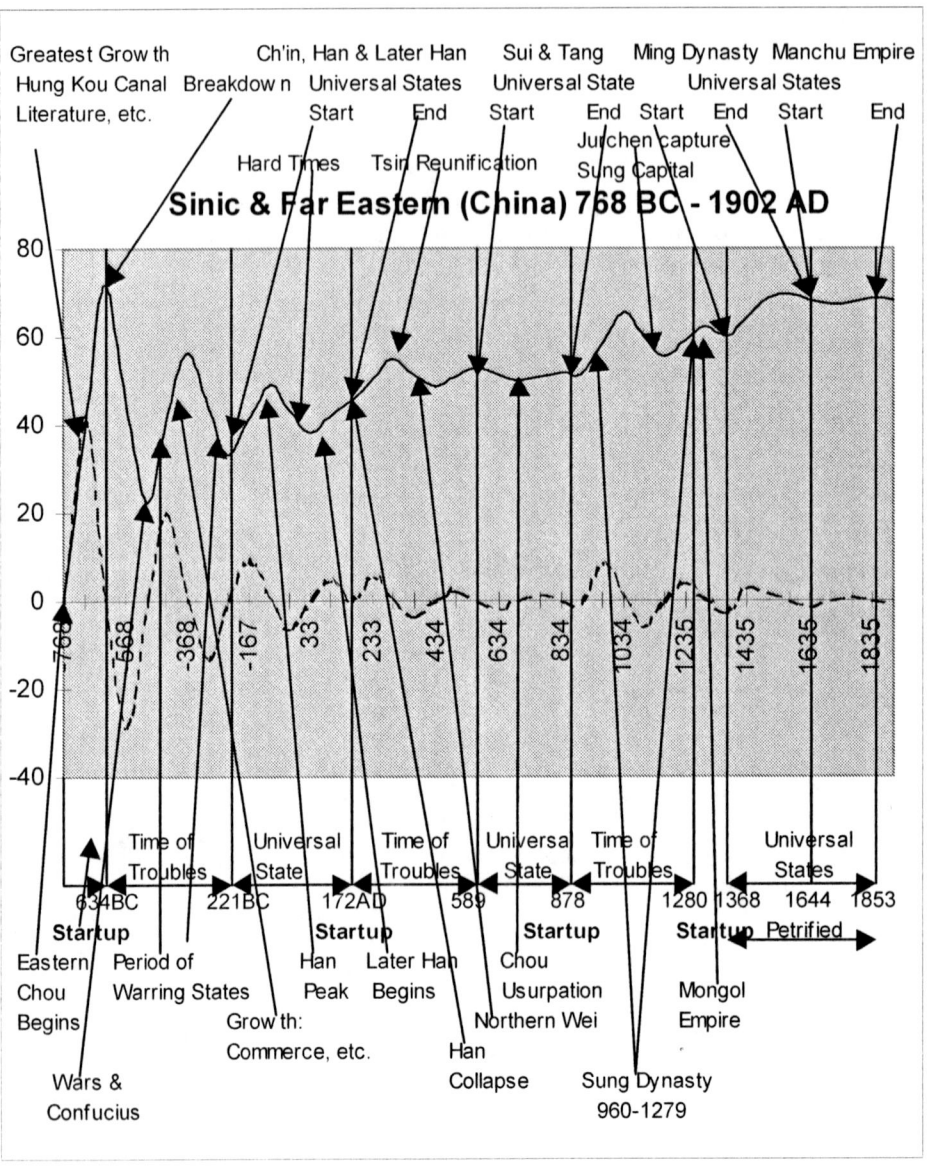

Figure 21. The pattern of Sinic, New Sinic, and Far Eastern civilizations.

Hellenic and Western Civilizations

Hellenic civilization is the parent of Western civilization. Hellenic civilization began in Greece and expanded throughout the Middle East and Europe due to the Greek Diaspora, the conquests of Alexander the Great, and the growth of the Roman Empire. Western civilization arose from the ashes of Hellenic civilization after the Dark Ages.

Exhibit 19. Cologne Cathedral. Perhaps the finest example of Gothic architecture.

The Life Cycle of Civilizations

In an earlier section we saw how our theory described the peaks and valleys of Hellenic civilization. We now extend the theory to encompass both Hellenic and Western civilization. We will then compare our extended theory with the historical events of these civilizations from 565 BC to modern times showing the continuity between them.

The initial startup of Hellenic civilization is taken to be 565 BC based on a breakdown occurring in 431 BC with the start of the Peloponnesian War.

A second startup occurred in 717 AD when Pepin the Short (father of Charlemagne) became King of the Franks marking the ending of the Dark Ages in Europe. The Carolingian Renaissance that developed after Charlemagne established his empire, together with other signs of revival, showed a major upswing in Western civilization was beginning.

A third startup occurred in 1781 due to the democratic explosion in the Western political scene delivered by the French Enlightenment and the success of the American Revolution. These events led to the French Revolution and the spread of liberal democratic ideas throughout Europe. The flowering of democratic thought provided the soil for the growth of the Industrial Revolution by opening men's minds to new ideas and promoting a sense of progress.

The choice of 1781 for the startup is based in part on the events of the American Revolution but more importantly on the breakdown in Western civilization that occurred 133.5 years later in 1914 with the start of World War I. Western civilization was largely at peace during much of the nineteenth century and a feeling of imminent universal peace was a common theme at the end of the nineteenth century. World War I destroyed the harmony of Europe and ushered in an age that can only be described as a time of troubles.

The year 1781 appears to be a reasonable choice for the startup since the American Revolution was in full swing at that point. Since it embodied the ideas of liberty, nationalism and democracy that were the rallying point of the French Enlightenment and European liberalism the American Revolution's success showed that ideas of liberty could be taken from the drawing rooms into the streets. The French Revolution that followed shortly thereafter and the sweep of its ideas across Europe in the wake of the Napoleonic conquests created a milieu in which the Industrial Revolution could flourish together with an upsurge in the rights of the working classes and a rise in nationalistic feelings. In turn the development of the ideas of liberty, democracy and nationalism eventually led to Sarajevo (an assassination by a Serbian nationalist) and World War I as well as the concept of the total war of populations.

The Life Cycle of Civilizations

Exhibit 20. Bed chamber of Catherine de Medicis at the palace of Fontainebleau, France.

Fig. 22 shows the curve of societal level S (and fifty times the change C) based on these three startups. The force used to generate C and S is:

$$F_{West} = F_0 + f_1 \delta(t - 717) + f_2 \delta(t - 1781) \qquad (43)$$

where f_1, and f_2 are constants, and F_0 is given by equation (7).

The total force specified in equation (43) results in an inhomogeneous differential equation using Newton's force law. The solution leads to the following expression for the total societal level S_{West}:

$$S_{West} = S(t + 565) + g_1 \theta(t - 717) S(t - 717) + g_2 \theta(t - 1781) S(t - 1781) \qquad (44)$$

where $S(t)$ is the standard societal curve (equation (20)) and where

$$g_1 = f_1/mb \qquad (45)$$

$$g_2 = f_2/mb \qquad (46)$$

Again we will set

$$g_1 = g_2 = 1/5 \qquad (47)$$

The plot of S_{West} in the following figure shows a close correlation between the shape of the curve and significant events in Hellenic and Western civilization.

Toynbee views Western civilization as having started before 700 AD and as having a time of troubles between roughly 1128 and 1526 for the "Western carapace" (part of Western civilization) against the Osmanli (Turk) onslaughts; and between 1378 and 1797 for the part of Western civilization derived from the "medieval cosmos of city-states".

In our view the pattern of events and our theory suggest a somewhat different picture. We see a Western civilization starting with the Carolingian revival in 717 with a subsequent time of troubles, and with a universal state in the Republica Christiana between 1250 and 1650. In 1781 we see the beginning of a new civilization that we have called Technic civilization.

Technic civilization appears to be in a time of troubles until 2314. The current societal level is predicted to decline until 2048AD when an upswing is expected. The difficulties in Technic civilization that are emerging at the time of this writing may therefore not disappear as quickly as many may hope. A universal state is predicted to appear around 2314. This state will probably include Europe and North America.

The Life Cycle of Civilizations

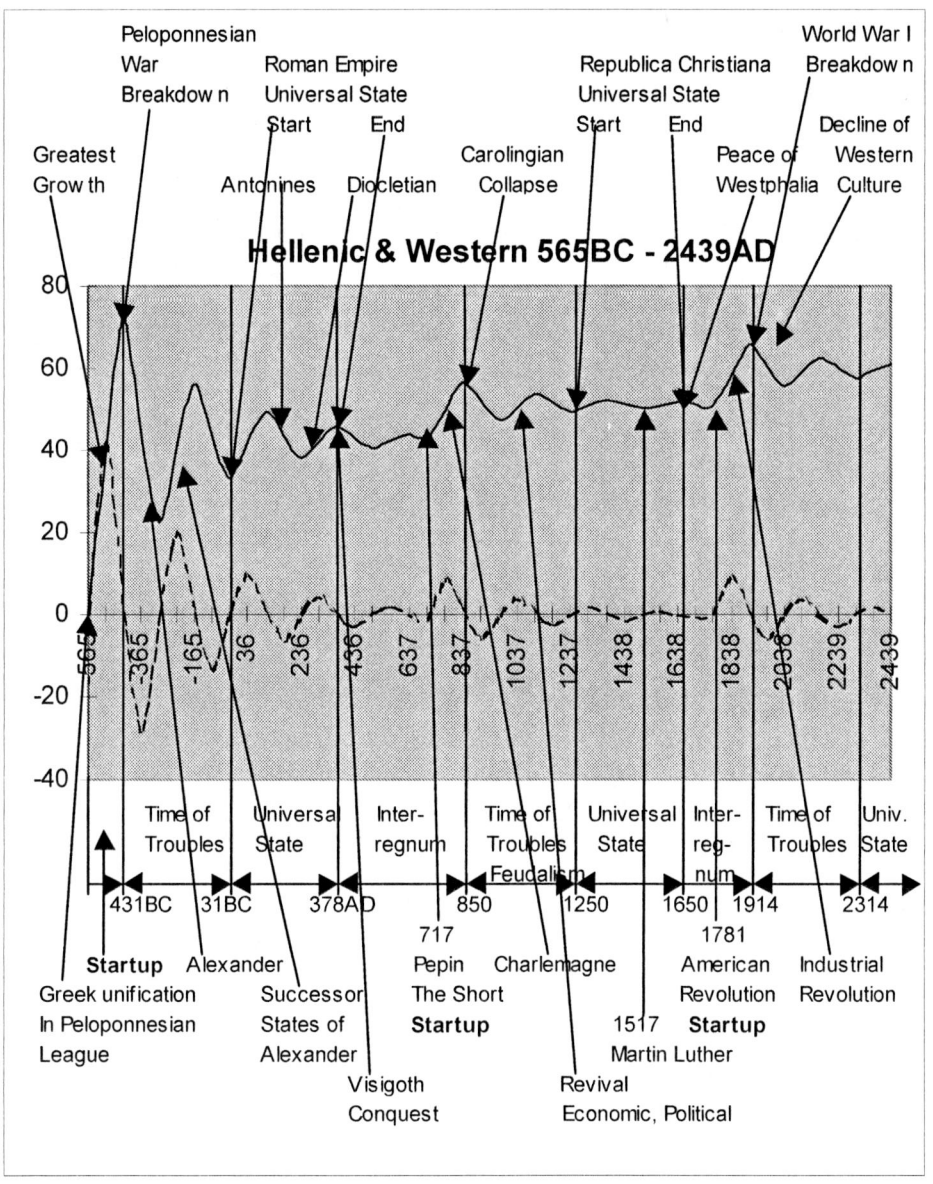

Figure 22. The pattern of Hellenic, Western and Technic civilizations.

Syraic and Arab Islamic Civilizations

Syraic civilization is the parent of Arab Islamic civilization. The original locale of Syraic civilization was Syria. But it expanded throughout Palestine and the Middle East. Arab Islamic civilization, one of its successors, was created through the conquests of Mohammed and his followers.

Syraic civilization and Arab Islamic civilization had the same region, Palestine and nearby Arabia, as their heartland. We suggest that there is a continuity between these civilizations because of the continuity of key parts of the populations of these civilizations. Therefore in this section we will apply our theory to the entire time span of Syraic civilization and Arab Islamic civilization. We will see the theory can encompass both Syraic and Arab Islamic civilization as a continuous stream of development (if proper account is taken of external forces).

The initial startup of Syraic civilization was 1060 BC based on a breakdown occurring in 937 BC with the breakup of King Solomon's empire.

A second startup can be placed at 107 AD – a date which is in the middle of a series of Jewish revolts (the Romano-Jewish Wars) against the Romans. These wars led to the permanent stationing of two Roman legions in Palestine. The significance of these wars is further underlined by the fact that the Jewish population of the Roman Empire is estimated to be approximately 12,000,000. The total population of the empire has been estimated to be approximately 120,000,000. The Jewish population was approximately 10% of the total population and thus a major factor in the affairs of the empire. (King Herod was raised in Rome.) The focus of Roman interest in Palestine led to Roman conquests in Arabia and the conquest of Mesopotamia.

The pattern of events starting in 107 AD and lasting until about 969 AD with a startup, a time of troubles and a re-imposition of a universal state suggest this period constitutes a civilization that we will call JudaeoPalestinic.

The third startup occurred in 1209 AD and was marked by the beginning of the Osmanli conquests that were to lead to the creation of the Ottoman Empire. It also was approximately the time that Muslims resumed control of Palestine.

Fig. 23 shows the curve of societal level S (and fifty times the change C) based on the three startups. The force used to generate C and S is:

$$F_{SyraicArab} = F_0 + f_1 \delta(t - 107) + f_2 \delta(t - 1209) \qquad (48)$$

where f_1, and f_2 are constants, and F_0 is given by equation (7).

The Life Cycle of Civilizations

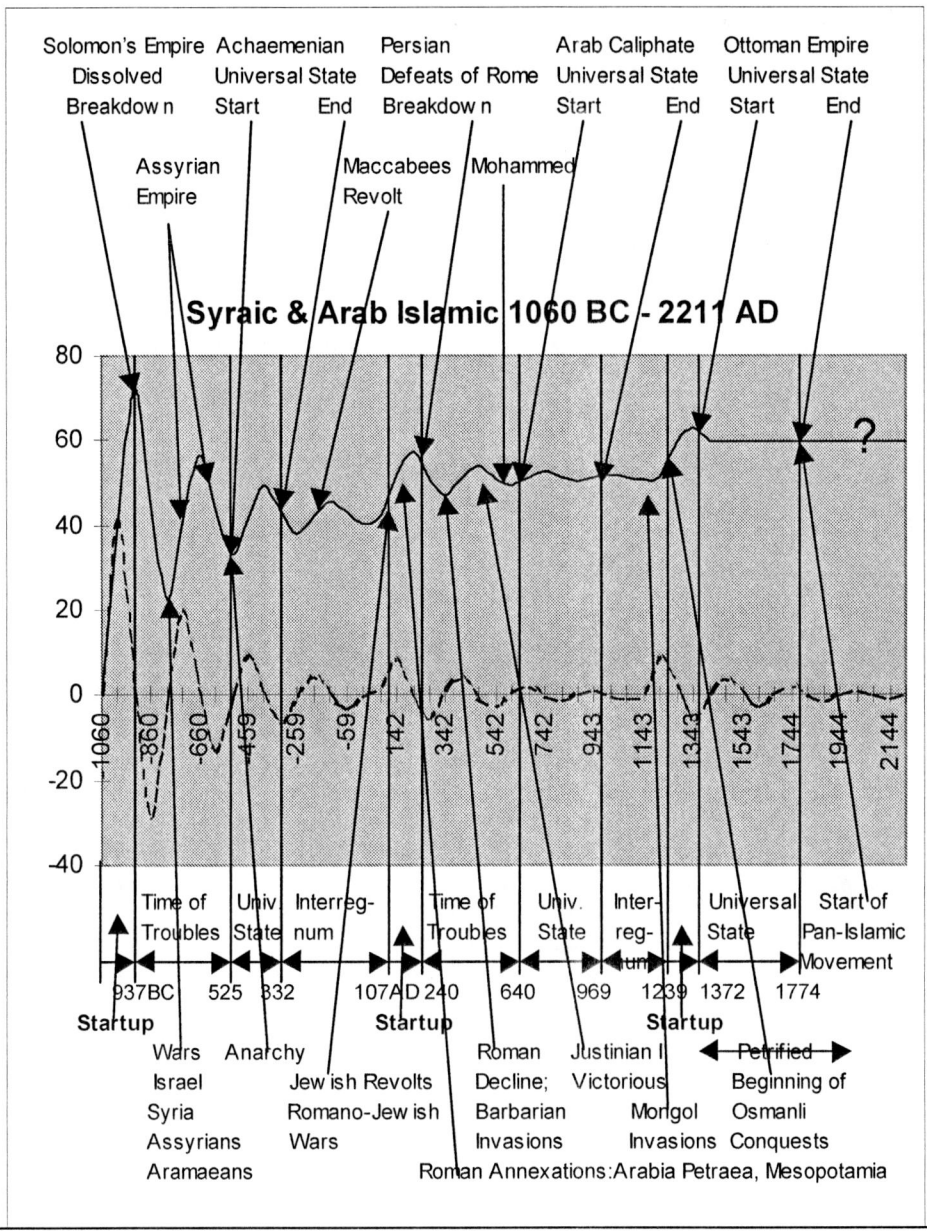

Figure 23. The pattern of Syraic, JudaeoPalestinic, and Arab Islamic civilizations.

93

The total force specified in equation (48) results in an inhomogeneous differential equation using Newton's force law. The solution leads to the following expression for the total societal level $S_{SyraicArab}$:

$$S_{SyraicArab} = S(t + 1060) + g_1 \theta(t - 107) S(t - 107) + g_2 \theta(t - 1209) S(t - 1209) \quad (49)$$

where $S(t)$ is the standard societal curve specified by equation (20) and where

$$g_1 = f_1/mb \quad (50)$$

$$g_2 = f_2/mb \quad (51)$$

Again we will set

$$g_1 = g_2 = 1/5 \quad (52)$$

The plot of $S_{SyraicArab}$ in Fig. 23 shows a close correlation between the shape of the curve and significant events in the Syraic and Arab Islamic civilizations.

The creation of the Israeli state in 1948 and the massive introduction of western technology in Islamic civilization due to Arab oil wealth raise the possibility that an Islamic civilization may be in a new startup phase. If the startup date is taken to be 1950 then a breakdown in growth may be expected in 2084. We will call this civilization PetroIslamic civilization.

Syraic and Iranian Islamic Civilizations

Syraic civilization is also the parent of Iranian Islamic civilization. Over the centuries Syraic civilization penetrated into what is now Iran. In addition, the conquests of Alexander the Great brought Hellenic civilization into Syria, the Middle East, Persia (now Iran) and India.

The Seleucid Empire was created by one of Alexander's successors Seleucus as a Greco-Persian empire. The Greek culture of this empire survived in the Parthian Empire that followed. The Parthian Empire did not have a direct, centralized government but rather consisted of provinces that were loosely organized in a feudal type of government. The provinces enjoyed a large measure of independence. They were ruled by local dynasties. The Parthian Empire can be viewed as existing in a time of troubles due to its continuous wars with Rome and the Scythians as well as internal conflicts and civil wars.

The Sasanian Empire that followed was a universal state that embodied a renaissance of Iranian culture together with a corresponding decline in Greek culture.

Arab Islamic civilization was brought to Iran through the conquests of Mohammed's followers. The Muslim conquest of Iran occurred in 641 AD. Iran was ruled by the Arab Abbasid Caliphate from 750 AD until roughly 870 AD. It was followed by minor Iranian dynasties until the mid eleventh century when the Ghuzz Turkmen tribes created a united empire consisting of Iran, Iraq and Syria under the leadership of Togrul and his successors. The next three centuries saw massive migrations of Turks together with Mongol invasions that transformed the croplands of a civilization to pastures and deserts, and reduced the cities to villages in a process that can only be called nomadization. This period constitutes an interregnum.

Shahruhk, son of Tamerlane, succeeded in uniting most of Tamerlane's empire, restored prosperity, and simulated a flowering of Persian culture in the period 1405 - 1447. This period represented a startup of Iranian civilization that led to the brilliant efforts of Shah Ismail I (1501 – 1524) to create a Persian nation. Subsequently, the Iranian universal state went through a complex series of developments as it journeyed to the twentieth century

In this section we apply our theory to Syraic civilization and its successor Iranian Islamic civilization. We will see the theory can encompass both Syraic and Iranian Islamic civilization as a continuous stream of development (taking account of external forces) in the region stretching from India to Palestine.

The initial Syraic civilization lasted from 1060 BC to Alexander's death in 323 BC. A startup began in 312 BC when Seleucus proceeded to conquer a vast empire extending through Iran and on to the Indus river.

The second startup began with the Muslim conquest of Iran in 641 AD and the establishment of the Abbasid Caliphate as ruler. Since the social structure and ruling classes under the Caliphate remained Iranian the conquest was not viewed as a foreign conquest. Local insurrections and internal discord developed as a time of troubles followed.

Starting in the tenth century massive migrations/invasions of Turks and then Mongols led to the end of this civilization in an interregnum that saw cities destroyed and cultivated land transformed to pastures and deserts.

A third startup occurred in 1405 that was led by Shahruhk. This startup eventually led to the Iranian nation of modern times.

The Life Cycle of Civilizations

Exhibit 21. Fourth Century AD Sasanian drinking bowl showing a king hunting stags.

The following figure shows the curve of societal level S (and fifty times the change C) based on the three startups. The force used to generate C and S is:

$$F_{SyraicIran} = F_0 + f_1 \delta(t+312) + f_2 \delta(t-641) + f_3 \delta(t-1405) \quad (53)$$

where f_1, f_2 and f_3 are constants, and F_0 is given by equation (7).

The total force specified in equation (53) results in an inhomogeneous differential equation using Newton's force law. The solution leads to the total societal level $S_{SyraicIran}$:

$$S_{SyraicIran} = S(t + 1060) + g_1 \theta(t + 312) S(t + 312) + \\ + g_2 \theta(t - 641) S(t - 641) + \\ + g_3 \theta(t - 1405) S(t - 1405) \quad (54)$$

where $S(t)$ is the standard societal curve specified in equation (20) and where

$$g_1 = f_1/mb \quad (55)$$

$$g_2 = f_2/mb \quad (56)$$

$$g_3 = f_3/mb \quad (57)$$

Again we will set

$$g_1 = g_2 = g_3 = 1/5 \quad (58)$$

The plot of $S_{SyraicIran}$ in Fig. 24 shows a close correlation between the shape of the curve and significant events in the Syraic and Iranian Islamic civilizations. It seems reasonable to identify the period from 312 BC to 641 AD as an Iranian civilization with strong Greek cultural influences. We will call this civilization Iranic civilization.

The period after 1950 saw a massive modernization drive in Iran that was only partially reversed by the revolt of the mullahs and the ouster of the Shah. This period may represent the beginning of a new civilization based on Islam and oil revenues that we will call PetroIslamic civilization.

The Life Cycle of Civilizations

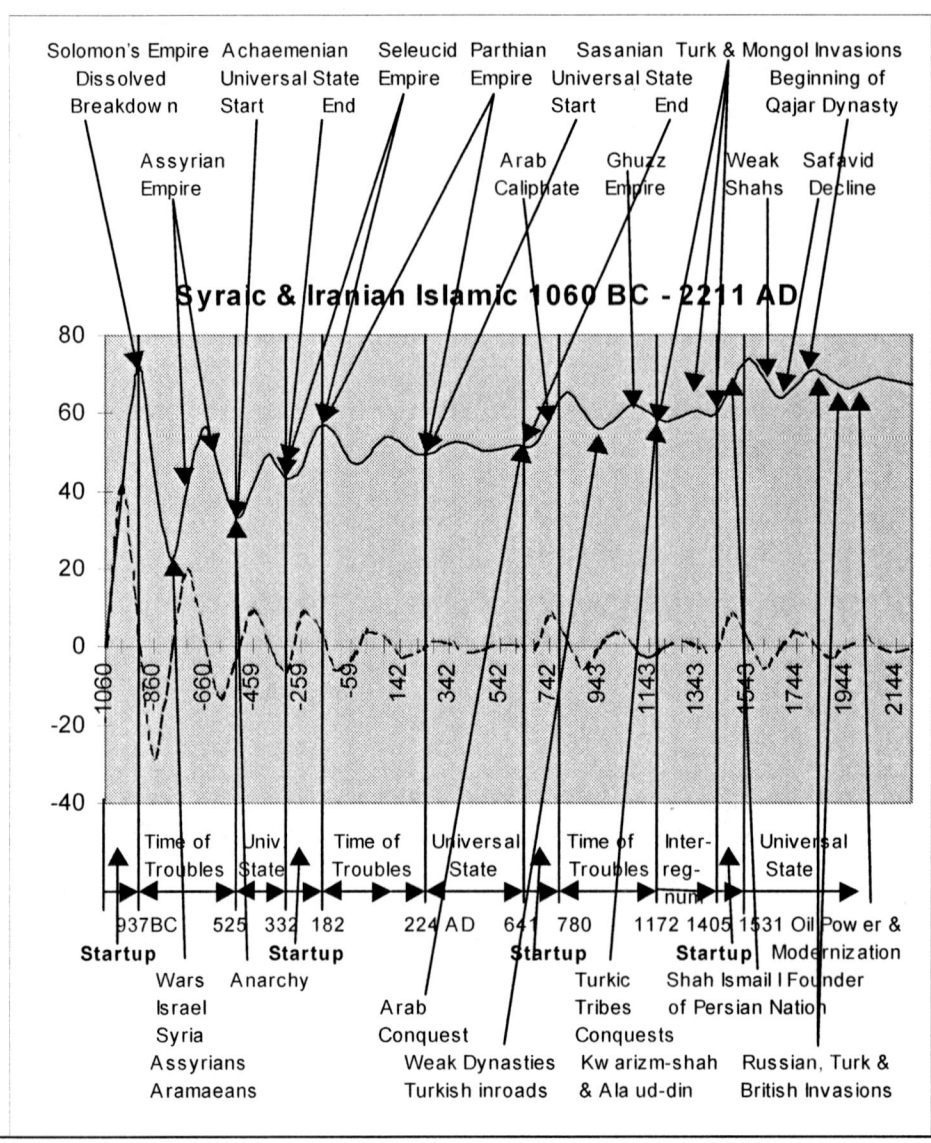

Figure 24. The pattern of Syraic, Iranic, and Iranian Islamic civilizations.

The Life Cycle of Civilizations

Exhibit 22. View of the Taj Mahal, India.

Indic and Hindu Civilizations

When[7] asked what he thought of Western civilization Mahatma Ghandi responded by saying, "I think that it is a wonderful idea." Civilization has a long history in India of which Indians can justifiably be proud.

Indian civilizations began with Indic civilization, the parent of Hindu civilization. In this section we apply our theory to Indic civilization and its successor Hindu civilization. We will see that the theory can encompass both Indic and Hindu civilization as a continuous stream of development (taking account of external forces).

The initial startup of Indic civilization was 855 BC based on a breakdown occurring in 722 BC and a succeeding 400 year time of troubles. The later Vedic period extends from the tenth century BC until the sixth century BC, which is consistent with an 855 BC startup of Indic civilization.

A second startup can be placed at 80 AD. A series of foreign invasions lasting from 185 BC until the first century AD provoked a startup that lead to the universal state of the Gupta Empire in 210 AD approximately 134 years after the startup. We have observed the general rule that a universal state appears after a startup provoked by foreign invasions. (A startup provoked by internal events is normally followed by a time of troubles.)

The third startup occurred in 1011 AD. This startup is placed 134 years before the beginning of the time of troubles of Hindu civilization beginning in 1175 AD.

Fig. 25 shows the curve of societal level S_{India} (and fifty times the change C) based on these three startups. The force used to generate C and S_{India} is:

$$F_{India} = F_0 + f_1 \delta(t - 80) + f_2 \delta(t - 1011) \qquad (59)$$

where f_1, and f_2 are constants, and F_0 is given by equation (7).

The total force specified in equation (59) results in an inhomogeneous differential equation using Newton's force law. The solution leads to the following expression for the total societal level S_{India}:

$$S_{India} = S(t + 855) + g_1 \theta(t - 80) S(t - 80) + \\ + g_2 \theta(t - 1011) S(t - 1011) \qquad (60)$$

where S(t) is the standard societal curve specified by equation (20) and where

---

[7] Anecdote provided by John K. Duncan, Esq.

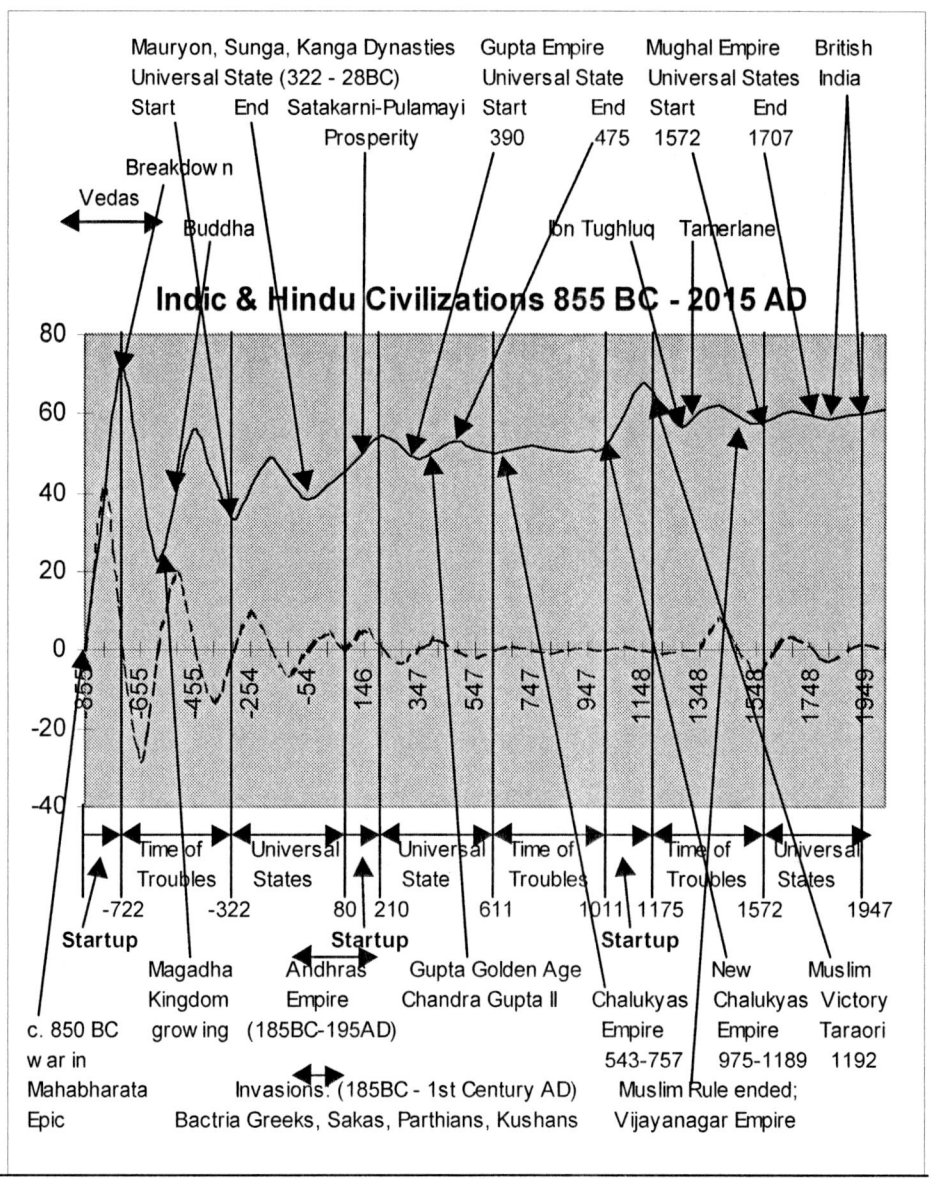

Figure 25. The pattern of Indic, Early Hindic, and Hindu civilizations.

$$g_1 = f_1/mb \qquad (61)$$

$$g_2 = f_2/mb \qquad (62)$$

Again we will set

$$g_1 = g_2 = 1/5 \qquad (63)$$

The plot of S_{India} in Fig. 25 shows a close correlation between the shape of the curve and significant events in the Indic and Hindu civilizations.

The period from 80 AD to 1011 AD appears to contain a civilization whose high point was the Gupta Empire. The Gupta Empire (the universal state in this period) is one of the peaks of Indian culture. We will call this civilization Early Hindic civilization.

Hellenic and Orthodox Christian (Main Body)

Orthodox Christian (main body) civilization developed in southeastern Europe and Anatolia from Hellenic civilization. Hellenic civilization has been described earlier. The Orthodox Christian civilization that emerged from it was based on the continuation of the eastern half of the Roman Empire. This continuation was based on two wise moves by the Eastern Empire's government. First a peace was arranged with Persia in 364 AD called the Peace of Jovian. This peace secured the eastern frontiers of the empire from an almost continuous war with the Parthians that had consumed major resources and manpower of the empire. A war with the Sasanian Empire over Armenia was also successfully ended with a peace treaty in 422 AD.

Secondly, the eastern half of the empire was protected from the invasions of the Visigoths and Ostrogoths after the disastrous battle of Adrianople (378) by arranging for their settlement in the Balkan provinces as allies. Later, in the fifth century, another German threat was eliminated through the use of strong Isaurian allies whose leader Zeno later became emperor. A renewed threat from the Ostrogoths in the Balkans was eliminated by encouraging their movement into Italy. As a result the Eastern Roman Empire was able to remove threats from the east, and from the Germans, and to survive for a thousand years beyond the Western Roman Empire.

We therefore take the startup for the continuation of the Eastern Empire to be 364 AD – the Peace of Jovian.

A second startup can be placed at 840 AD due to the revival of the Byzantine Empire by Michael III. This revival included the renunciation of the destructive iconoclasm movement.

Fig. 26 shows the curve of the societal level $S_{HellenicOrthodox}$ (and fifty times the change C) based on these startups. The force used to generate C and $S_{HellenicOrthodox}$ is:

$$F_{HellenicOrthodox} = F_0 + f_1 \delta(t - 364) + f_2 \delta(t - 840) \qquad (64)$$

where f_1, and f_2 are constants, and F_0 is given by equation (7).

The total force specified in equation (64) results in an inhomogeneous differential equation using Newton's force law. The solution leads to the total societal level $S_{HellenicOrthodox}$:

$$S_{HellenicOrthodox} = S(t + 565) + g_1 \theta(t - 364) S(t - 364) + \\ + g_2 \theta(t - 840) S(t - 840) \qquad (65)$$

where S(t) is the standard societal curve specified by equation (20) and where

$$g_1 = f_1/mb$$

$$g_2 = f_2/mb$$

Again we will set
$$g_1 = g_2 = 1/5 \qquad (66)$$

The plot of $S_{HellenicOrthodox}$ in Fig. 26 shows a close correlation between the shape of the curve and significant events in the Hellenic and Orthodox Christian (main body) civilizations.

In addition it appears reasonable to identify the period from 364 AD to 840 AD as an intermediate civilization which we will call Byzantine civilization. This civilization ended with the end of the convulsive Iconoclasm movement in 840 AD.

The Life Cycle of Civilizations

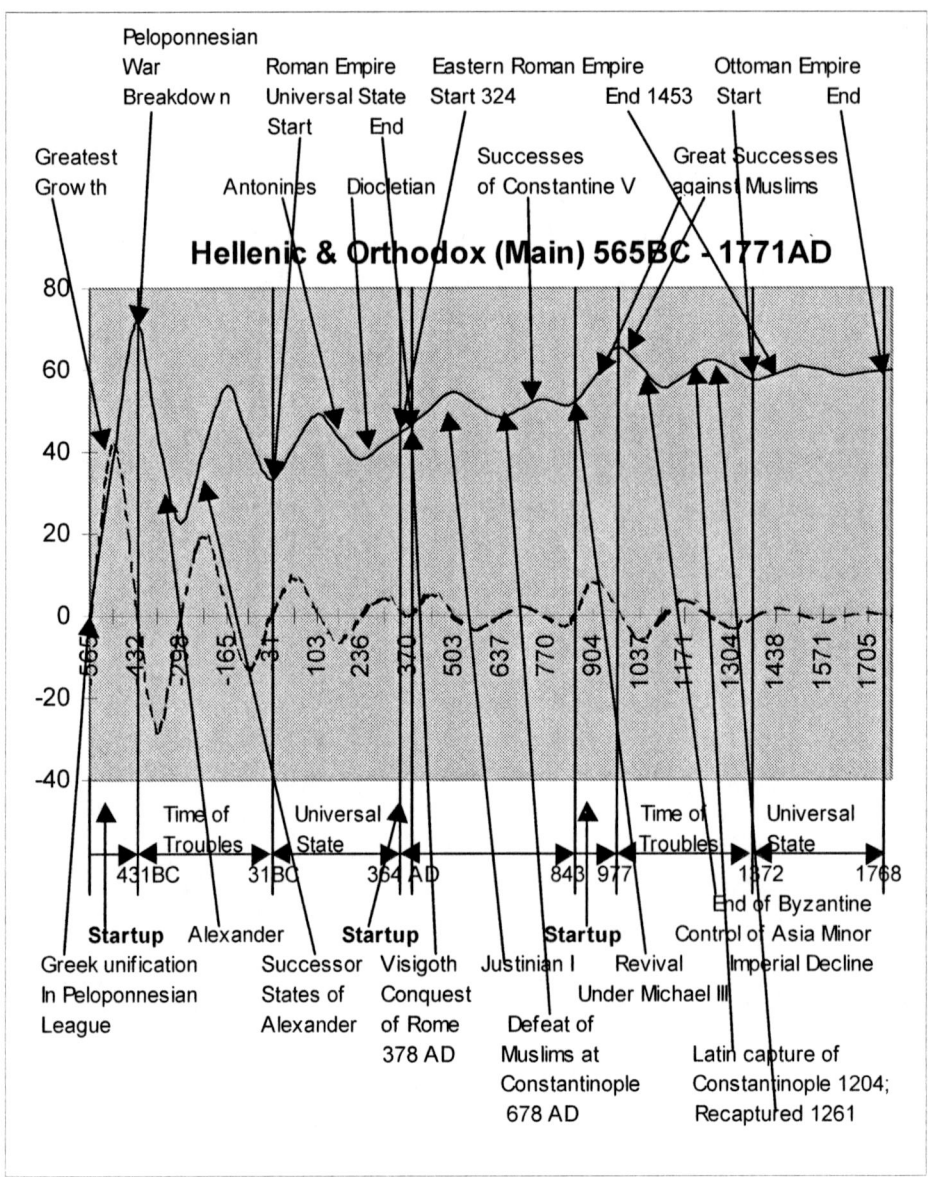

Figure 26. Hellenic, Byzantine, and Orthodox Christian (main body) civilizations.

Hellenic and Orthodox Christian (Russian)

Orthodox Christian (Russian) civilization is a branch of the Orthodox Christian (main body) civilization that had a startup around 941 AD with Byzantine successes in wars with the Bulgars and Russians.

Fig. 27 shows the curve of societal level $S_{HellenicRussian}$ (and fifty times the change C) based on the following startups: a startup in 364 due to the Peace of Jovian and a startup in 941 due to the Byzantine successes with the Bulgars and Russians. The force used to generate C and $S_{HellenicRussian}$ is:

$$F_{HellenicRussian} = F_0 + f_1 \delta(t - 364) + f_2 \delta(t - 941) \qquad (67)$$

where f_1, and f_2 are constants, and F_0 is given by equation (7).

The total force specified in equation (67) results in an inhomogeneous differential equation using Newton's force law. The solution leads to the following total societal level $S_{HellenicRussian}$:

$$S_{HellenicRussian} = S(t + 565) + g_1 \theta(t - 364)S(t - 364) + \\ + g_2 \theta(t - 941)S(t - 941) \qquad (68)$$

where S(t) is the standard societal curve specified by equation (20) and where

$$g_1 = f_1/mb$$

$$g_2 = f_2/mb$$

Again we will set

$$g_1 = g_2 = 1/5 \qquad (69)$$

The plot of $S_{HellenicRussian}$ in Fig. 27 shows a close correlation between the shape of the curve and significant events in the Hellenic and Orthodox Christian (Russian) civilizations. As before, it appears reasonable to identify the period from 364 AD to 840 AD as an intermediate civilization which we will call Byzantine civilization. This civilization ended with the end of the convulsive Iconoclasm movement in 840 AD.

The Life Cycle of Civilizations

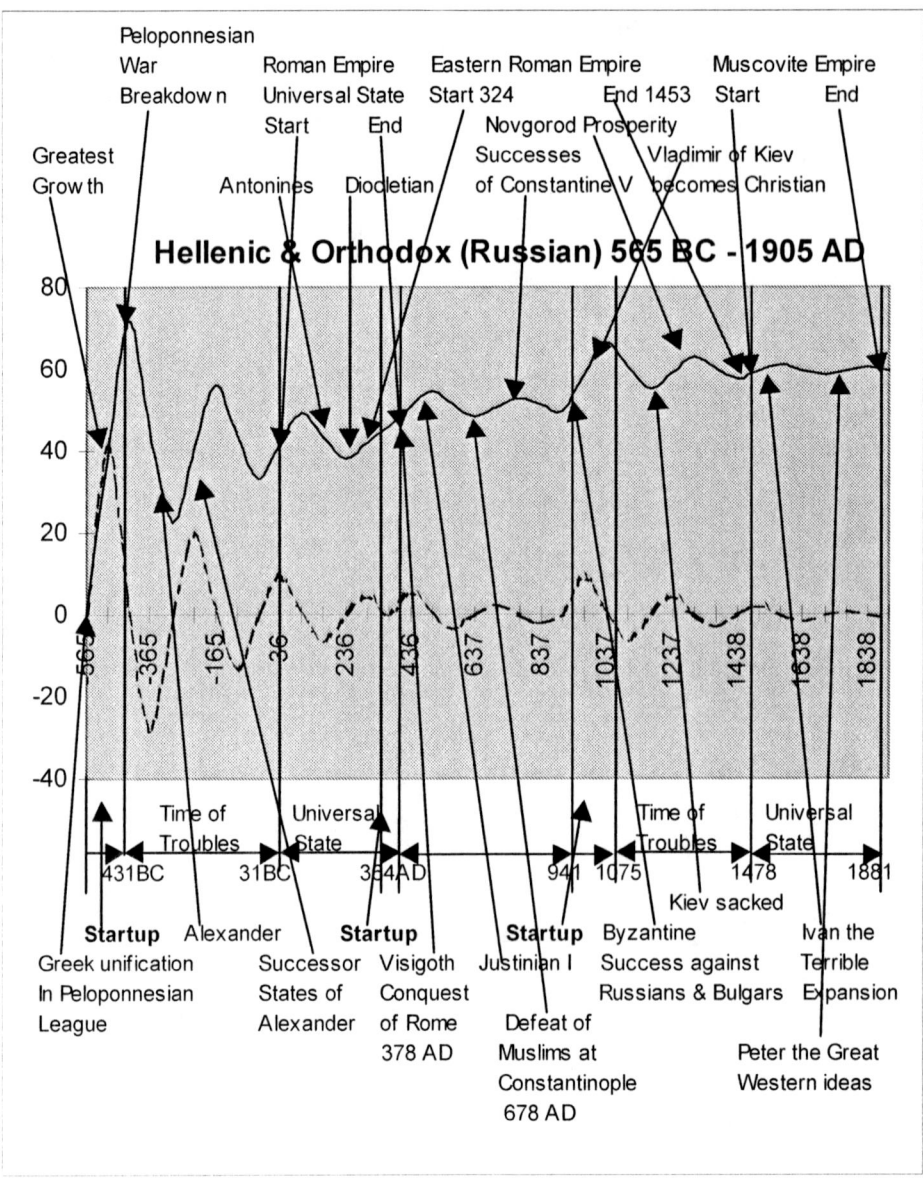

Figure 27. Pattern of Hellenic, Byzantine, and Orthodox Christian (Russian) civilization.

General Features of the Theory's Parameters

The preceding figures show that our general theory of civilizations can account for the peaks and valleys of civilizations over broad expanses of time. Some general conclusions emerging from this investigation are:

1. The value of b = .0235 appears to be the same for all human civilizations. It specifies the time period T of oscillations to be approximately 267 years using equation (16).

2. The value of the parameter a can vary from civilization to civilization. It sets the rate of decline in a civilization as the civilization disintegrates. The three and a half beat pattern which is fairly consistently seen in civilizations corresponds approximately to a value of .75 for the parameter d which, in turn, gives a value for a of 0.00281 using equation (19). This value of a corresponds to a decline in the peaks of a civilization from peak to peak of a factor of 2.117 using equation (17). Roughly speaking, each time a civilization reaches a new peak in its disintegration phase the peak is half the previous peak.

3. In a given geographical region the history of successive civilizations can be described by our theory if we include the idea of startups due to internal or external events. At certain points in the history of a region an internal or an external event can occur that causes a "revival" of civilization. We call these events startup points. If a startup event is internal then a period of growth ensues followed by a time of troubles and a universal state in that order. If the startup event is external (such as a conquest by a foreign power) then a universal state and a time of troubles follow in that order.

Since we are unable to numerically determine societal levels experimentally we have taken the strength of each startup after the initial startup of the first generation civilization to be one-fifth (the value of the g parameter) of the value of the initial startup. This choice of value seems to produce an overall pattern for a series of successive civilizations that looks reasonable.

4. The natural application of the patterns in China and Japan suggest that the period between Sinic and Far Eastern civilization (172 AD – 878 AD) in China contains a civilization as well that we will call New Sinic; and the early period (58 BC to 876 AD) in Japan contains a civilization that we will call Early Japanese. In addition recent Japanese history suggests a new western-style technological civilization (based on Japanese culture) started in 1868. Recent Chinese history, especially the reorganization of the country begun in 1900, suggest China is also at the beginning of a Western-style technological

The Life Cycle of Civilizations

civilization based on Chinese culture. We take the startup point for SinoTechnic civilization to be 1950.

5. The portrayal of the dates of civilizations given by Toynbee and others may need revision based on the patterns displayed in the preceding figures. The figures showing Hellenic and Western civilization, Syriac and Arab Islamic civilizations, Syraic and Iranian Islamic civilizations, and Indic and Hindu civilizations suggest the existence of other unrecognized civilizations (listed below).

6. A theory often gives form to data that previously looked unstructured or fragmented. The theoretical analysis presented in the preceding equations and figures suggests the following ordering of civilizations with newly recognized civilizations marked "NEW".

Hellenic-Western civilizations:
    565 BC – 378 AD   Hellenic civilization
    717 AD – 1650 AD   Western civilization
    1781 AD – 2715? AD   Technic civilization (NEW)

Hellenic-Orthodox Christian (main body) civilizations:
    565 BC – 378 AD   Hellenic civilization
    364 AD – 840 AD   Byzantine civilization (NEW)
    840 AD – 1768 AD   Orthodox Christian (main body)

Hellenic-Orthodox Christian (Russian) civilizations:
    565 BC – 378 AD   Hellenic civilization
    364 AD – 840 AD   Byzantine civilization (NEW)
    941 AD – 1881 AD   Orthodox Christian (Russian)
    1917 AD – 2851? AD   RussoTechnic (NEW)

Syraic-Palestinian civilizations:
    1060 BC – 332 BC   Syraic civilization
    107 AD – 969 AD   JudaeoPalestinic civilization (NEW)
    1209 AD – 2172? AD   Arab Islamic civilization
    1950 AD – 2884? AD   PetroIslamic civilization? (NEW)

Syraic-Iranian civilizations:
    1060 BC – 332 BC   Syraic civilization
    312 BC – 641 AD   Iranic civilization (NEW)
    641 AD – present   Iranian Islamic (with interregnum)

1950 AD – 2884? AD	PetroIslamic civilization? (NEW)

Indian civilizations:

855 BC – 80 AD	Indic civilization
80 AD – 1011 AD	Early Hindic civilization (NEW)
1011 AD – 1947 AD	Hindu civilization
1950 AD – 2884? AD	IndoTechnic (NEW)

Chinese civilizations:

768 BC – 172 AD	Sinic
172 AD – 878 AD	New Sinic (NEW)
878 AD – 1853 AD	Far Eastern (main body)
1949 AD – 2883? AD	SinoTechnic (NEW)

Japanese civilizations:

58 BC – 876 AD	Early Japanese (NEW)
1048 AD – 1868 AD	Far Eastern (Japan)
1868 AD – 2802? AD	JapoTechnic (NEW)

7. The preceding list of civilizations can be displayed as a family tree consisting of four (or perhaps five) generations of civilizations. The four generation view of civilizations appears to be logically more satisfying than Toynbee's three generation view since, for example, the Far Eastern civilizations, both in the main body and in Japan, become third generation civilizations as they appear to be when comparing their characteristics with other civilizations. In this view the proposed appearance of higher religions between the second and third generations is no longer true. The loss of this proposed regularity is not of importance since it was not logically explainable—merely an accidental regularity at best.

8. The mass parameter of a civilization m was not discussed in the previous examples because it always appeared in ratio with other parameters. Since the value of b, and to a large extent a, are the same for almost all civilizations (except petrified civilizations) we can view the parameters that specify resistance to change as proportional to m:

The Life Cycle of Civilizations

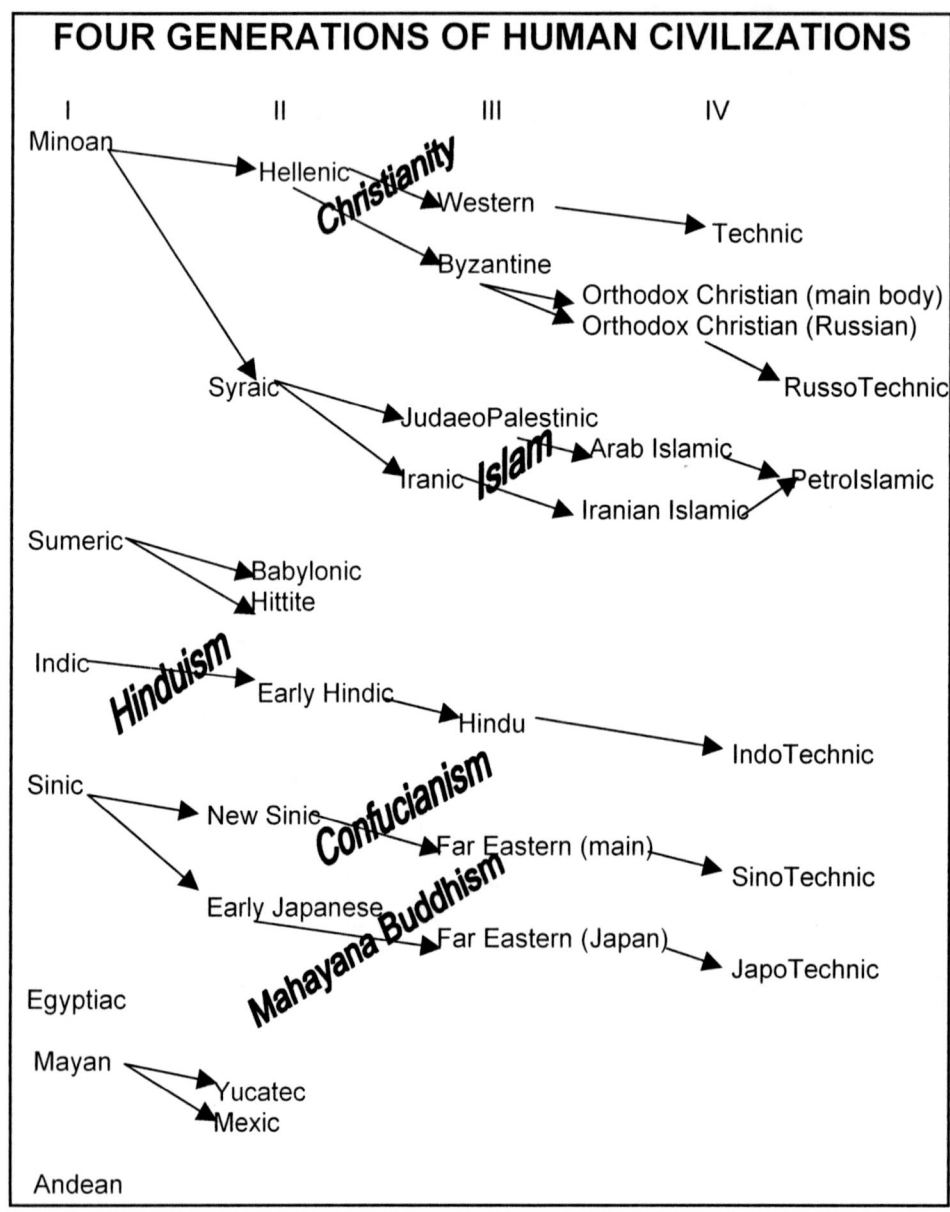

Figure 28. A New Family Tree of Human civilizations based on the theory.

$$r = m\, r_0 \tag{70}$$

$$s = m\, s_0 \tag{71}$$

where $r_0 = 1/178$ and $s_0 = 1/1923$ are independent of the civilization. However the mass of a civilization is important in setting the strength of a startup (which we arbitrarily set to 1/5). The larger the mass of the civilization the smaller the effect of an external or internal startup event. This observation is in agreement with our common notion that "it takes a big event to change a big civilization." Elephants ignore fleas. Thus a large mass m imparts stability to a civilization against the effects of major events.

By setting each g parameter equal to 1/5 we are implicitly assuming that the major events that generated startups were so significant that the effect on the civilization was largely independent of the civilization's mass. We can qualitatively picture the value of g in relation to the magnitude of events as "jumping" to 1/5 after a certain threshold level of event size (set to level 8 in our "Richter Scale" of events below). "Jumps" in vibratory phenomena are not uncommon. (See page 102 of Joos)

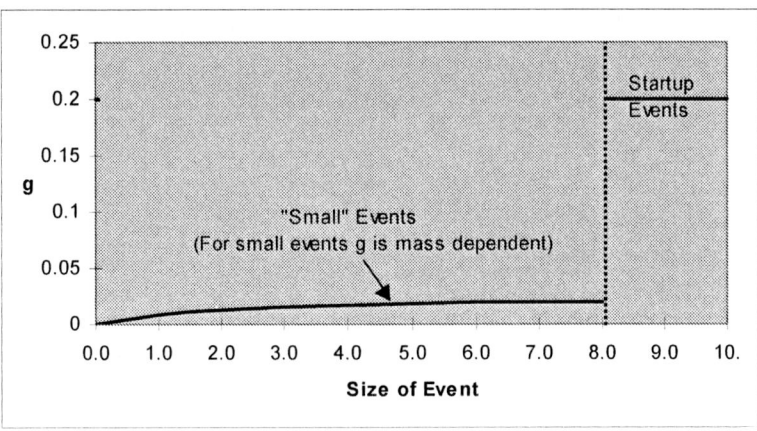

8. General Considerations on the Theory of Civilizations

What is Waving?

When Quantum Mechanics was being invented by de Broglie, Schroedinger, Heisenberg and others an apparently major question that was raised was "What is waving?" Waves were somehow associated with matter but it was not clear of what the waves consisted. Later physicists came to understand these waves to be waves of probability.

We face a similar problem in the theory that we have developed. The societal S curves have an oscillating, cyclic form when we plot them—they are similar to damped waves that decline in size with time—just as we see when we drop a stone in a puddle of water.

We cannot specify precisely what is waving when we look at these societal waves, and we do not know how to numerically measure these waves. The only thing that is clear is that the peaks and valleys of the waves appear to correspond to historical events and situations. Thus historical events seem to be indicators of these peaks and valleys. This fact gives our societal curves a reality. Just as a doctor uses the symptoms of a disease to identify a disease, historians can use historical events to identify the routs and rallies of a civilization and develop a view of the societal curve of the civilization.

What shall we think of these societal waves? First it is clear that the S waves are a measure of some overall social feature of a civilization. Second it is clear that this feature is not a material feature such as population size, or geographical area or wealth. Instead it appears to be a measure of the inner "temper" of the people of the civilization as a whole. For example, towards the end of the Western Roman Empire the common feeling was that the world (namely their civilization) was approaching an end. Philosophers talked of "cosmic senescence" setting in. Ordinary people noted the decline of the population, poor harvests, bad weather and the attacks, and increasing dominance, of the barbarians. This universal feeling of the people of a civilization probably comes closest to corresponding to the societal level S.

We have seen a similar development of a universal feeling in the United States in the aftermath of the September 11, 2001 World Trade Center attack. For several months most of the population of the United States appeared to have a common feeling of disaster, a feeling that life had changed in a permanent way for the worst, and a fear of more bad news to come. The United States had a temporary "loss of nerve." "What will happen next?" Similarly some historians have commented that the Roman Empire fell due to a continuing "loss of nerve" after a series of setbacks. Thankfully, the United States seemed to have recovered and resumed its confident progress into the future.

Thus it seems best to view the societal level S as a measure of the joint feeling of the people of a civilization. It grows when a challenge has a successful response. It declines if a challenge is not successfully met. Civilizations may say as Cassius said, "The fault, dear Brutus, is not in the stars but in ourselves."

The societal level S can be expected to fluctuate from day to day, month to month, and year to year. In the absence of a detailed theory for short time scale fluctuations we can only view our theory for S as a time average of S over some appropriate time. Since the periodicity in S appears to be related to the dynamics of human generations (next section), and since a reasonable length for a human generation is about thirty years, we can perhaps view the values of S as averaged over approximately five-year time periods. Five years seems long enough to "wash out" the effects of transitory events and yet short enough to capture the details of major trends in a civilization. Simply put the value of S at a time t can be taken to be the average of S over the period starting 2.5 years before time t to 2.5 years after time t.

Origin of the Periodic Oscillations

Having seen the success that we have had in matching historical events with our S curves it is natural to inquire into the origin of the societal oscillations, and into the reason why all civilizations appear to have the same period of oscillation.

The Length of a Cycle

Our initial selection of 267 years as the approximate period of oscillation was based on Toynbee's observations that the time of troubles of a civilization was roughly 400 years as was the time interval of the universal state that typically followed a time of troubles. Toynbee also pointed out that in this 800 year time interval there were oscillations normally amounting to three and a half beats. The time of troubles was not entirely a downward move. It usually had a rally within it. The universal state was most often not just a rally. It often had a rout within it. Consequently Toynbee's basic picture of a time of troubles was rout-rally-rout, and of a universal state as rally-rout-rally. Each phase therefore

The Life Cycle of Civilizations

was more than one period of oscillation. One period would be the time required for a rally-rout or a rout-rally cycle. Thus Toynbee implicitly suggested that each phase was one and a half cycles:

$$400 \text{ years} = 1.5 \, T \qquad (72)$$

with the result

$$T = 267 \text{ years} \qquad (73)$$

The next issue was the length of the initial interval of growth before the breakdown. Toynbee was uncertain on this point stating that the growth phase did not have a discernible structure unlike the following time of troubles and universal state did.

This author felt that the periodicity seen in both the time of troubles and universal state phases (which incidentally smoothly meshed) should be extrapolated backwards to the growth phase. By definition the growth phase was the interval from the beginning of growth of the civilization to the breakdown point which was defined as the first point where the growth ended and the societal level started to decline. This definition of the growth period together with the reasonable extrapolation of the periodicity to the growth period implies the growth interval is half the period .5T or 134 years. The resulting cyclic pattern is embodied in the next figure. (The relative magnitude of the peaks and dips are not set by these considerations.)

A growth period of 134 years is a relatively short time period. The shortness of this time interval would explain why Toynbee failed to find a structure in the growth period. He thought the growth period was of much greater length. The events of these longer intervals of time had no pattern. Either the longer interval was in part an interregnum, or partly a time of slow growth of ordinary societies – not civilizations.

An example of our view is the American experience that led to the formation of the United States. Englishmen and others started migrating to the British North American colonies in the mid-1600's. There was a slow growth in the colonies over a period of a century or so. Then the American Revolution took place and the United States was formed. After a successful financial and political structure were put into place (around 1800) the United States began a period of rapid growth that lasted until the 1930's when the Great Depression occurred – a period of approximately 130 years. Major growth seems to occur in spurts of the order of 100 years or so in length. Thus the growth phase of 134 years for a civilization in our theory appears quite reasonable.

The Life Cycle of Civilizations

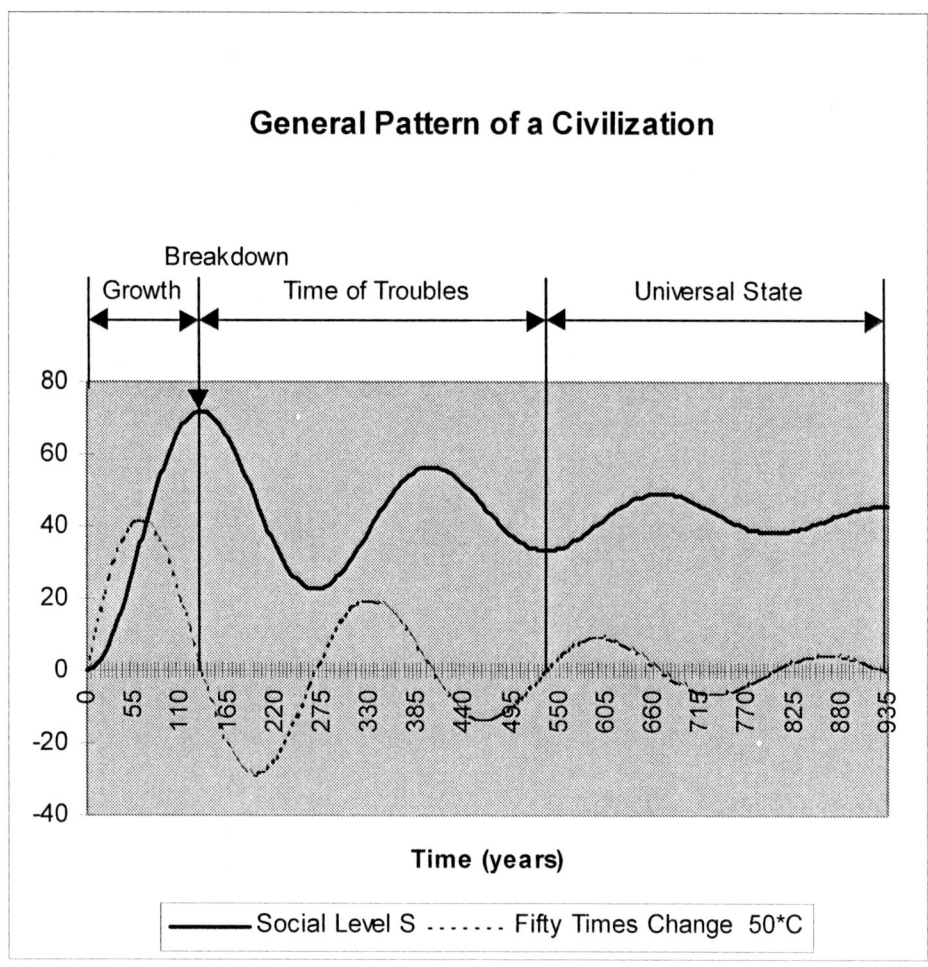

Figure 29. General pattern of a civilization's routs and rallies a la Toynbee.

Some may think this is a rather short time period for a civilization to grow. However it should be noted that the transition from a static society to a dynamic civilization requires a period of growth BEFORE the civilization starts. For example when the ancient Egyptians entered the Nile valley they had to clear the swamps and bring the soil into cultivation before civilization could begin. In this early time interval survival was the goal—not the development of a civilized society. After this phase was completed and sufficient surplus time and labor was available a civilization could develop. This point marks the beginning of the civilization and the start of societal growth of a civilization. In Egypt this point marks the beginning of the age of the great pyramids. These pyramids were built in a remarkably short interval of about a hundred years. This period ended with the breakdown of Egyptaic civilization and the following time of troubles. Egyptaic civilization conforms to our view of a 134 year time interval of civilized growth.

The other first generation civilizations also conform to this picture of a short time interval of civilized growth. A glance at the preceding figures shows major societal growth in all first generation civilizations in the 134 year growth phase. Greek civilization developed a political climate and a league that enabled it to withstand the Persian invasion and set the stage for a burst of Greek culture in the Periclean Age. Syraic civilization saw the greatness and prosperity of the kingdom of David and Solomon. Chinese civilization made great strides in its 134 year growth period starting major canals as well as developing literature and the arts. More recently, Japan has grown in four generations (134 years) starting in 1868 from an illiterate, backward country to the second largest economy in the world.

The Reason for the Periodicity

After seeing the pattern of civilizations and the successful match of the pattern with historical events in well-documented civilizations we now address the question: Why is the period of oscillation approximately 267 years?

Since the 267 year period appears to apply to all civilizations and since the oscillations are not synchronized with each other in any discernible way we must attribute the 267 year period to the internal structure of all civilizations. This period does not depend on the environment, barbarians, religions or any other obvious environmental factor or combination of factors.

The only common feature of all civilizations is that they are composed of human beings. Therefore we can only conclude the origin of the roughly 267 year oscillation in civilizations is in the nature of mankind, and, in particular, the social nature of mankind.

The length of a rally, or a rout, is approximately 134 years if the period is 267 years. This length of time is approximately four generations of about 33.5 years each.

Numerous authors, including Toynbee[8], have pointed out the existence of long term social trends lasting generations. Evidence exists for three generation social effects in nationality, religion and class changes. Paul Ligeti in his work

---

[8] Toynbee, abridged version, volumes VII – X, pp. 281 – 288.

Der Weg aus dem Chaos suggests a 130 year repeating pattern of architecture, sculpture and painting.

Toynbee, and others, have suggested that a four-generation interval may be required to effect a change in international politics. It appears that a four-generation pattern of routs and rallies applies to civilizations as well. The initial period of growth is four generations. The strain of this growth causes a breakdown and brings on a rout that lasts for four generations followed by a rally for four generations and so on.

The question now becomes why four generations? This question cannot be answered in any definitive way. One can argue that a rally eventually runs out of steam. The motivations that led a civilization to build enormous pyramids may fade after four generations.

One can also argue that a rout eventually peters out when "all is lost" in the view the people of a civilization.

But the question is not really answered by these observations. The real answer lies in the transmission of experience and information from generation to generation. Parents transmit their hopes and fears, their knowledge and ignorance, to their children. In some manner the transmission of a trend, a rout or a rally, peters out in four generations. Certainly we see patterns of this sort in many situations. For example, a common pattern in the United States:

1. Great Grandparents come to America and improve their lot a bit
2. Grandparents prosper as blue-collar workers
3. Parents go to college and prosper as white-collar workers
4. Children drop out of college feeling prosperity is not the real purpose of life and accept less rewarding jobs

Thus a financial rally in a family of four generations peters out.

So we can conclude that a long term, multi-generation social mechanism appears to be the basis of the observed periodicity of 267 years or eight generations. This conclusion is supported by the results of the next section which show the 267 year period is not limited to civilizations but also applies to the only large, well documented, long lifetime, social organization of which we are aware—the Roman Catholic Church.

Ultimately, the origin of the four-generation interval for routs and rallies must be more solidly based on the development of the social nature of mankind hundreds of thousands of years ago. There must have been some subtle evolutionary advantage to a four-generation interval for routs and rallies in the earliest human societies.

The Life Cycle of Civilizations

Universality of the Periodic Oscillations

We have seen the appearance of oscillations in civilizations with a period of approximately 267 years. These oscillations appear to be the result of the inherent social nature of mankind.

If the social nature of mankind is truly the source of these oscillations then we should see evidence of this phenomenon in other organizations of mankind. To verify the universality, or generality, of this phenomenon we should see it appear in other large, organized, social institutions over a sufficiently long time period of at least a thousand years.

The only large social organization that appears to meet these requirements is the Roman Catholic Church. Other religious bodies and religions are too small, or too short in duration, or too close to a government or too diffuse in their organization to detect changes in societal level. Buddhism, for example, is a "diffuse" religion with many sects spread over many countries It would be difficult to analyze Buddhism for changes in "societal level." Islam, Hinduism, and Confucianism are also difficult to analyze in terms of societal level. Some religions such as Shintoism and Orthodox Christianity are closely intertwined with governments and their societal level would be strongly influenced by the history of the governments which are in turn part of civilizations. Thus they would not provide as clean a test of the oscillation phenomena.

Theory Applied to the Roman Catholic Church

The Roman Catholic Church has existed for two thousand years, has maintained its independence of governments for the most part, has a well-defined social structure, and has a well-documented history. (For those who might be offended by the application of this theory to the Roman Catholic Church we wish to say it is done respectfully and conforms to the Church's view that it is in part an earthly organization.)

We will apply our theory to the Church using the same parameters that were used for a three and a half beat civilization.

Fig. 30 shows the curve of societal level S_{RCC} (and fifty times the change C) resulting from the application of the theory. It has an initial startup in 590 AD (when the western church solidified its organization and began major growth) and a subsequent startup in 1870 when the Church entered a period of renewal and major growth. The force used to generate C and S is:

$$F_{RCC} = F_0 + f\,\delta(t - 1870) \qquad (74)$$

where f is a constant and F_0 is given by equation (7).

Exhibit 23. View of the Vatican and St. Peter's Cathedral in 1900.

The Life Cycle of Civilizations

The total force specified in equation (74) results in an inhomogeneous differential equation using Newton's force law. The solution leads to the following expression for the total societal level S_{RCC}:

$$S_{RCC} = S(t - 590) + g\, \theta(t - 1870)\, S(t - 1870) \qquad (75)$$

where the societal curve $S(t)$ is specified by equation (20) and where

$$g = f/mb \qquad (76)$$

As we did for civilizations, we will set

$$g = 1/5 \qquad (77)$$

The agreement between the peaks and valleys of S_{RCC} and historic events of the Roman Catholic Church is remarkable. The startup in 1870 suggests the large growth of the Church during the startup period will end in 2004 and a period of decline will ensue. Recent events suggest that the Church may be entering a time of troubles. We note the decline in priestly vocations, the sizable falling away of Catholics, major financial problems of the Church and a rise in major scandals that will severely challenge the faith of the laity.

The Life Cycle of Civilizations

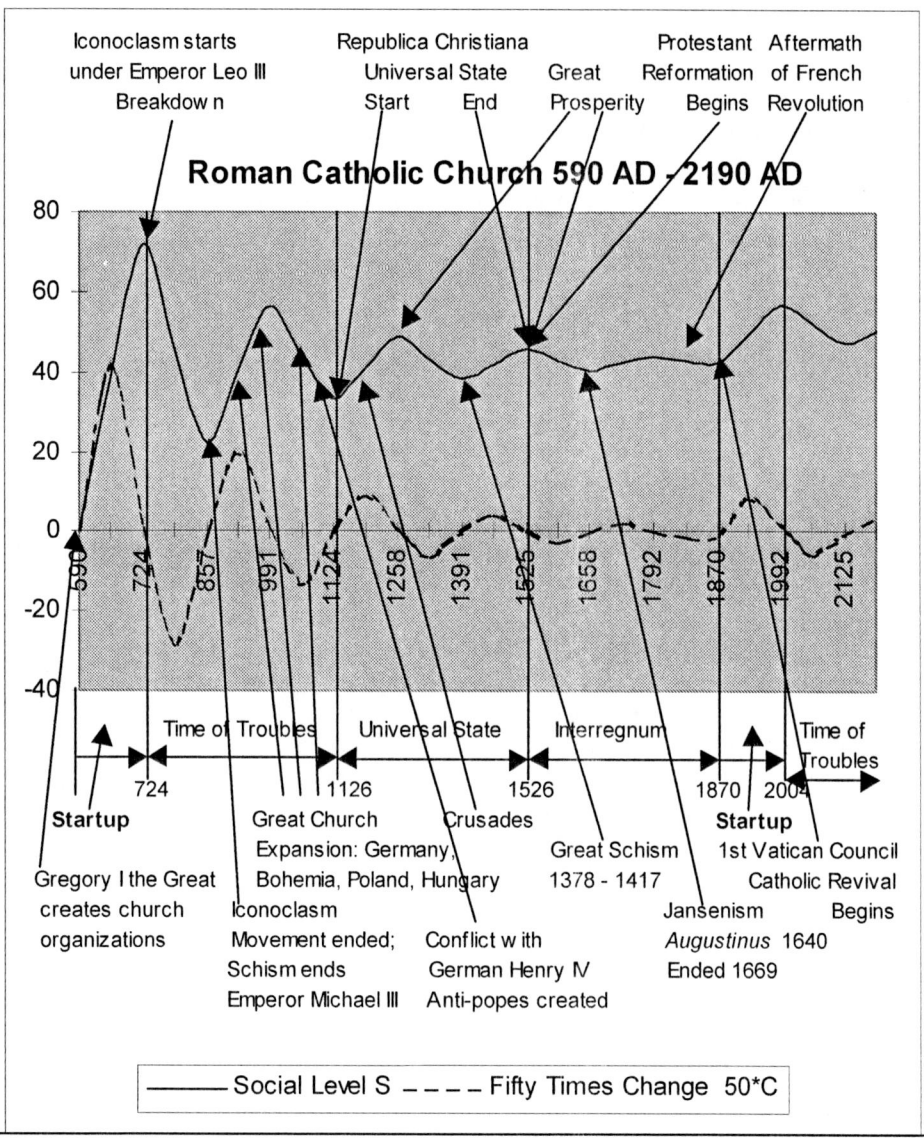

Figure 30. The theory applied to the Roman Catholic Church showing the theory is based on the long-term social nature of mankind.

Multi-generation Social Effects

Our theory suggests that mankind has a built-in four generation social periodicity. This periodicity does not appear to be related to weather cycles or environmental factors in the current epoch. It appears to be an inherent part of mankind's social makeup. As Toynbee has noted humans were social animals before they were humans. In addition, it appears that mankind emerged from a small original ancestral group that must have lived in a specific location for a long period of time amounting to perhaps hundreds of thousands of years.

If there were consistent weather cycles of approximately 134 years for a time interval of hundreds of thousands of years, then a social cycle of 134 years may have been induced in the human group through selective evolution. Environmentally based cycles have been known in mankind and animals for some time. Multi-generation social cycles have been proposed by Sorokin and others. And the Kondratieff cycle of 50 – 60 years appears to apply to recent economic events.

A Model of World History

The success that we have seen in applying our theory to sequences of affiliated civilizations suggests that a model for world history in the past 6,000 years could be constructed. The model would be similar in concept to detailed econometric models of the United States and other countries that have been constructed and simulated on computers.

A model for world history would contain the theory of civilizations that we have developed with the startups generated within the model directly from environmental effects and the activities of external societies (such as the Nomads). For example, the dry spells on the Eurasian Steppes that stimulated Nomadic invasions of civilizations would be inputs rather than arbitrarily specified startup dates as we have done in our dynamical equations. In addition the effects of the interactions of civilizations with each other, and with other societies, would be specified through a coupled set of differential equations. A model of world history based on these considerations could be easily studied with computer simulations.

The existence of a successful model of world history and a knowledge of important current trends such as global warming, and its effects on agriculture, would enable projections into the future that could provide guidance as to the proper course of action required of world governments.

9. Implications for the Future of Civilizations

The Immediate Future of Current Civilizations

The theory we have developed enables us to make some general predictions about the near term prospects of current civilizations. These observations are subject to change due to chance historical events, environmental effects such as global warming or major volcanic eruptions, events such as plagues and epidemics, and the appearance of singular individuals such as a Napoleon who might have a temporary but major impact on history. Despite these possibilities the overall pattern of political and economic events that represent parts of long-term trends are embodied in the predictions of the general theory.

We will first look at the present state and near term prospects of individual civilizations. Then we will examine the combined effect of these prospects on the future.

The next figure shows the current phases of some major contemporary civilizations: the startup phase, the breakdown, and the "rout" phase after the breakdown based on the following data.

Dates of Phases in Contemporary Civilizations

	Technic	JapoTechnic	RussoTechnic	SinoTechnic	IndoTechnic	PetroIslamic
Startup	1780	1868	1917	1950	1950	1950
Breakdown	1914	2002	2051	2084	2084	2084
Rout End	2048	2136	2185	2218	2218	2218

The Life Cycle of Civilizations

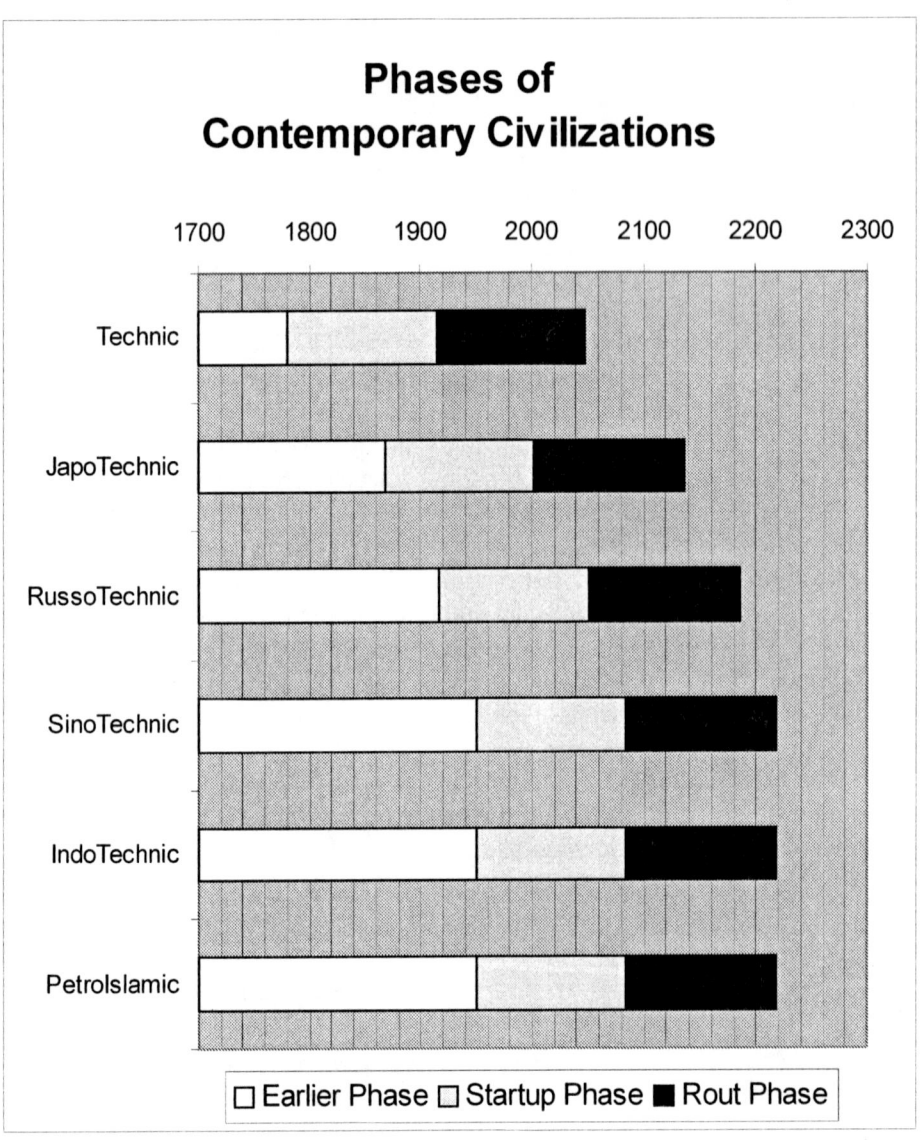

Figure 31. A comparison of the phases of contemporary civilizations.

Western Technological (Technic) Civilization

Technic civilization appears to have had a startup in approximately 1780. The rapid industrialization of the western world and the growth of democratic ideas both occurred during the 134 years that followed. An apparent side effect of both of these trends was the development of the concept of the total war of populations that started with the breakdown in 1914 of the peace of Europe. Before that war Europe was more or less at peace and citizens of the leading countries enjoyed an international culture and a belief in a developing universal peace. World War I shattered that hope and began a time of troubles that contains both world wars as well as the Cold War with its threat of massive nuclear destruction that lasted until roughly 1990.

Writing in the year 2002 we see a new threat of nuclear destruction from nuclear proliferation to secondary powers and, potentially, to well-financed terrorists.

The period from 1914 to 2048 represents a "rout" within a time of troubles. A "rally" is projected to begin in 2048. What do these phases represent? The rout reflects a decline in the overall "spirit" of Western civilization. Since 1914 the western world, and particularly Europe, has seen the disappearance of vast empires created in the Third World: Asia, Africa and South America. The attitudes of Western civilization have also changed from a feeling of cultural and political superiority to a sense of equality and, perhaps, due to the cultural and immigration invasion from former colonies, and subject states, to a feeling of disadvantage in certain areas such as philosophy and the arts. This decline, which may be a welcome change towards an egalitarian world, nevertheless represents a rout for Western civilization. The population declines being experienced by many European countries also reflects this "spiritual" decline. People are having fewer children partly because they realize that their economic horizons are limited and having children represents a major expense. The rout in Western civilization is predicted to end in approximately 2048. Then a rally is predicted for 134 years with a corresponding revival in the spirit of Western civilization.

Contemporary Japanese Civilization

Japan experienced a startup in 1868 due to the opening of Japan by the United States. The shock of western technology led Japan to totally reorganize itself to meet a new future. This reorganization was depicted internally as a restoration of ancient Japanese values and called the Meiji Restoration.

Japan rapidly progressed during this growth phase. Japanese literacy progressed from near zero to one hundred per cent literacy in little more than one generation. Japanese industrial and military progress led to the defeat of a major European power Russia in the Russo-Japanese War of 1904-5.

Despite a complete defeat and occupation in World War II Japan resumed impressive growth afterwards that led to its position as the second largest economy in the world by the late 1980's.

The events since 1868 happened within an extraordinary growth period that is scheduled to end in roughly 2002 according to our theory. Interestingly, Japan has been experiencing difficulties in this last generation of four generations of growth. Starting around 1988 Japan has experienced increasing economic difficulties. In addition Japan is starting to experience social difficulties associated with a rapidly aging population and low birth rate. As of this writing (March, 2002) it appears that Japan must undertake major financial reforms in order to restore its economy. Under present conditions Japan's economy is expected to contract by over four per cent in the next year by financial analysts. The financial reforms necessary to make Japan's economy healthy again will undoubtedly cause serious economic dislocations. The effects of these reforms may initiate the breakdown projected by our theory. Afterwards Japan is projected to enter into a time of troubles lasting four hundred years.

Contemporary Chinese Civilization

China was unified for the first time since the Manchu Dynasty in 1949 with the complete takeover of mainland China by the Communists. The Communists embarked on a program of education and economic and industrial development that led to a Chinese nuclear bomb in 1964 and a Chinese space program in 2000. The rapid development of China as an industrial power and as a technological power—particularly in the 1990's, and its unification of the majority of the Chinese people suggest that 1950 be taken as the point of a startup of 134 years of growth that may be expected to continue until roughly 2084 when a breakdown is projected to occur. We will identify 1950 as the beginning of a technological society based on Chinese culture that we will call SinoTechnic civilization.

At the time of this writing in March, 2002 China is experiencing growth pains in the form of financial problems. Our analysis suggests that China will emerge from these issues and continue strong growth until 2084 when it will enter a time of troubles.

Contemporary Indian Civilization

India received independence from Great Britain in 1950. Since receiving independence India has made great strides in technology and industry including the development of a sizable computer industry, the development of nuclear energy including a nuclear bomb and the development of rocket technology. Despite an enormous population increase modern India has made great strides in its standard of living for the westernized component of its population. Based on this recent history, and especially in comparison to the preceding hundred years, it appears that India is in a major growth phase that we will take to have begun in 1950.

If the growth startup did indeed begin in 1950 then a breakdown can be expected in roughly 2084 when India will enter a time of troubles. The new Indian civilization of over a billion people combines technology and Indian culture. We call this civilization IndoTechnic.

The cause of the anticipated breakdown can only be conjectured at this time. But it may well be the result of a conflict between traditional Indian society of which the vast majority of Indians are members and modern, technological India consisting of a hundred million or so individuals. The breakdown may be similar to the Iranian revolution of the 1980's which was a reaction of traditional Islamic culture to rapid modernization.

Contemporary Arab Islamic Civilization

The Arab Islamic civilization of the last 800 years is projected to end in approximately 2172. If so, then an interregnum or new startup is possible at that time.

It is possible that a startup has already occurred due to the oil wealth of the Arabs, the end of western colonial dominance and the creation of Israel in a major religious center of Islam. It seems reasonable to date the beginning of this probable startup at roughly 1950 based on these factors.

Since 1950 there has been a massive infusion of technology into the Middle East purchased with Arab oil wealth that has lead to industrial growth, atomic power, and scientific and engineering prowess. This growth phase raises the question whether a new civilization has started in this region – a new civilization grounded in Islam but committed to technological progress. Since the basis for this growth is petroleum resources it seems reasonable to call this proposed new civilization the PetroIslamic civilization.

The growth phase of PetroIslamic civilization (if it indeed has started) is projected to end in 2084 according to our theory. The growth phase will be followed by a time of troubles lasting four hundred years. After the time of troubles the creation of an Islamic universal state is projected realizing the dreams of the Pan Islamic Movement.

Contemporary Russian Civilization

The Russian branch of Orthodox Christian civilization ended in 1881. In 1917 the Russian Revolution began a phase of rapid industrialization. Ultimately this led to brilliant Russian technical achievements in science and in space. While the empire that the USSR built has been disbanded, Russia remains an empire in terms of its geographical size and in terms of its military capabilities.

The enormous growth of Russia since 1917 raises the question whether it entered a startup phase for the development of a technically based civilization within the Russian cultural experience. The question is one that cannot be answered definitively for at least several hundred years. We will provisionally assume Russian civilization did undergo a startup in 1917 and call that civilization RussoTechnic civilization. If so, the growth phase should end in a breakdown around 2051.

The Mix of Contemporary Civilizations 2002

An observer of the international scene in 2002 sees a new interplay of civilizations taking place. The United States and other nations of Western civilization have shifted from the relative complacency of the 1990's when war appeared to be a thing of the past to an open-ended war on terrorism. In the last twenty years of the twentieth century Western civilization developed a largely peaceful relationship with other important civilizations on earth with the exception of Islamic civilization. Islamic civilization has been engaged in a covert expansionism that is evidenced by conflicts in Nigeria, the Philippines, Indonesia, and the Sudan among others. The Saudi government sponsors this expansionism through an extensive program of mosque building, education and other forms of support in the western world, particularly in the United States. Islam has an active grass roots program with a goal of converting the world to Islam.

The peoples of Islam are generally poor and part of Third World poverty. They see the West, and particularly the United States, as engaged in a conspiracy to prevent them from emerging from poverty.

Most importantly, they see the West as the main support of Israel. In the Islamic view Israel is an occupier of sacred Islamic ground that was won by conquest. In view of the inability of Islamic governments to win a conventional war with Israel, elements within the Islamic peoples have formed terrorist groups to fight Israel and it greatest supporter the United States. While the United States was basking in the afterglow of its successful war with Iraq terrorist groups were training and preparing for a widened terrorist offensive against their perceived enemies. The events of September 11, 2001 are one of the results of their worldwide preparations.

The response of the United States to September 11th was an attack on the al Qaeda terrorist organization and their Afghan Taliban allies. This attack was widely viewed in the Islamic world as part of a war between Western civilization and Islamic civilization. The West tried to portray this conflict as a war on terrorism.

The Life Cycle of Civilizations

The analysis that we have presented shows the West to be in the latter stages of a decline of societal level. On the other hand Islamic civilization may well be in a growth phase. Certainly its oil resources which are of vital importance for the economy of the West give Islam a major card to play against western military strength.

A historical perspective suggests the terrorist activities correspond to barbarian attacks on a civilization. Barbarian attacks are a familiar part of the history of civilizations. The immigration of large numbers of Muslims to western countries is similar to the migration of barbarians into the Roman Empire in the latter days of the empire. These analogies, and the crucial role of the great oil wealth of the Islamic world for the Western industrial democracies, would appear to be a bad portent for the future. It must be remembered that the terrorist leadership of al Qaeda came from the affluent Arab community—not from poor Arabs. It came from Arabs who were most acquainted with the West.

However there is an important difference between the Islamic-Western situation and the Roman-barbarian conflicts. The barbarians only became a serious threat to Rome towards the end of western Hellenic civilization. Today it appears that Western civilization is barely past a new beginning that started in 1780. The societal level of Western civilization gives it the internal strength to turn back the attacks of barbarians into the foreseeable future. Later in the twenty first century when western Technic civilization begins a rally and Islamic civilization perhaps enters a time of troubles the West should enjoy an even stronger position.

Another important current situation is the continuing Japanese financial crisis. By our analysis Japanese civilization is nearing the end of its growth phase and approaching a breakdown. If this analysis is correct and Japan does have a catastrophic event, the effect on the world's financial condition could be profound. Therefore the West should make a major effort to ease the Japanese through its financial difficulties.

China is still in the midst of the growth phase of SinoTechnic civilization that should last until a breakdown that is projected to occur in 2083. China is aggressively moving forward in science and technology with a major space program, and major scientific programs including the development of a larger nuclear arsenal. China is also trying to instill bravery and courage in its children as part of their educational programs. Further China is promoting economic development and the exploitation of natural resources at the maximum possible rates. It is particularly trying to exploit less developed regions such as western China and developing a major presence along its Siberian border with Russia. These trends suggest China may attempt to press its claims for parts of Siberia if Russia should become weaker.

Russia experienced a major dip in its development in the 1990's due to its changeover to a capitalist economy. Russia appears to be beginning to move forward. Its massive natural resources and agricultural potential give it a great potential for further growth. Its growth phase is projected to end in about fifty years (2051) with a breakdown. Global warming may act to benefit Russia agriculturally, and in the development of Siberia. Russia has the potential to exploit the growth phase for maximum benefit. An improved economy and health care system could lead to an increase in Russian population growth. A democratic, vibrant Russia could also expect immigration from Germany and other parts of western Europe as well as the Third World. With a resurgent China eyeing Siberia Russia can be expected to continue good relations with the West.

India has made great strides in development in the 1980's and 1990's particularly in the computer industry. Having created a dynamic technology sector IndoTechnic civilization is enjoying a major growth phase. A breakdown in growth is projected for 2084. The nature of this breakdown is societal. It could be the result of a major conflict between the westernized technologically oriented Indian sub-society and the Hindu fundamentalist sub-society that has emerged in recent years.

India is clearly trying to establish itself as a major world power. It has a continuing conflict with Pakistan that will result in a de facto concession by Pakistan that India is the overwhelmingly dominant power on the Indian subcontinent. The latent conflict with China in common border regions will likely result in a continuing stalemate.

The Mix of Contemporary Civilizations 2050

An observer of the international scene in 2050 will see a much changed world. Not only will the effects of global warming be very evident, but there may be major changes in the status of the various civilizations.

Russia, China, India and the Islamic world will have enjoyed major growth phases bringing them all to new levels of prosperity as civilizations. In such a situation one can expect that there will be temptations for all parties to exploit their strength and prosperity by aggressive activities economically, politically, or in space. Russia, China and India all have major space programs. The next fifty years are likely to be more or less peaceful (in the sense that there will not be a world war) due to the overwhelming strength of the United States.

The growth of these countries in a general atmosphere of peace, and the drain on the United States in its role as a world leader, will lead the world to a situation reminiscent of Europe before World War I.

Rather than being a great hope for the future, widespread affluence may actually promote conflict and war.

The Mix of Contemporary Civilizations 2100

An observer of the international scene in 2100 may see a much changed world from 2050. With all major civilizations having undergone a breakdown in the previous century, all civilizations will be simultaneously in a time of troubles. It is natural to think that this confluence of phases cannot be a happy portent. While the breakdowns are individual according to our theory since they stem from the social nature of mankind, a confluence of routs would seem to lead to a period of turmoil.

Will it Ever End?

Mankind has seen war, famine and hardship since human life began. Will the pains and sorrows of human existence ever end? Can we hope for a lasting peace based on the brotherhood of mankind? Can we see an end to ceaseless striving? It appears the record of human history says that conflict will continue, and the rise and fall of civilizations will continue. Until a remote future when the meek shall have inherited the earth or until some issue arises (such as a major worldwide environmental crisis) that forces all men to unite.

Does that mean we are doomed to be mindless armies warring in the night? The conflicts, and routs and rallies of civilizations, may perform a necessary role in the further development of humanity. As Toynbee observes civilizations grow, and mankind grows, in response to challenges. The social conflicts that cause so much suffering and grief may be a necessary adjunct to future growth. This view could be described as a cruel view of mankind's history. But mankind began in the cruelty of mindless evolution. We do not complain of the cruelty of the period of "the survival of the fittest" that led to mankind. Should we complain too loudly of the apparent cruelty that advances mankind to the future?

10. The Effect of Shocks on Civilizations

The Effect of Shocks on Civilizations

Every civilization is at risk. Shocks can arise that may cause it to change dramatically in a short period of time. The sources of civilizational shocks may be environmental such as a long drought or a volcanic eruption, or may be of human origin such as a brutal conquest.

We have looked at the shock to Egyptaic civilization delivered by the Hyksos conquest. The Egyptian people reacted to this hateful conquest with a revolt that led to the New Kingdom. The Hyksos generated a strong reaction through their harsh rule and caused the societal level of Egyptaic civilization to rise as the people unified.

We were able to simulate the effect of the Hyksos Conquest on Egyptaic civilization with a Dirac delta-function force that caused the societal level to increase significantly as the Egyptian New Kingdom was formed.

Another effect that we noticed in the case of the Hyksos shock was the entry of Egyptaic civilization into a universal state phase immediately rather than passing through a time of troubles. This phenomenon led to the formulation of a rule that a shock delivered by an invasion of an external enemy will cause a startup with a reversal in the usual order of a time of troubles phase followed by a universal state phase. There is a natural explanation for the direct entry into a universal state. The external enemy causes the people of the civilization to unite against them as the Egyptian people united against the Hyksos creating a universal state.

The Hyksos shock was a positive shock in the sense that it stimulated Egyptaic civilization. The other shocks that we have considered up to now have also been positive shocks due to external or internal events that stimulated societal growth.

It is possible that a shock could occur that would be so overwhelming that it would have the reverse effect of lowering the societal level of a civilization. One possible form of this type of shock is a massive natural catastrophe. For example Minoan civilization is believed to have been destroyed by a massive volcanic eruption in 1645 BC. (There is some disagreement over the date of this eruption which some have placed at a later date. We will assume a date of 1645 BC. If the true date is different then the dates in the following figure should be shifted by the amount of the difference from 1645 BC.)

Unlike preceding earthquakes and volcanic eruptions, the palaces were not rebuilt after this eruption with the exception of the palace at Knossos which was rebuilt apparently by Achaean invaders. The failure to rebuild indicates the destruction inflicted on Minoan civilization was truly catastrophic.

Minoan Civilization

We can model Minoan civilization and take account of the destructive events of the Theran (Santorini) volcanic eruption using a Dirac delta-function force to simulate the impact of the volcanic eruption (as we did in equation (28) for the Hyksos):

$$mC'' + rC' + sC = -f\,\delta(t + 1645) \qquad (78)$$

with one difference: a minus sign appears before the delta function in equation (78) to represent the *destructive* effects of the volcanic eruption. Equation (78) is an inhomogeneous differential equation with a solution that leads to the following expression for the total societal level S_{Minoan}:

$$S_{Minoan} = S(t + 2430) - g\,\theta(t + 1645)\,S(t + 1645) \qquad (79)$$

where $S(t)$ is the standard societal level S specified in equation (20) and where

$$g = f/mb \qquad (80)$$

The value of the constant f (and thus g) is difficult to specify based on rational grounds. In the previous cases, which were all positive startups, we consistently assigned g a value of one-fifth. In the case of Minoan civilization, where the shock had an enormous negative impact from which the civilization never recovered, it seemed reasonable to choose

$$g = 1/2 \qquad (81)$$

with the result that S_{Minoan} diminished to a value that was below previous lows (when building and rebuilding was going on) and was close to the value of S_{Minoan} at the beginning of the Minoan's civilization's growth phase.

The Life Cycle of Civilizations

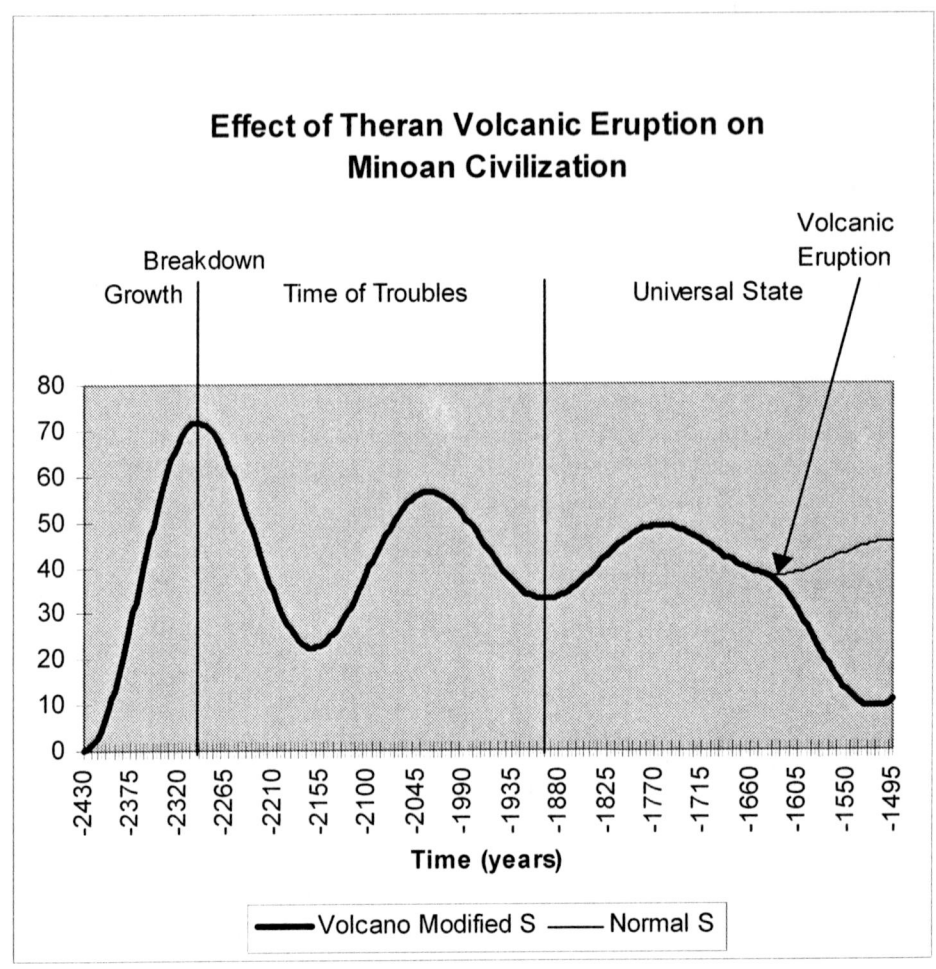

Figure 32. The effect of the Theran volcanic eruption on Minoan civilization. The dates are based on a widely accepted date of 1645 BC for the eruption.

The g Coupling Constants and their Relation to the Initial Startup of a Civilization

At this point it is worthwhile to explore the reasonableness of our choices for g. We will call the g parameters that we have encountered *coupling constants* since they represent the strength of the coupling (or interaction) of the civilization with an external force. The larger the value of g, the stronger the impact on the civilization. The external force is "coupled" to the civilization and can raise it up or drag it down.

The values for g that we have used of one-fifth (for positive startups) and one-half (for disasters) are reasonable from the point of view of the form of the S curve that we created for first generation civilizations. The S curve for a first generation civilization can be viewed as generated from the force equation:

$$mC'' + rC' + sC = f\delta(t) \qquad (82)$$

The initial impetus to the growth of a civilization can be represented by a delta-function force that, in effect, kick starts it. Equation (82) is an inhomogeneous differential equation with a solution that leads to the following expression for the societal level S_{tot}:

$$S_{tot} = g\,\theta(t)\,S(t, r) \qquad (83)$$

where r is specified by d = .75 for our standard societal level S and

$$g = f/mb \qquad (84)$$

In our previous discussions we have set g = 1 (or f = mb) and did not display the step function in order to keep the presentation simple. It was understood in all the discussions that only positive values of time were of interest thus implicitly recognizing the step function.

Consequently g values of one-fifth or one-half are reasonable since they are in the "same ballpark" as the value of g for first generation civilizations.

11. The Effect of Technology on Civilizations

Technical Progress as a Driving Force for Civilization

Technical progress in science and engineering has become increasingly important in the last two hundred years. It has reshaped society and is an important source of power and prosperity in modern Western civilization. Its importance has led us to propose that a new civilization, Technic civilization, effectively started in the eighteenth century with its first major concrete growth sign being the nineteenth century Industrial Revolution.

Technical progress was an occasional phenomenon in early civilizations and often the result of folk technology: an improved bow, improved smelting techniques, advances in architectural techniques, and new military formations and strategies. Ancient Egypt and classical Greece developed relatively advanced architectural techniques and the Romans were master builders. The first and perhaps the greatest architect was Imhotep the architect of the design of the great pyramids.

The first state sponsored research appears to be the work of Archimedes who developed "burning mirrors" for the defense of Syracuse against the Romans.

The first major group research efforts seem to have been in Alexandria, Egypt where the great Museum and Library had an associated group of investigators who, among many major developments, invented a steam boiler, and made great progress in mathematics and astronomy. This group effectively disappeared with the destruction of the Ptolemaic Dynasty by the Romans. Afterwards technological development endured a long dry spell although significant advances appeared from time to time. The nineteenth century began the modern phase of large-scale technological development.

Technology has been a crucial factor in improving the societal level of civilizations – particularly in recent civilizations. A comparison of societal levels in 1800 and in 1900 would show a significant rise in societal level based in part on the tremendous growth in the middle classes in Great Britain, Germany, France, other countries of Western Europe and the United States. This growth was founded on the benefits of the Industrial Revolution.

Exhibit 24. Nineteenth Century sailing-steamer ship.

The Life Cycle of Civilizations

A comparison of societal levels in 1900 and 2000 would show major growth in the prosperity of the working classes in these countries as well as a higher standard of living for the middle classes. There can be little doubt that these improvements in society are the results of technological progress as represented by the Industrial Revolution of the nineteenth century and the Electronic Revolution of the twentieth century.

Exhibit 25. Nineteenth century railroad train.

In view of the major impact of technology on Western civilization we have suggested a new phase of western history began around 1780 with the startup of a new civilization that we call Technic civilization – a civilization based on democratic principles and growing through an increasing mastery and application of technology.

Since technological progress has had a significant impact on societal level we must extend our theory to include a technological driving force. There appear to be three reasonable general forms for this force (bearing in mind that we are necessarily working at the level of the "big picture" and not at a detailed level.)

A Constant Technological Driving Force

The simplest technological force that one can imagine is a constant force that begins at a certain time t_0:

$$F_{tech} = \alpha \, \theta(t - t_0) \qquad (85)$$

where α is a constant and $\theta(t - t_0)$ is the step function with value 1 if $t > t_0$. This force leads to a contribution to the societal level S given by

$$S_{tech} = \alpha \, (t - t_0) \, \theta(t - t_0) / (m \, b^2) \qquad (86)$$

$$S_{tot} = S + S_{tech} \qquad (87)$$

where b and m are defined as previously and S represents the societal level due to all other forces. S_{tech} is a linearly rising function of time and can be expected to rise until technological progress ends. It starts with the value zero at $t = t_0$. The linear rise in S_{tech} is possibly a valid approximation for the initial time period of technological progress but is obviously not acceptable for the distant future. Nothing rises forever.

In order to get an appreciation of the effect of a constant technological force on civilization we have plotted it as an addition to S as specified by equation (44) for the Hellenic and Western civilizations. We chose $t_0 = 1800$ and set

$$\alpha = 2 \, m \, b^3 \qquad (88)$$

with $b = .0235$ as previously. This choice of α produces reasonable values of S_{tech} of the same order of magnitude as S. As a result

$$S_{tot} = S + 2b \, (t - t_0) \, \theta(t - t_0) \qquad (89)$$

with S given by equation (44). Equation (89) is plotted in the next two figures.

The Life Cycle of Civilizations

A Linearly Increasing Technological Driving Force

We often hear about the accelerating pace of technology. Some observers even claim technology is growing exponentially. These considerations motivate us to also consider a linearly growing technological change driving force.

$$F_{tech} = \alpha \, (t - t_0) \, \theta(t - t_0) \qquad (90)$$

where α is a constant and $\theta(t - t_0)$ is a step function as before. This force leads to a contribution to the societal level S given by

$$S_{tech} = \alpha[\, t^2 - t_0^2 - 2(t_0 + 2a/b^2)(t - t_0)]\theta(t - t_0) / (2mb^2) \qquad (91)$$

where a, b and m are defined as previously. S_{tech} in this case is a quadratic rising function of time. Notice the effect on the societal level is to add a quadratically increasing term that will quickly grow large as time increases.

This linear force also cannot be taken as realistic indefinitely into the future. However it does have one interesting feature. For times near t_0 it is actually negative. It is negative due to the term rC' expressing the resistance of civilization to change. This resistance to change causes the change C to be negative from $t = t_0$ until $t = t_0 + r/s$. It is amusing to note that there was a significant societal reaction *against* the industrial revolution in its early days (the Luddites and so on). The quantity r/s is roughly 10 years using our values for r and s (see equation (21)). Interestingly, the first card driven loom was developed in 1801, the Luddite outbreak began in 1811 with the breaking of looms, and the Luddites were ultimately completely destroyed by the British government by 1815 by hanging seventeen workers among other measures.

The period from the invention of the card driven loom to the beginning of the repression in 1813 was twelve years – not much different from the ten years predicted by the preceding S_{tech} curve. This close agreement would merit further investigation if a more detailed theory were available. It may be that the technological driving force is approximately linear near the beginning of the Technic civilization.

To get an appreciation of the effect of the linear technological force on civilization we have also plotted it as an addition to S as specified by equation (44) for the Hellenic and Western civilizations. We chose $t_0 = 1800$ and set

$$\alpha = m \, b^4 \qquad (92)$$

with b = .0235 as previously. This choice of α produces reasonable values of S_{tech} in the beginning near t_0. We plot

$$S_{tot} = S + S_{tech} \qquad (93)$$

with S given by equation (44) in the next two figures.

A Bounded Exponential Technological Driving Force

The effect of technology on the societal level of a civilization should be more pronounced in the earlier stages of the civilization's technological development then in the latter stages. The rationale behind this observation is the decreasing benefits of a rising technology level for a civilization's societal level. After a certain point the benefits of technology do not improve the morale or the spirit of a civilization. When the technology of a society has reached a point where the vast majority of the citizenry is "happy" and feels secure (and is secure) from foreign attack a further growth in technology will not improve the societal level. Consequently we can expect further increases in technology will not drive the societal level appreciably higher.

As a result it seems reasonable to consider a bounded exponentially decreasing technological driving force.

$$F_{tech} = \alpha \, e^{-\beta(t-t_0)} \, \theta(t-t_0) \qquad (94)$$

where α is a constant and $\theta(t - t_0)$ is a step function as before. This force leads to a contribution to the societal level S given by

$$S_{tech} = g[\, 1 - e^{-\beta(t-t_0)}\,]\theta(t-t_0) \qquad (95)$$

where g is

$$g = \alpha/[m\beta(\beta^2 - 2a\beta + b^2)] \qquad (96)$$

with a, b and m defined as previously. The determination of α and β is an issue. Since technological progress is still ongoing two hundred years after the beginning of the Industrial Revolution it seems reasonable to assign

$$\beta = 1/267 = b/(2\pi)$$

so that the force is still appreciable until about 267 years after the start of the technological impact at t_0. The result of this choice of β on g is

The Life Cycle of Civilizations

$$g = 8\pi^3\alpha/[mb^2(4\pi^2 b + b - 4\pi a)] \qquad (97)$$

If we let

$$\alpha = \pi m b^3 \qquad (98)$$

we obtain g = 19.7 which results in an S_{tech} that appears to have values that produce a reasonable looking curve for S_{tot} with S given by equation (44) for the Hellenic and Western civilizations. We chose $t_0 = 1800$.

$$S_{tot} = S + S_{tech} \qquad (99)$$

Figs. 33 and 34 show S_{tot} for a bounded exponentially decreasing technological driving force.

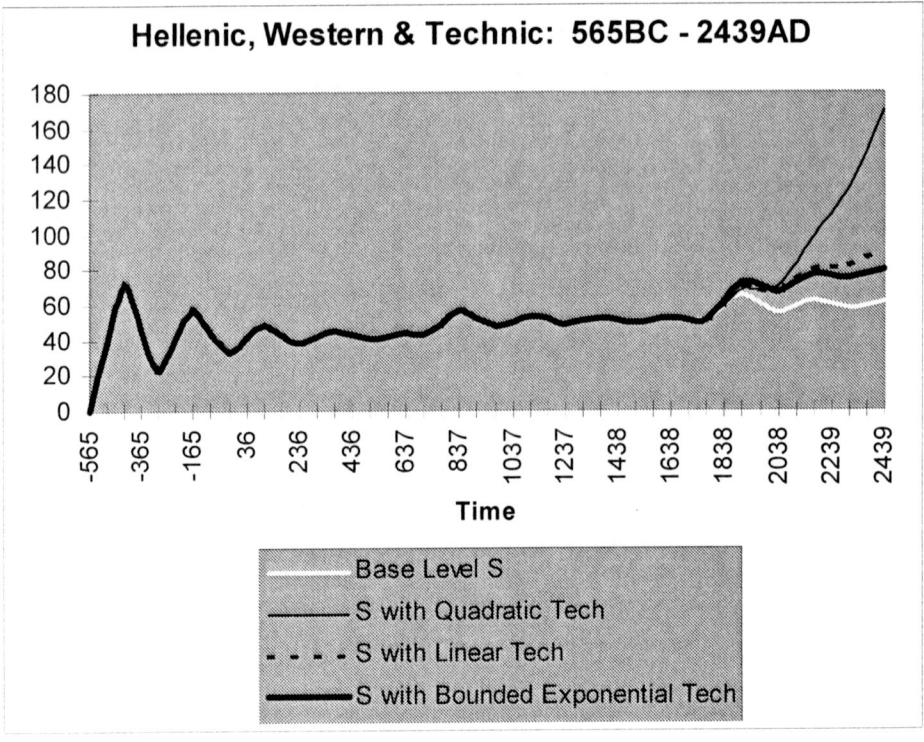

Figure 33. Effect of technology on western civilizations: 565 BC to 2439 AD.

The Life Cycle of Civilizations

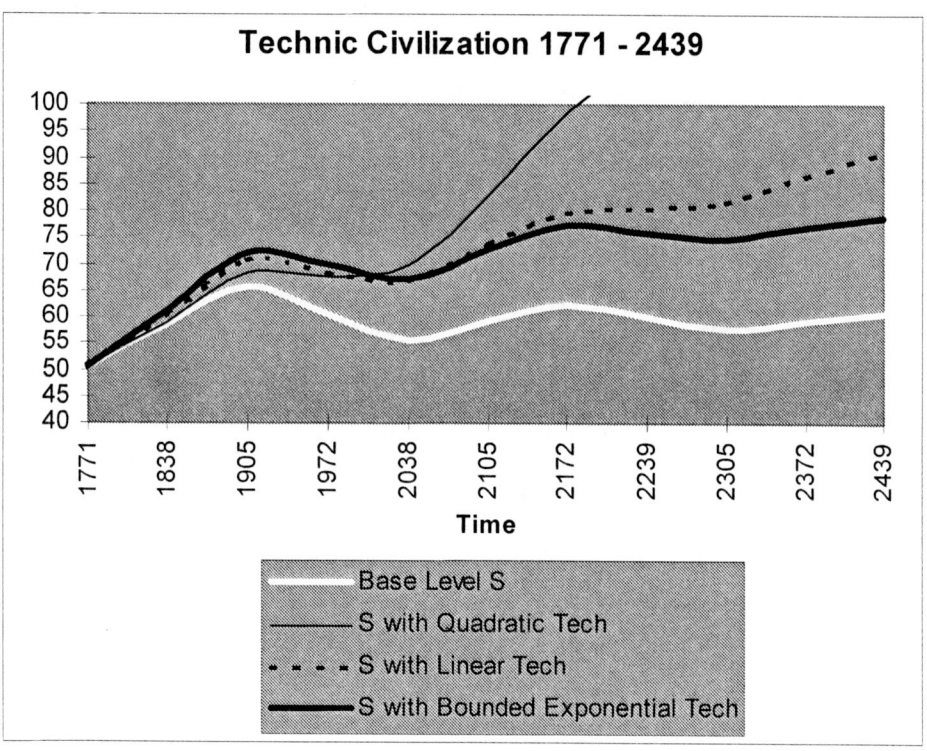

Figure 34. Expanded view of the recent impact of technology on the West.

An examination of these figures shows that there is little difference (at the level at which we are working) in the effects of the three models for the technological driving force in the first two hundred years after the onset in roughly 1800. The quadratic driving force is least effective at the beginning of this period and then "takes off" in roughly 2000. The linear driving force is also less strong in the beginning and does not begin a large upsurge until around 2300. The bounded exponential driving force has the most pronounced effect of the three forces at the beginning of the period. It then gives a constant addition to the baseline value of S after roughly 2150.

The bounded exponential driving force seems to be the most reasonable choice. One reason supporting it was the great upward thrust that the early nineteenth century experienced as a result of the initial technological advances.

The Life Cycle of Civilizations

The second reason is the saturation of the societal effects of technological advances. At some point when human needs are well satisfied and a civilization has a large measure of security the effect on the societal level of new *incremental* technological advances can be expected to be much reduced. (A major technological advance such as time travel or inexpensive, ultra-fast space travel would of course totally change civilization and, as such, would produce a major technologically based startup boost to civilization.)

A major effect of all the technological driving forces is the near elimination of the "rout" in Western (Technic) civilization expected between 1914 and 2048. The societal level in 2048 is somewhat above the level of the baseline societal level of 1914. Thus technology may have enabled the West to overcome the loss of its colonial empires and other societal problems such as two world wars and advance into the future with prosperity and strength.

The beneficial effects of technology have also driven the Japanese to new heights despite a disastrous defeat in World War II. China and India also are starting to see major benefits from technology although they are to some extent "late comers to the game."

12. Barbarians and Civilizations

Barbarians and Civilizations

Barbarians have been viewed as the cause of the disintegration of civilizations since well before the famous remark of Gibbon on the decline of the Roman Empire as "the triumph of Barbarism and Religion." While barbarians often administer the final *coup de grâce* to a disintegrating civilization, there is usually a long interaction between a civilization and a group of barbarians before the barbarians conquer the civilization.

In this chapter we will develop a quantitative theory describing a barbarian culture interacting with a civilization. Then we will apply the theory to the onslaught of the German tribes that eventually ended the Western Roman Empire.

There are two extremes in the interaction of a barbarian culture and a civilization. One extreme is a rapid total conquest of the civilization. The Hyksos and Mongol conquests illustrate this type of interaction. This type of interaction is handled by delta-function startups as in previous chapters. The other extreme is one of gradual interchanges (warlike and peaceful) between a barbarian culture and civilization over a period of centuries resulting in the rise of the barbarians as the civilization disintegrates. We address this type of interaction in this chapter.

The general picture of the history of a long-term interaction of a barbarian culture with a civilization begins with the first (usually warlike) encounters between the civilization and the barbarians with the civilization in a dominant position. Then the barbarians become admiring allies of the civilization and often enter the civilization's service as workers and soldiers. The barbarians obtain an education through their interactions with the civilization and become familiar with the civilization's wealth and weaknesses. In time the civilizations increasing vulnerability, and wealth, tempt the barbarians to attack the civilization for booty and land. Eventually the civilization disintegrates with the barbarians playing a leading role in the successor states if not creating and ruling them.

The Life Cycle of Civilizations

The barbarians are not the cause of a civilization's disintegration in this view. The civilization disintegrates due to internal causes. The barbarians can only accelerate and take advantage of the disintegration of a civilization.

Following our usual approach we assume the barbarian culture starts in a state where the societal level is minimal or zero, $S = 0$ and the change $C = 0$ correspondingly. There is internal resistance to change and so we start with an equation like equation (8):

$$mC_b'' + rC_b' + sC_b = 0 \qquad (100)$$

in the absence of external forces where C_b is the change in the barbarian civilization and S_b is the societal level of the barbarian culture:

$$S_b = \int dt' \, C_b(t') \qquad (101)$$

In the absence of forces $C_b = S_b = 0$ is a solution of these equations. Thus the barbarian society is static and not growing societally.

We now assume that the barbarian culture comes into contact with a civilization. The civilization is much stronger in the initial encounters and little affected by the barbarians. The barbarians are affected by the civilization's society and wealth, and the barbarian culture reacts to these encounters by growing. We represent the force exerted by the civilization on the barbarian culture with

$$F_{bext} = \gamma \, S_c(t) \, \theta(t - t_0)\theta(t_1 - t) \qquad (102)$$

where γ is a constant and S_c is the societal level of the civilization. The time t_0 is the time of the first significant encounters between the barbarians and the civilization. The time t_1 is the time at which the civilization has disintegrated to the point that the barbarians are intermixed with the peoples of the civilization and have assumed leadership of successor states to the empire. The time t_1 marks the end.

We will assume that S_c is a first generation civilization such as Hellenic civilization described by equation (13) with $c_1 = 1$. (The analysis is extendible to civilizations with several startups such as equation (38) using simple but tedious mathematics.)

The solution of

$$mC_b'' + rC_b' + sC_b = \gamma \, S_c(t) \, \theta(t - t_0)\theta(t_1 - t) \qquad (103)$$

leads to

$$S_b = \gamma b[\, t - t_0 + (s(t) - s(t_0))/(2b^2)](m(a^2 + b^2)^2) \qquad (104)$$

where

$$s(t) = e^{-at}[\, t((b^2 - a^2)\cos(bt) + 2ab\sin(bt)) +$$

$$+ ((2a^3 b - ab^3)\cos(bt) + (a^4 - b^4)\sin(bt))/(b(a^2 + b^2))] \qquad (105)$$

with a and b defined as in equations (10) and (11). We use our standard values for a and b: a = .00281 and b = .0235 since both the civilization and the barbarians are human. The constant γ we define with

$$\gamma = 4mb^4 \qquad (106)$$

because it gives reasonable values for S_b. Later we will suggest that this choice appears to be consistent with similar choices in the application of the theory to the interactions of civilizations. Thus there may be a deep reason for our choice of γ in equation (106).

Gothic Barbarians and Hellenic Civilization

We now apply these results to the interaction of the Gothic tribes with Hellenic civilization in the west. We set t_0 = 113 BC the date the Cimbri and Teutones defeated a Roman army at Noreia and t_1 = 378 AD the date the Visigoths conquered Rome. After $t = t_1$ we set $S_b = S_c$ since the Gothic tribes were thereafter intermixed with the population of the empire with the Roman courts administering justice and the military consisting of members of the Gothic tribes. The result is an intermixed society that was still dominated (except militarily) by the societal values of Hellenic civilization due to the much larger numbers of Roman people compared to the relatively small numbers in the tribes.

The next figure shows the growth of Gothic barbarian culture due to the interactions with Hellenic civilization. The culture shows an initial period of rapid growth followed by a pause that probably represents a backlash of the civilization to the strong growth of the barbarian's power. In history this backlash was represented by the appearance of a strong Roman military presence. Afterwards as Roman military power

The Life Cycle of Civilizations

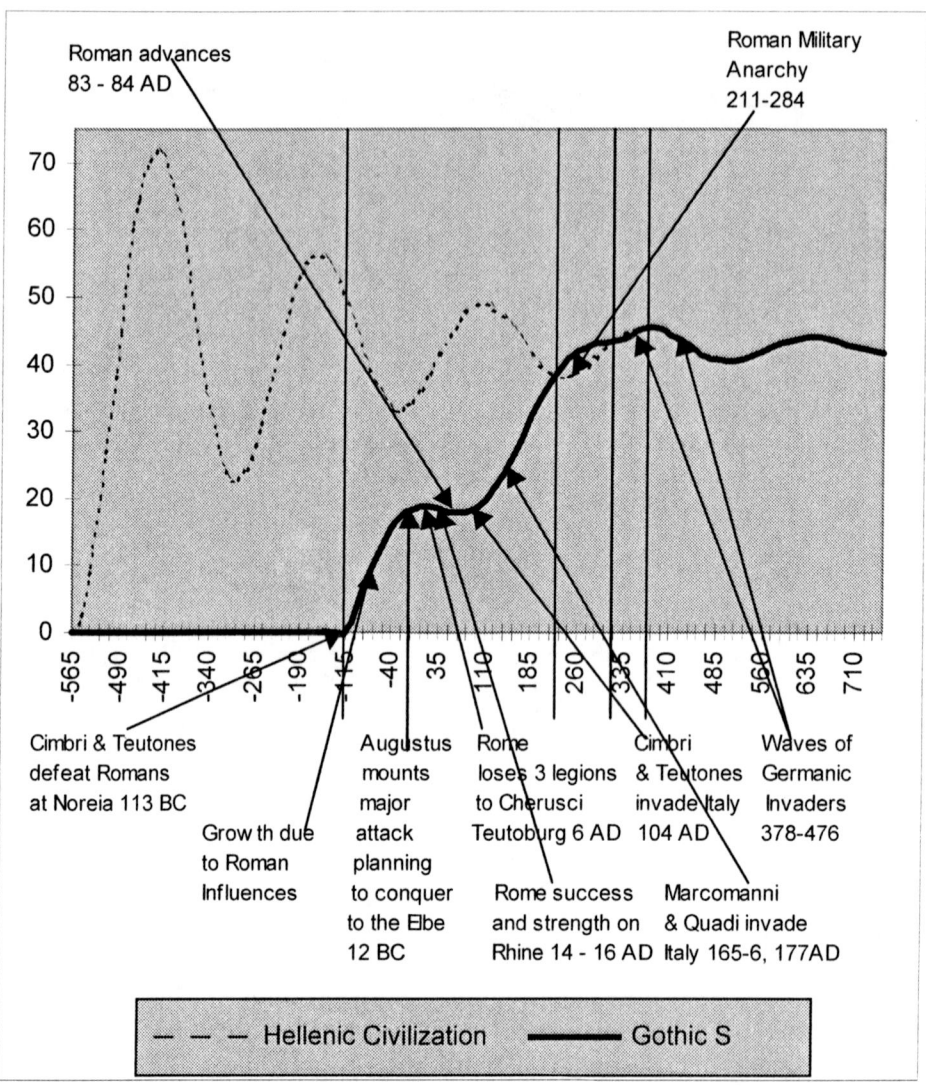

Figure 35. Gothic barbarian culture and Hellenic civilization.

again declined the barbarians resumed growth. They appropriated Roman land as well as military and social values. Eventually the barbarian culture rose to the level of the disintegrating Hellenic civilization in the west until they were, for all practical purposes, integrated. Afterwards their fates were united.

The Life Cycle of Civilizations

As Fig. 35 shows our theory of the interaction of Gothic barbarian culture and Hellenic civilization seems to match the historical events of the period quite well. Thus it appears we have a successful theoretical approach to the long-term interaction of a civilization and a barbarian society.

If one were to develop a more detailed theory of the interaction of a barbarian society with a civilization then one would have to take account of the "back reaction" of the barbarians on the civilization – particularly in the later stages of the civilization's disintegration. It is known that the leaders and the people (the dominant minority and the internal proletariat) are often influenced by the barbarians. They often adopt the dress of the barbarians, their modes of combat, and their ideas including their religious ideas in the latter stages of disintegration.

A step in the direction of a more detailed theory would be to modify the civilization's differential equation for its change C_c to include a term due to the barbarian's influence (force):

$$mC_c'' + rC_c' + sC_c = -\gamma_b S_b(t)\, \theta(t - t_2)\theta(t_1 - t) + F_{rest} \quad (103a)$$

where C_c is the change in the civilization's societal level, t_2 is the time at which the barbarians start to significantly influence the civilization, γ_b is a constant representing the strength of the coupling between the barbarians and the civilization (or, in other words, the influence of the barbarians on the civilization), and F_{rest} represents the other forces on the civilization. Notice the minus sign in front of γ_b which results in the barbarian force "pulling down" the civilization.

13. Interactions Between Human Civilizations

Interacting Civilizations

In the previous chapter we looked at the interaction of a barbarian culture with a civilization. In this chapter we will examine the interaction between two civilizations.

There are several possible scenarios for two civilizations in interaction:

1. An interaction between a "low" civilization and a "high" civilization with a one way transfer from the high civilization to the low civilization. The previous chapter on the interaction of a barbarian culture and a civilization falls into this category. (The barbarian culture can be viewed as a "static civilization in miniature.") The chapter on the interaction of a human civilization with an advanced extraterrestrial civilization describes a more general case in which the constants a and b of the "high" civilization are different. It presumes the earth civilization will receive a one way transmission from the extraterrestrial civilization.

2. A two way interaction between roughly equal civilizations with the same a and b values. The interaction brings them to parity in societal level. This possibility is discussed in this chapter.

3. A two way interaction between roughly equal civilizations with different a and b values. This case is qualitatively similar to case 2.

4. A one way interaction between roughly equal civilizations with different a and b values. This case is also within the framework of the discussion on a human civilization in interaction with an extraterrestrial civilization (item 1 above).

5. A one way interaction between roughly equal civilizations with the same a and b values. This case is mathematically the same as the

barbarian culture interaction with a civilization discussed in the previous chapter.

We will now consider case 2 with "civilization 1" having a societal level S_1 and a change C_1, and with "civilization 2" having a societal level S_2 and a change C_2. We will assume S_1 is greater than S_2 ($S_1 > S_2$).

When unequal civilizations come into contact we assume the lesser civilization will rise as it acquires the cultural traits of the higher civilization. Correspondingly the higher civilization may acquire aspects of the culture of the lesser civilization. This observation, which may seem strange to some, can be seen in history. For example in the latter stages of the Roman Empire the people and leaders (including the Emperor) began to emulate barbarian dress, manners and styles of combat. A similar phenomenon occurred in China when ambitious Chinese affected Manchu manners and spoke with the manners and gestures of their Manchu conquerors. Thus there is an element of reciprocity in the relations of civilizations.

In developing our theory of the interaction of two standard civilizations we will assume the force on each civilization is proportional to the difference between the other civilization's societal level and the civilization's societal level. Each civilization experiences a driving force "pushing" it to the level of the other civilization. When the civilizations' societal levels become equal the force disappears.

Therefore our force equations are

$$mC_1'' + rC_1' + sC_1 = \gamma (S_2(t) - S_1(t)) \theta(t - t_0) \qquad (107)$$

and

$$mC_2'' + rC_2' + sC_2 = \gamma (S_1(t) - S_2(t)) \theta(t - t_0) \qquad (108)$$

where γ is a constant and t_0 is the time at which the civilizations start interacting.

The solution of these equations gives:

$$S_1(t) = [S_1(t_0) + S_2(t_0) + (S_1(t_0) - S_2(t_0))e^{-f(t-t_0)}]/2 + gS_h \qquad (109)$$

$$S_2(t) = [S_1(t_0) + S_2(t_0) - (S_1(t_0) - S_2(t_0))e^{-f(t-t_0)}]/2 + gS_h \qquad (110)$$

for $t > t_0$ with f and g being constants, and S_h being a solution of the homogeneous equation (equation (8)) which we will take to be (equation (13))

$$S_h(t) = [b - e^{-at}(a \sin(b(t - t_0)) + b \cos(b(t - t_0)))]/(a^2 + b^2) \quad (111)$$

and f being the real positive solution of the equation:

$$f(mf^2 - rf + s) = 2\gamma \quad (112)$$

$S_1(t_0)$ and $S_2(t_0)$ are the societal levels of the respective civilizations at time t_0 when they first start influencing each other. Using the standard values of a = .00281 and b = .0235 which set r and s by equations (10) and (11) we can approximately solve equation (112) to obtain

$$f \approx (2\gamma/m)^{1/3} \quad (113)$$

Equations (109), (110) and (111) are partly determined by the requirement that the societal levels be continuous at $t = t_0$. (The symbol $\approx$ means "approximately equal to.")

The remaining issue is to determine γ. In an attempt to be consistent with the barbarian – civilization case of the previous chapter we will set γ using equation (106) with the result:

$$f \approx 2(b)^{4/3} \quad (114)$$

At this point we are now in a position to see the implications of our solutions for societal levels. We will consider the case of the last stages of Egyptaic civilization when it came into contact with Hellenic civilization at the beginning of the Roman Empire. The preceding Ptolemaic Dynasty period of Egypt was characterized by a Hellenic ruling group superimposed on an Egypt that was largely indifferent to the alien Hellenic rulers. Hellenic civilization largely ignored Egypt during this period with the exception of some technical and religious borrowings.

Interaction between Hellenic and Egyptaic Civilizations

During the Roman occupation Egypt came to Rome in the form of Cleopatra, and in the form of a war led by Cleopatra and Mark Anthony against Octavius. Egyptian religious practices were introduced into Rome and elsewhere in Italy and Greece. Egyptian grain fed the Roman people. Rome, for its part, directed major attention to Egypt to maximize grain exports and tax collection.

The Life Cycle of Civilizations

The close interactions between Egyptaic civilization and Hellenic civilization, as represented by Rome, produced a cross-fertilization that drove the civilizations to a common level. Equations (109) and (110) show the coming together of societal levels—as time progresses the difference between them decreases exponentially.

There are two general cases to consider: $g = 0$ the case with no homogeneous term, and the case of a non-zero g where the homogeneous term S_h contributes to S_1 and S_2 in equations (109) and (110). The case with $g = 0$ has the virtue of simplicity.

In the case of a non-zero g, we will set $g = 1/5$ (a value we have consistently used for startups). The homogeneous part S_h can be viewed as a startup due to the cross-fertilization of cultures. We will assume that serious interchanges between the Hellenic and Egyptaic civilizations began around $t_0 = 20$ BC shortly after the start of the Roman Empire by Augustus (31 BC). Prior to that point Egyptaic civilization was in a petrified state. (The interaction between Greeks and Egyptians in Ptolemaic times was restricted to a limited group of individuals concentrated primarily in Alexandria. This exchange did not have a broad societal impact on either civilization although it stimulated significant intellectual progress.)

The following figures show the change in societal levels as the Hellenic and the Egyptaic civilizations interact for the $g = 0$ case (Figures 36 and 37), and for the case $g = 0.2$ (Figures 38 and 39).

These figures show the civilizations are driven to the same societal level in roughly two hundred years by the force of the interaction. At the end of the two hundred year period Egyptaic civilization had essentially merged with Hellenic civilization. This period of roughly six generations provided the time necessary for a change of mentality in the Egyptians from being Egyptians to being part of the Hellenic Roman Empire.

The Life Cycle of Civilizations

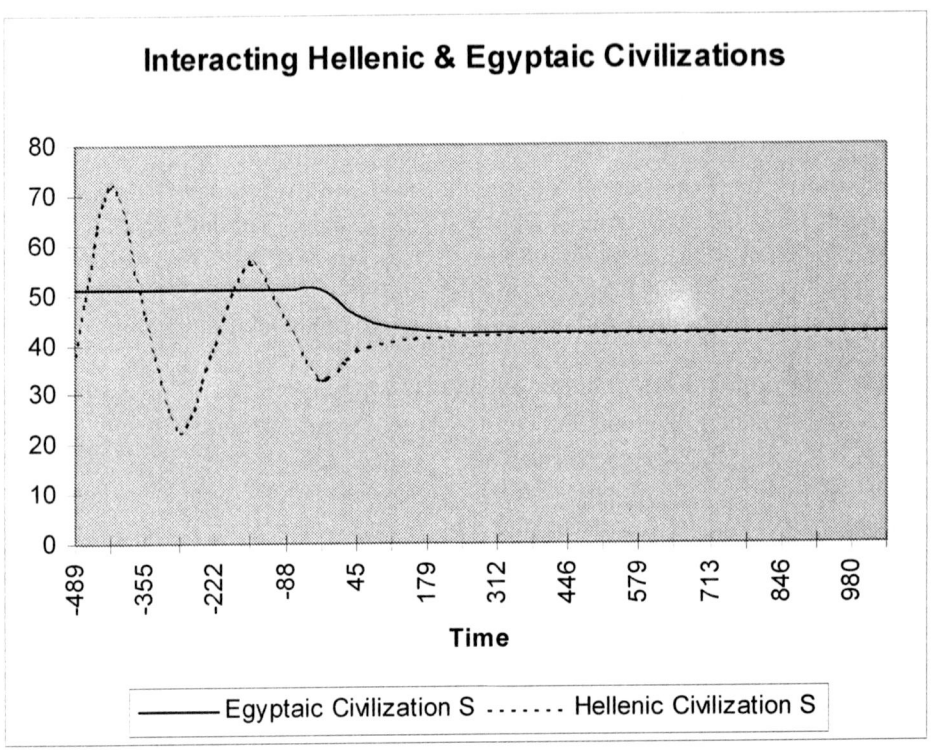

Figure 36. Interacting Hellenic and Egyptaic civilizations with g = 0.

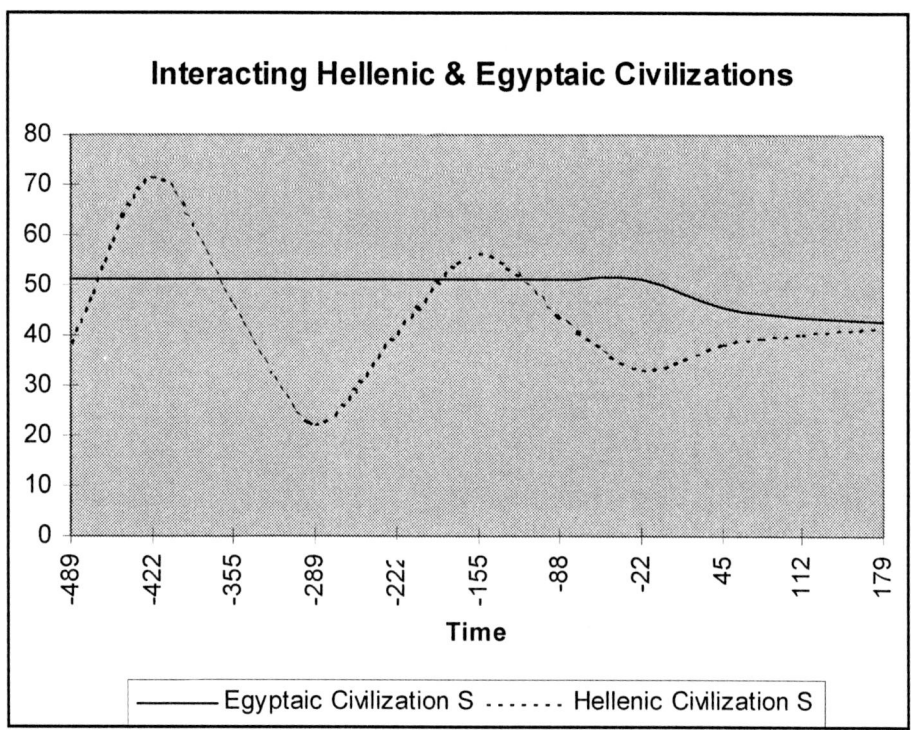

Figure 37. Close-up of interacting Hellenic & Egyptaic civilizations with g = 0.

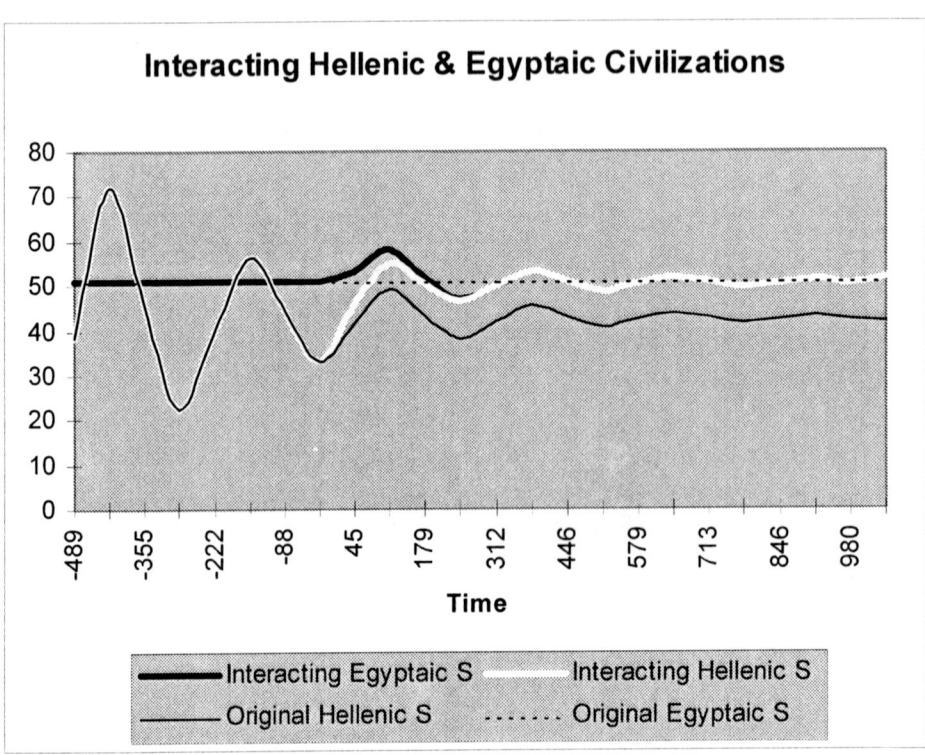

Figure 38. Interacting Hellenic & Egyptaic civilizations with g = 0.2. The interacting Hellenic and Egyptaic civilizations have the same S level after 246 AD.

The Life Cycle of Civilizations

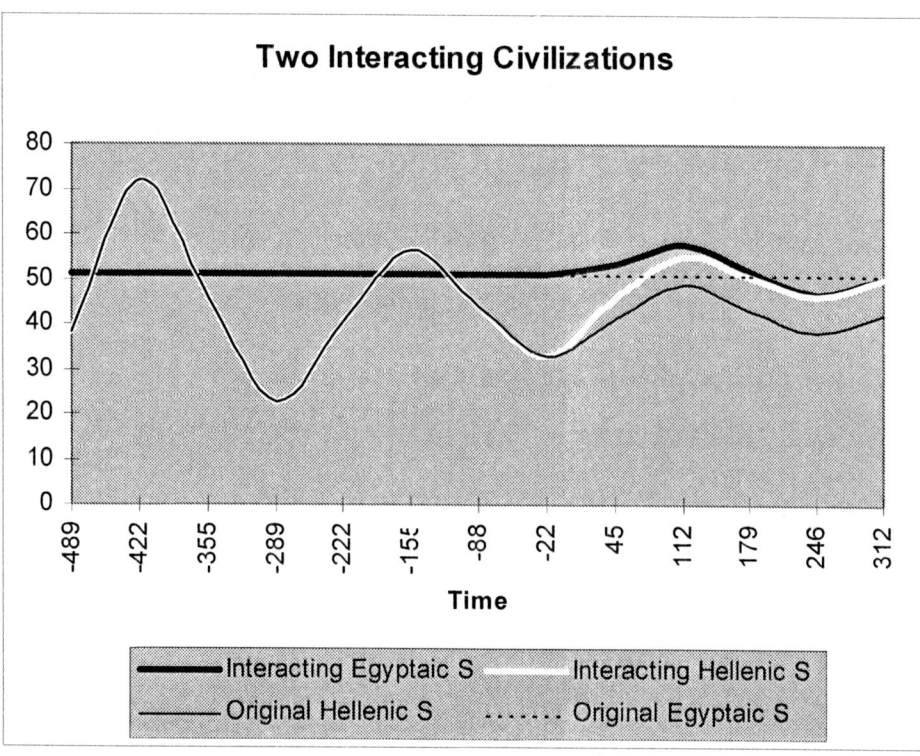

Figure 39. Close up of Hellenic - Egyptaic interaction with g=0.2. Egyptaic civilization had a flat petrified S curve. It begins "oscillating" due to the interaction with Hellenic civilization.

The S curve with the homogeneous term (g = 0.2) appears to be a better choice as a description of the evolution of the interacting Hellenic and Egyptaic civilizations since it conforms to the shape of the dominant Hellenic civilization. The net effect of the interaction was to combine the Egyptaic civilization with the Hellenic civilization not only politically as part of the Roman Empire but also societally. Hellenic civilization received a boost of ten units in its societal level. In addition to massive grain imports, Hellenic civilization utilized many religious and technical contributions from Egypt including plumbing improvements.

14. Interactions with Possible Extraterrestrial Civilizations

The bulk of technical civilizations in the universe may be immensely more advanced than ours ... enormous, almost unbelievable, quantities of information can be communicated over immense distances, if such civilizations exist.
Carl Sagan

Extraterrestrial Civilizations

The search for extraterrestrial life has not as yet uncovered definitive evidence of life "out there." But recently evidence has appeared for many of the preconditions for life as we know it. Water has been found in large quantities on Mars as well as on some Jovian satellites (which may have extensive liquid water oceans beneath their surfaces.) Water and organic compounds have also been detected in interstellar regions suggesting that the preconditions for life may be fairly widespread in the universe. Lastly, life seems to have appeared on earth about five hundred millions years after it was formed – rather quickly from the point of view of astronomical times. These considerations suggest extraterrestrial life will eventually be found (and perhaps very soon if the proposed Mars expeditions are successful.)

New Searches for Extraterrestrial Life

Several other major initiatives will start in the next eight years to identify earth-like planets within 4,000 light years of the earth. The National Aeronautics and Space Administration hopes to launch spacecraft that will systematically search for earth-like planets in 2007 (the Kepler Spacecraft Mission) and in 2009 (the Space Interferometer Mission - SIM). The Kepler mission will observe up to 100,000 stars over a period of two to three years. It will be capable of detecting earth-sized planets circling stars up to a distance of 4,000 light years away by sensing the dimming of a star's light as an earth-sized planet rotates around it casting a shadow. After this survey is completed we will have an idea of the number of earth-like planets in the galaxy. We will also have an idea of where to point antennas to attempt to receive radio and/or laser transmissions from these planets.

In 2009 the Space Interferometer Mission (SIM) will start measuring the wobbles of nearby stars within a radius of 50 light years of earth. It will be sensitive enough to detect earth-sized planets that are orbiting a star at a distance of 0.5 AU to 10 AU from the star. (An AU is about 93,000,000 miles – the distance of the earth from the sun.)

A third spacecraft, the Terrestrial Planet Finder (TPF), is scheduled to be launched around 2015. Its goal is to chemically analyze the atmospheres of promising planets found in preceding space flights to search for evidence of life. The TPF will gather light reflected by a candidate planet and analyze the light for evidence of water, carbon dioxide, oxygen or methane in the planet's atmosphere. The presence of these chemicals would suggest the possibility of life on the planet.

The net result of these three missions will be to identify the extent of life in the galaxy and to identify earth-like planets in the general vicinity of earth. With this knowledge it would be possible to target likely planets that might harbor intelligent life and then attempt to detect radio and laser transmissions from these planets. Ultimately, probes could be sent to nearby planets to explore them and perhaps return. These probes would take hundreds of years to reach planets circling nearby stars.

Communicating with Extraterrestrial Civilizations

After extraterrestrial life is found the next step will be the detection of extraterrestrial civilizations and the establishment of communication with them. The imaginative Project SETI represents an inspiring example of efforts in this area—particularly with its exciting use of ordinary individual's personal computers to analyze data for signals. When evidence for extraterrestrial civilizations is found there will still be the formidable technical challenge of establishing a practical form of communication with them. (Beyond that is the problem of fast interstellar travel for communication, trade and exploration.) The apparent limiting factor of the speed of light is the major impediment to effective communication. Ordinary radio and TV-style communication would take years to communicate with potential nearby civilizations.

There have been suggestions that the limitation of the speed of light might be evaded through the use of quantum effects. Some buzz words in this area of study are quantum teleportation, quantum communications and quantum entanglement. Such efforts are currently highly speculative.

In this chapter we will extend our study of civilizations to include extraterrestrial civilizations. We will base our analysis on a common assumption behind much of the work in the biological and social sciences, that our knowledge of current times and nearby places can be extended to other times and other places. Nature uses similar methods everywhere and no place has a special significance or special treatment by nature. This assumption is true in the natural sciences and would seem to be true of social institutions as well since they are the result of natural events.

With this as our starting assumption we observe that the most intelligent species on earth tend to have long lifetimes. We think of man or elephants or whales with lifetimes that can be over a hundred years. In addition the more intelligent species tend to have a longer period of adolescence before they become mature adults. We also note that as mankind has advanced the average lifetime of mankind has increased significantly. For these reasons it seems reasonable to assume that civilizations that are much more advanced than earthly civilizations have populations with much longer life spans. The period for routs and rallies of earthly civilizations seems to be eight generations or approximately 267 years.

Forms of Extraterrestrial Civilizations

An extraterrestrial civilization at about the same level as Western Technic civilization might thus have a population with a similar lifetime as humans and perhaps a similar period for routs and rallies.

A very advanced extraterrestrial civilization might have a much longer average lifetime for their population and a much longer period of oscillation. Therefore we will look at the societal levels of civilizations with periods of 800, 8,000 and 20,000 years. The choice of these periods was motivated by simple considerations:

> 1. The choice of a period of 800 years was based on the concept of a civilization that had a period roughly three times longer than earthly civilizations. The average lifetime of a person in Western civilization has doubled in the last century. Recent medical advances suggest that a significantly longer lifetime for humans is feasible in the near future. If humanity's average lifetime triples with a corresponding tripling of the length of generations then an 800 year oscillation in human civilizations may be attainable in the future. An extraterrestrial civilization with an 800 year period thus seems reasonable as well.

> 2. The choice of an 8,000 year period was simply an extrapolation by a factor of ten. It seemed suitable for a very advanced civilization. Earth has species (trees and shrubs) with lifetimes of thousands of years. So the possibility of intelligent creatures with very long lifetimes is worth considering.

The Life Cycle of Civilizations

3. The choice of a 20,000 year period was motivated by a curiosity to see how a civilization with a universal state of 30,000 years duration would look. The motivation was to compare it to the Galactic Empire of Isaac Asimov's Foundation series of books. Asimov's Empire had a 30,000 year lifetime. It appears Asimov's Empire is not consistent with the theory of civilizations presented herein. The population of Asimov's Empire has the same life span and social characteristics as the populations of current earth civilizations. Therefore a 30,000 year lifetime for a universal state is very unlikely. In addition, the discussions of the nature of the Empire, its decline, and the following barbarous period also differ from our theory and Toynbee's (and other historians') observations.

Setting the Parameters of Extraterrestrial Civilizations

The period T sets the parameter b of our theory of civilizations directly due to equation (16):

$$T = 2\pi/b \qquad (115)$$

The following table lists values of b and the lengths of the phases of a civilization for each choice of period. The generation length is based on eight generations per period as seen on earth. It is only meant to convey an idea of time scales.

Period (years)	Generation Length (years)	b (years^{-1})	Startup (years)	Time of Troubles (years)	Universal State (years)	Total Lifetime (years)
267	33.38	.0235	134	400	400	934
800	100	.00785	400	1,200	1,200	2,800
8,000	1000	.000785	4,000	12,000	12,000	28,000
20,000	2500	.0000785	10,000	30,000	30,000	70,000

Figure 40. Possible time periods of extraterrestrial civilizations.

The other parameter that describes a civilization is the parameter a. The value of a sets the rate of the decline of a civilization. While some might hope that a sufficiently advanced civilization might not decline like earthly civilizations, the decline of all complex entities with time is a universal fact of nature. So we shall assume that extraterrestrial civilizations will also decline with time. The rapidity of the decline is not something that we can at present determine. Therefore we will consider a range of possibilities based on earthly experience extrapolated (adapted) to extraterrestrial civilization time scales.

The Life Cycle of Civilizations

The successive peaks of a civilization decline by the *factor*:

$$e^{-d}$$

where

$$d = aT \tag{116}$$

with T being the period measured in years by equations (18) and (19).

For human civilizations we found d = .75 and thus a = .00281 were able to describe all the human civilizations that we studied except for petrified civilizations where d = 5 (and thus a = .0187) was used. For extraterrestrial civilizations we will consider a range of d values from .5 to 5. The values of the parameter a that we examined are:

d = e^{-d} = Period	.5 .607	.75 .472	1 .368	2 .135	5 .00674
267	.00187	.00281	.00375	.00749	.0187
800	0.000625	0.000938	0.00125	0.0025	0.00625
8,000	0.0000625	9.38E–05	0.000125	0.00025	0.000625
20,000	0.000025	3.75E–05	0.00005	0.0001	0.00025

Figure 41. Possible values of a for extraterrestrial civilizations.

Using the above values of a and b, and the universal expression for S given in equation (13) with $c_1 = 1$:

$$S(t, r) = [b - e^{-at}(a \sin(bt) + b \cos(bt))]/(a^2 + b^2) \tag{117}$$

We obtain the following figures displaying the societal level S for extraterrestrial civilizations.

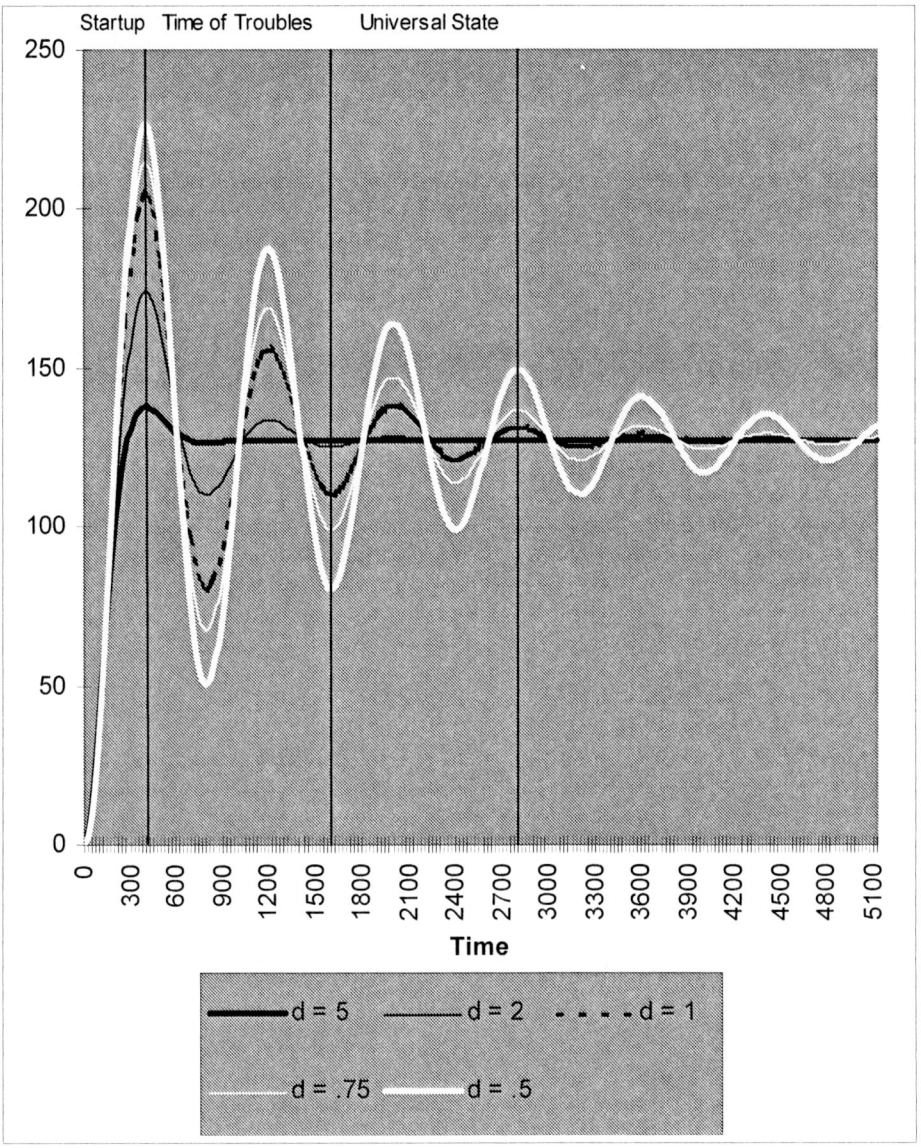

Figure 42. S for extraterrestrial civilizations with an 800 year period.

The Life Cycle of Civilizations

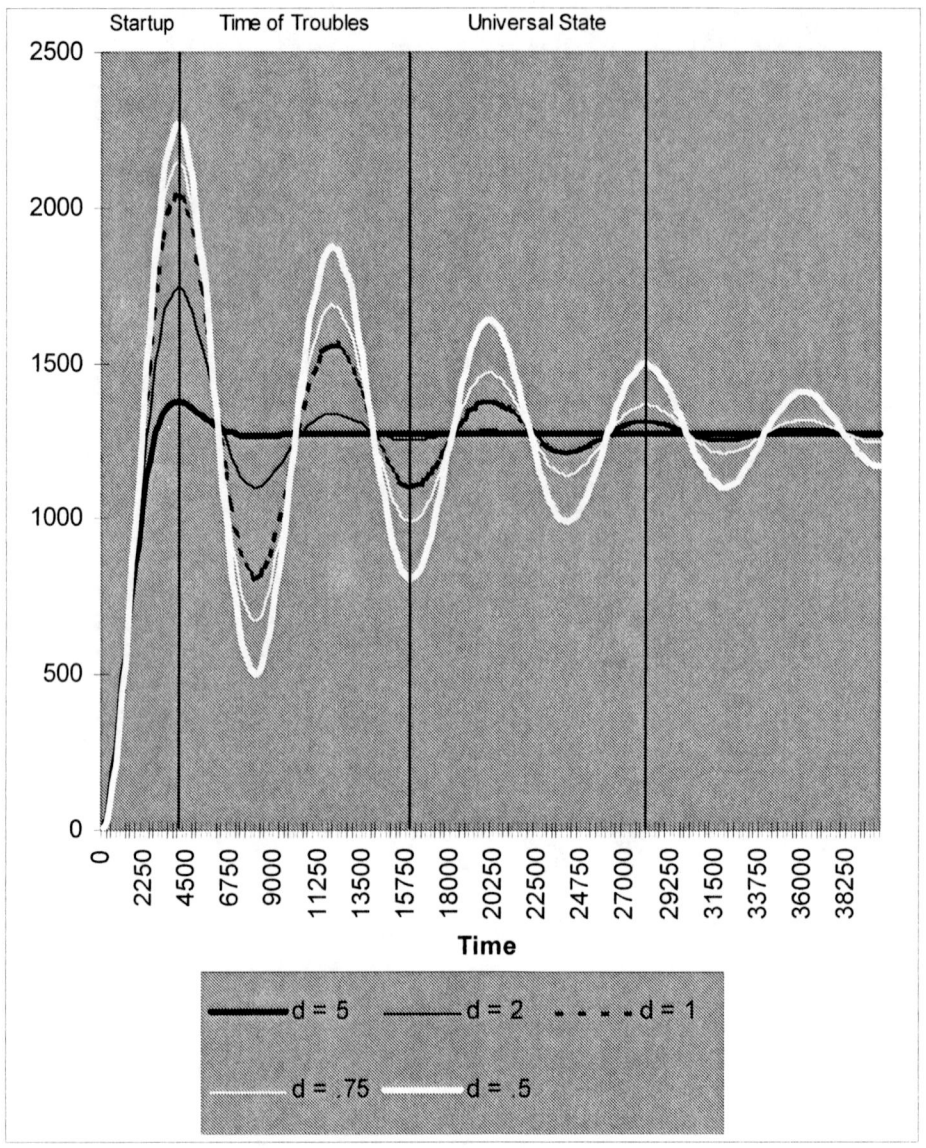

Figure 43. S for extraterrestrial civilizations with an 8,000 year period.

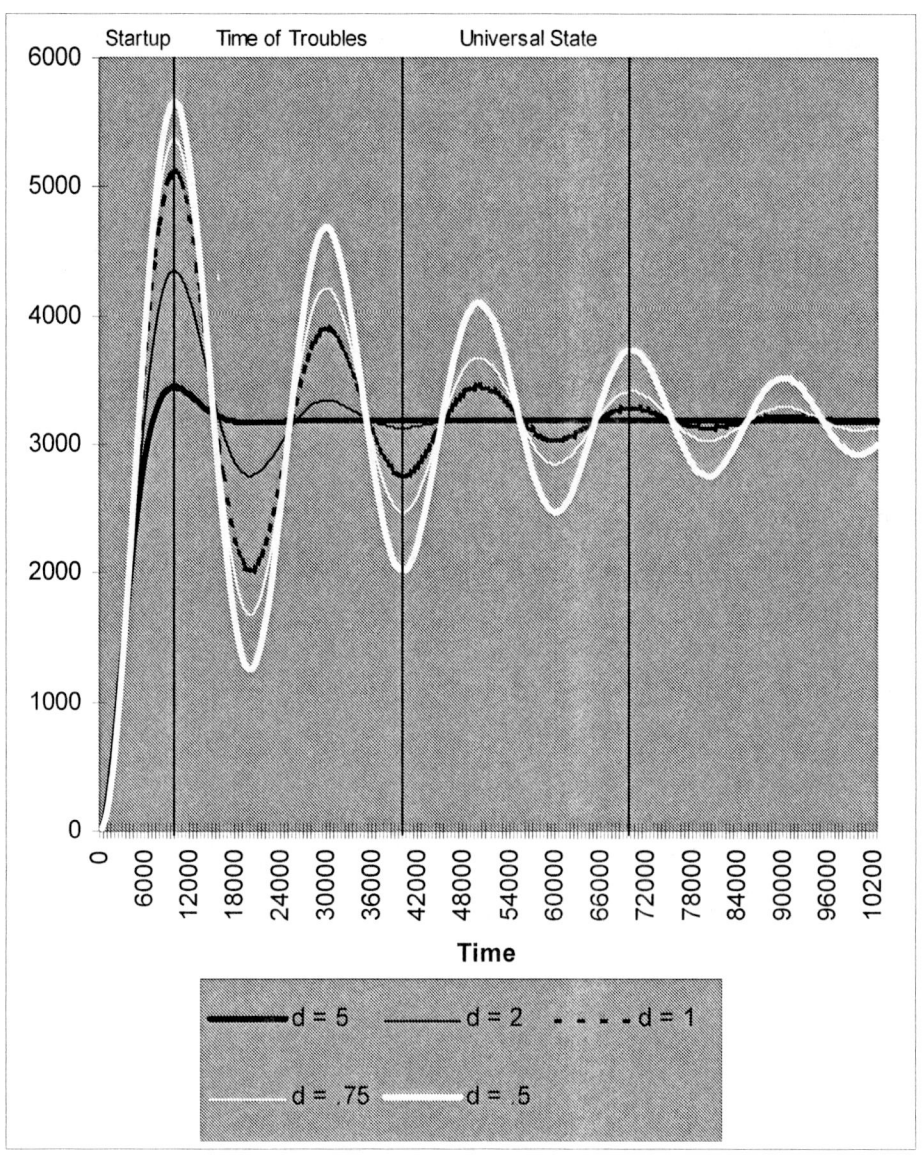

Figure 44. S for extraterrestrial civilizations with a 20,000 year period.

Extraterrestrial Civilization Interacting with a Human Civilization

The interaction between an extraterrestrial civilization and an earth civilization such as Western Technic civilization is an interesting question to investigate. The first issue to address is how can an earth civilization interact with an extraterrestrial civilization. There does not appear to be any extraterrestrial civilizations in this solar system although the possibility of hidden civilizations beneath the surface of Mars has not been ruled out. There is also a possibility of life on Jupiter and Saturn's satellites that might have evolved into intelligent species with civilizations. But all these possibilities are unlikely. We have not detected any electromagnetic radiation from these bodies that would signal a civilization. So if a civilization exists within our solar system it must either be primitive or completely different in nature from our technological civilization.

Thus we expect that any extraterrestrial civilization must be located in another solar system(s) in our galaxy or in other galaxies. Interaction with a civilization at these great distances will be difficult due to the limitations on communication and travel imposed by the speed of light. No message can travel faster than the speed of light. No body can travel faster than the speed of light. These laws of nature severely limit interactions with extraterrestrial civilizations. (The situation would change dramatically if methods can be found by future science to evade these restrictions. Then our discussion would become very relevant.)

For the moment we will assume that an extraterrestrial civilization can transmit vast amounts of cultural and technical knowledge to earth via conventional means over a period of years. Current data compression technology makes the transmission of large amounts of information in a short time feasible. Why would an extraterrestrial civilization transmit such knowledge? There are a number of reasons one could envision: a strong sense of altruism, a pride in their own civilization, a hope that other civilizations might reciprocate, a sense of loneliness after their own solar system is explored and found empty, and/or a knowledge that other civilizations would not be a threat due to the vast distances and the limitations of the speed of light.

So we will assume an extraterrestrial civilization may transmit advanced knowledge to earth that may be a driving force for the advancement of earth civilizations.

We will further assume that the extraterrestrial civilization is described by equation (13) using extraterrestrial values for a and b which we will denote as a_e and b_e. (e is for extraterrestrial.)

$$S_e(t, r) = c_1[b_e - e^{-a_e t}(a_e \sin(b_e t) + b_e \cos(b_e t))]/(a_e^2 + b_e^2) \quad (118)$$

with $c_1 = 1$. (Actually S_e could be a superposition of terms like equation (117) and the results would be qualitatively similar to the solution below.)

We will see the impact of an extraterrestrial civilization on Western Technic civilization in the effects of the extraterrestrial civilization's force. (We assume the interaction will be peaceful and constructive. The possibility of the obliteration of human civilizations also exists.) We will represent the force exerted by the extraterrestrial civilization on a human civilization starting at time $t = t_0$ by:

$$F_{etext} = \gamma\, S_e(t)\, \theta(t - t_0) \quad (119)$$

where γ is a constant. The time t_0 is the time of the first significant exchanges between the extraterrestrial and the human civilization.

The solution of

$$mC'' + rC' + sC = F_{ext} + \gamma\, S_e(t)\, \theta(t - t_0) \quad (120)$$

(with F_{ext} containing all other forces) leads to

$$S = S_0(t) + \gamma b_e(t - t_0)/(mD) + S_1(t) \quad (121)$$

$$S_1(t) = -\gamma b_e[(s(t) - s(t_0)]/m \quad (122)$$

with

$$s(t) = e^{-a_e t}[A_e \cos(b_e t) - B_e \sin(b_e t)]/(b_e(b_e^2 + a_e^2)^2 E) + \\ + e^{-at}[A\cos(bt) - B\sin(bt)]/(b(a^2 + b^2)^2 E) \quad (123)$$

where

$$A_e = 4a_e b_e^3 - 2ab_e^3 - 2a_e^2 b_e(a_e - a) - 2a_e b_e[b^2 + (a_e - a)^2] \quad (124)$$

$$A = 4ab^3 - 2a_e b^3 - 2a^2 b(a - a_e) - 2ab[b_e^2 + (a_e - a)^2] \quad (125)$$

$$B_e = b_e^2(b_e^2 - b^2) + a_e^2(a_e - a)^2 - 6a_e b_e^2(a_e - a) - a^2 b_e^2 + a_e^2 b^2$$

$$B = b^2(b^2 - b_e^2) + a^2(a_e - a)^2 + 6ab^2(a_e - a) + a^2 b_e^2 - a_e^2 b^2 \qquad (126)$$

$$(127)$$

$$D = (a_e^2 + b_e^2)(a^2 + b^2) \qquad (128)$$

$$E = [(b_e^2 - b^2)^2 + (a_e - a)^4 + 2(b_e^2 + b^2)(a_e - a)^2] \qquad (129)$$

where $S_0(t)$ is the Western Technic societal level in the absence of the extraterrestrial force, and a and b are the parameters describing an earthly civilization. This solution applies unless $a_e = a$ and $b_e = b$. (In the unlikely case that the extraterrestrial civilization has the same a and b values as earth civilizations the solution for the barbarian - civilization interaction would apply (equation (104)) with the earth civilization being the "barbarians".)

The parameters a and b are defined as in equations (10) and (11). We use our standard terrestrial values for a and b: a = .00281 and b = .0235. We will consider the cases of an extraterrestrial civilization with a period of 800 years and an extraterrestrial civilization with a period of 8,000 years. In each case we will use d = .75 to set a_e (see the previous section). The value of b_e is set by the period of the civilization as in the previous section.

Period (years)	a_e	b_e
800	.000938	.00785
8000	.0000938	.000785

We will choose the time that serious interactions begin in the not too distant future: t_0 = 2038. It is conceivable that Project SETI or other efforts will result in contact within the next thirty-six years.

The interaction constant γ should depend on the earth civilization's receptivity to transmissions from other cultures. While γ could be an arbitrary constant that differs in an unpredictable way from interaction to interaction, we will assume that it depends on the receiving civilization's internal characteristics. In particular we set

$$\gamma = 4mb^4 \qquad (130)$$

where b is the b value of the receiving earth civilization in this section. We shall see that this choice leads to what appears to be reasonable results for both the 800 year and 8,000 year extraterrestrial civilization cases. The following figures show the plots of equation (121) for each case.

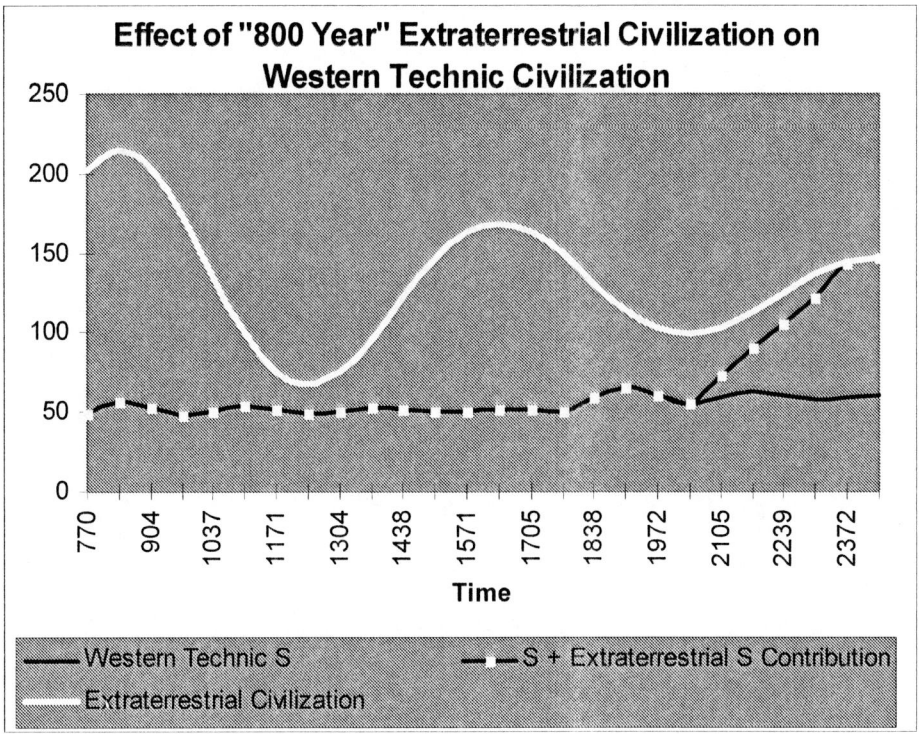

Figure 45. Effect of an extraterrestrial civilization with an 800 year period on Western Technic civilization.

The Life Cycle of Civilizations

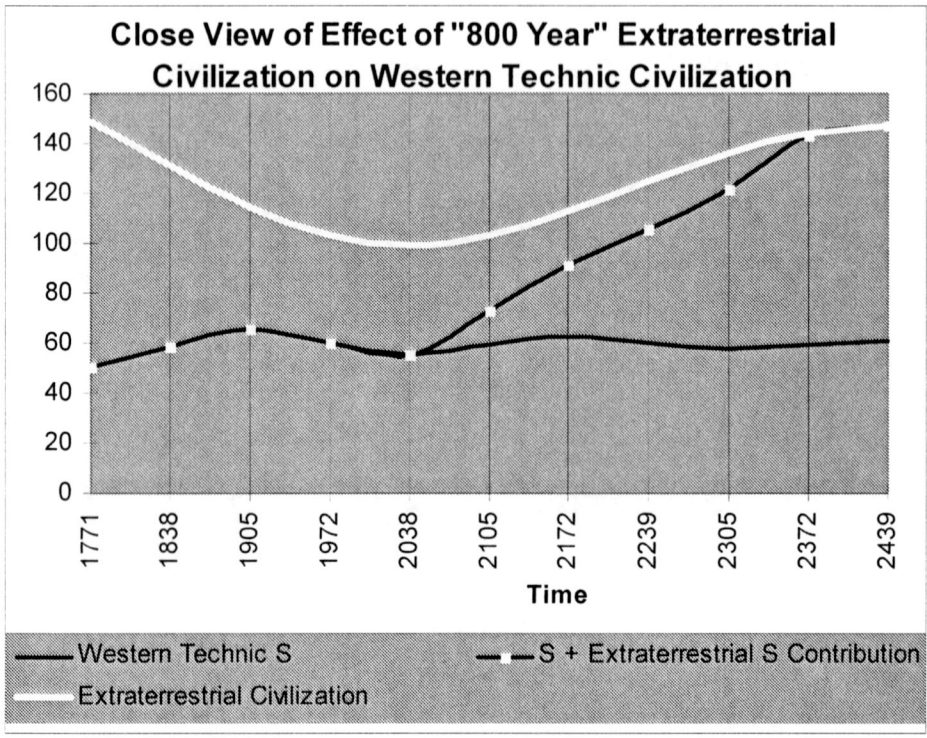

Figure 46. Close view of the effect of an extraterrestrial civilization with an 800 year period on Western Technic civilization.

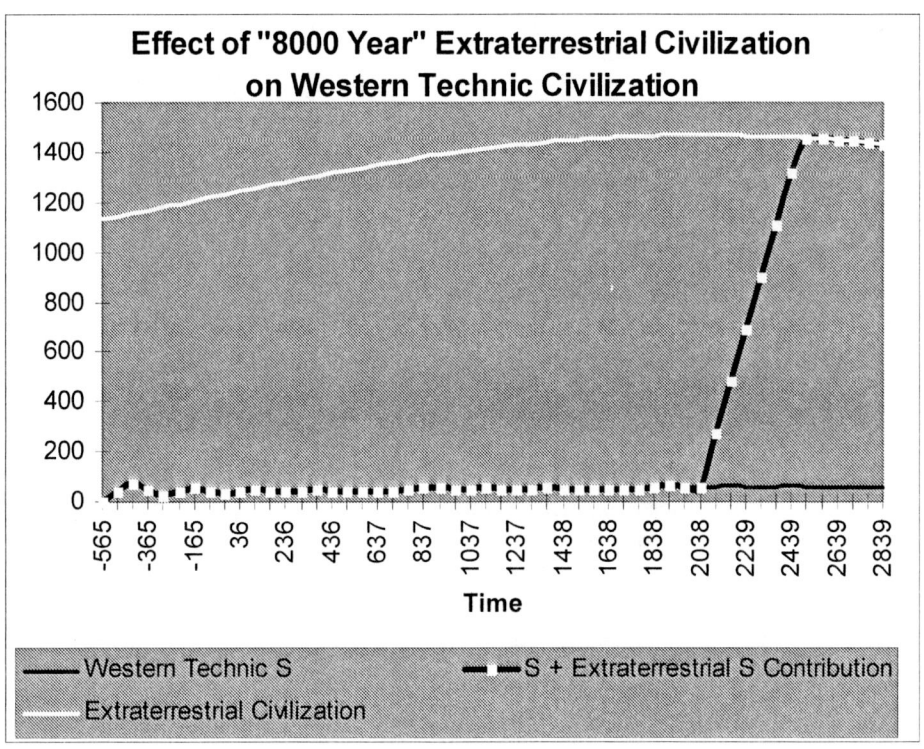

Figure 47. The effect of an extraterrestrial civilization with an 8,000 year period on Western Technic civilization.

The Life Cycle of Civilizations

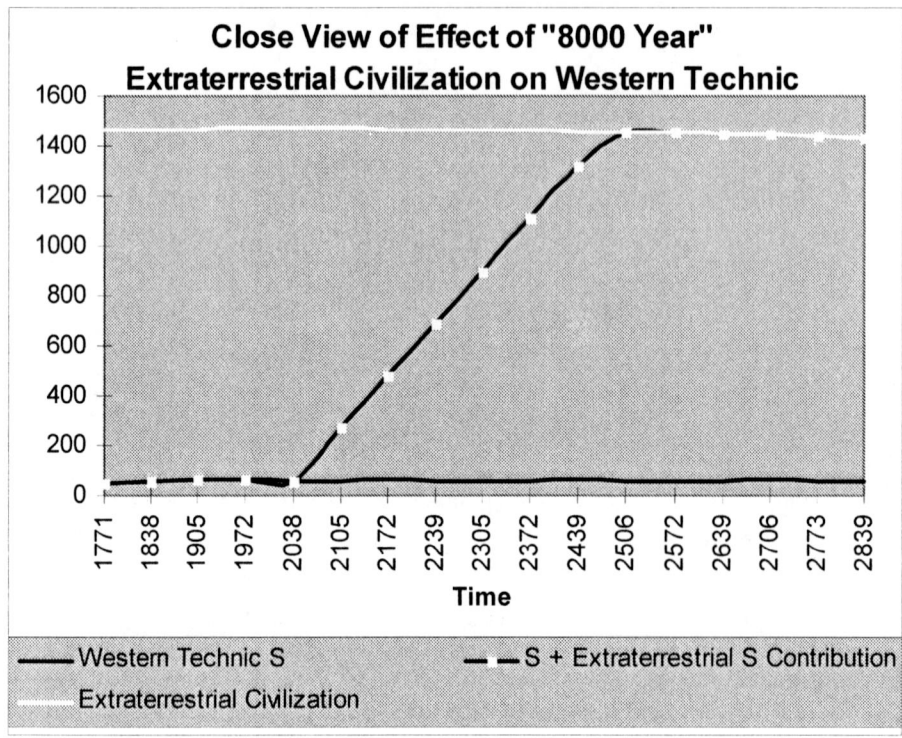

Figure 48. A close view of the effect of an extraterrestrial civilization with an 8,000 year period on Western Technic civilization.

The Resulting Rapid Rise of Human Civilizations

If an advanced extraterrestrial civilization made contact with earth civilization, then the preceding figures suggest that earth civilizations would progress upwards relatively rapidly to the level of the extraterrestrial civilization. The form of contact could be as simple as a one-way transmission of the scientific and cultural knowledge of the civilization via radio waves or laser beams. Earth scientists could decipher the incoming data via some "Rosetta stone" perhaps in the form of mathematics. The following table shows the transition time for technical earth civilization to reach the level of advanced extraterrestrial civilization is of the order of a few hundreds of years.

Extraterrestrial Civilization	Time Required By Earth Civilization To Reach its Level (years)
800 Year Period	334
8,000 Year Period	468

Figure 49. The time required by earth civilization to reach the level of various extraterrestrial civilizations in our theory.

Although the time required for the transition is not long on the scale of human history it can expect to be punctuated by massive civil disturbances unless carefully managed.

Dominant Term in Societal Level Transition

The dominant term in the transition expression for S given by equation (121) is the linear term in time:

$$\gamma b_e (t - t_0)/(mD)$$

which emanates from a constant term in the change C that, in turn, has its source in the constant term in the force exerted by the extraterrestrial civilization on the earth civilization.

Consequently any extraterrestrial civilization that has a roughly constant societal level during the period of contact with earth civilization can be expected to generate such a linear term in the societal level of the earth civilization. Thus our results have some generality and do not depend on the precise form of the extraterrestrial civilization's societal curve S.

Stimulus via an Extraterrestrial Information Burst

The force exerted by the extraterrestrial civilization may take place in a short time interval: for example in the form of a massive burst of information sent to earth over a period of days or weeks, and containing the "entire" accumulation of knowledge of the extraterrestrial civilization. There are two extremes of response that one can envision:

    1. This burst of data could have the same overwhelming effect on Western Technic civilization that the Hyksos conquest had on Egyptaic civilization: but as a conquest of knowledge and ideas rather

than a physical, military conquest. The result could be a revulsion against the influx of knowledge (while perhaps accepting some of the technical parts) and the entry of Western Technic civilization into a petrified state that, perhaps paradoxically, could continue to progress technically. In this case we would expect a startup to result similar to that seen in the Egyptaic case in equations (26), (27) and (28).

2. This burst of information could have the same effect on Western Technic civilization that the influx of classical Greek knowledge and culture had on early Western civilization: a Renaissance. This response requires that the earth civilization be in a receptive state that is capable of assimilating the influx of knowledge. As Toynbee has pointed out earlier infusions of Greek learning into Europe at the end of the Dark Ages fizzled out because the society of the time was unable to understand and appreciate the knowledge.

Perhaps a better analogy for the impetus given to earth civilization by a burst of knowledge from an extraterrestrial civilization would be the Japanese response to the "opening of Japan" in 1868. The Japanese totally reorganized their government (Meiji Restoration) and society to accommodate a transformation to an advanced industrial economy. The response in this case would be modeled as in equations (32) and (33) that describe the Japanese case with a delta-function force representing the knowledge infusion.

Thus the detection of an extraterrestrial civilization via radio or laser beam signals and the subsequent reception of massive amounts of information in a short time period could have a profound effect on earth civilizations even if there is no "back and forth" communication or physical contact.

15. Universality of interactions Between Civilizations

A Universal Interaction Constant

The study that we have made of the interactions of civilizations and cultures suggest that the interaction constant γ may have the same form in all of these situations. In the case of barbarians and civilizations, the case of the interaction of two civilizations, and the case of the interaction of an earth civilization with a vastly different extraterrestrial civilization we found that

$$\gamma = 4mb^4 \qquad (131)$$

leads to reasonable results in all cases including interactions with very different extraterrestrial civilizations with periods of 800 years and 8000 years. It thus seems reasonable to suggest equation (131) may have some deep significance.

Another regularity that leads one to suspect that there might be some deeper significance present is the value

$$f = mb/5 \qquad (132)$$

(g = 1/5) which we used for all positive startups in our study of human civilizations. It may be coincidental but the expression for f can be approximated numerically with

$$f = mdb/\pi = 2ma \qquad (133)$$

or

$$g = 2a/b$$

to within 20% if d = .75 as d is for all but petrified human civilizations. Using equation (133) for f, and thus g, would not significantly alter our results.

The Life Cycle of Civilizations

The resolution of these issues requires a more detailed, and deeper, theory of civilizations. Nevertheless, the fact that we can describe very disparate interactions and civilizations with similar values for parameters suggests that our approach may be valid and may be a good approximation to a detailed fundamental quantitative theory of societies.

16. Human Progress through the Progression of Civilizations

The Societal Progress of Mankind

When we look at history we see the creation of civilizations, their growth, their decline and eventually their disintegration. What rays of hope can we see in this cycle of growth and decay? Are we doomed to an indefinite future of "mindless armies clashing in the night?"

Modern societies have become conditioned to an expectation of progress. The growth of technology and knowledge, and improving living standards in the Western world, have led us to believe that the future will be better than the present. Yet when we look at history we do not see improvements in the happiness or the situation of mankind as represented by their civilizations. The twentieth century has been described by some observers as the bloodiest century in human history. Only the Mongols practiced the wholesale murder of large civilian populations in previous centuries.

When we examine the Arts or culture in general it is far from obvious that one can assert that we have progressed upwards from the Arts and culture of Athens at its peak. Nor can we see a growth in culture in the last two centuries that compares with the growth of the Athens of Pericles.

Yet there appears to be three general areas where there is evidence of human progress that show increases from civilization to civilization as world history evolves: science, technology, and religious/moral concepts. As Toynbee points out, "The history of Religion appears to be unitary and progressive by contrast with the multiplicity and repetitiveness of the histories of civilizations." And the growth in Science and Technology is self-evident.

Civilizations have a lifetime of approximately a thousand years. As we have seen their lifetime can be extended by external and internal forces. Their effects can be further extended in successor civilizations that arise from their ashes. If we compare contemporary civilizations with the civilizations of past millenniums we see that the general standards of behavior and conduct are much improved. More people are living better and longer. Educational and cultural levels are higher and more widely diffused among the people. So we sense an ill-defined progress towards a better world—particularly in the West and the nations in Asia that are participating in rising standards of living through modern technology.

A Quantitative Definition of Progress

With these considerations in mind we would like to define a measure, or variable, that quantifies progress in some general sense. We realize that we cannot measure the values of this variable experimentally at this time in the absence of a detailed quantitative theory of civilizations. Nevertheless it is important to see if a sensible measure of progress can be defined. Since we view progress as the cumulative result of the generations of civilizations we will start with the simplest possible definition (Ockham's Razor) of the total human progress at time t, $P(t)$, as the sum of the societal levels $S_i(t)$ of all civilizations at time t:

$$P(t) = \sum_i S_i(t) \qquad (134)$$

where the sum is over civilizations, labeled by i, existing at time t in all parts of the world and $S_i(t)$ is the ith civilization.

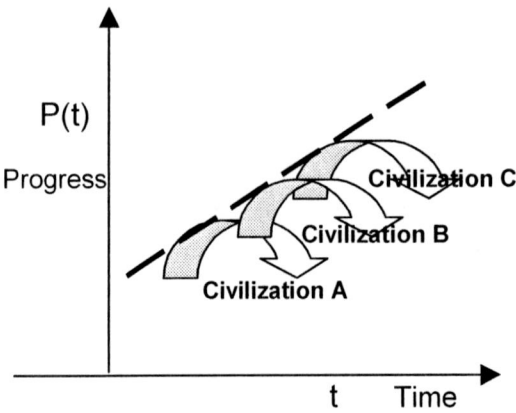

Figure 50. Man progresses through a series of civilizations that are born and die.

We expect progress to be revealed if P(t) increases with time indicating a worldwide growth of societal level.

In the last six thousand years of human history we have seen many civilizations grow and disintegrate. The regions and population of civilized areas have also changed. While the definition of progress P(t) appears straightforward, the calculation of P(t) raises the question of double counting due to overlaps of civilizations in time and location. One example of this problem is the cases of Iranic civilization and Arabic civilization which fused together to create an Islamic civilization. The population of the Islamic civilization is the sum of the populations of the preceding Iranic and Arabic civilizations. Should we add the societal levels of the extensions in time of the Iranic and Arabic civilizations to obtain the societal level of Islamic civilization? It seems that a more accurate result would be obtained if we treated civilizations by region and added civilizations region by region to calculate progress. We have followed this procedure in the following figures.

Another issue is the major effect of technology on contemporary civilizations. It appears that technology is a major new factor in the evolution of civilizations and human progress. The first two of the following figures show the progress of civilizations without taking account of an additional technological contribution. The third figure includes the effect of technology. Remarkably this figure shows an almost straight-line growth in progress P(t) with time. The contributions of technology are required to obtain a straight line due to the flattening of progress (without technological effects) in the centuries after 1800.

The Calculation of Mankind's Progress

The following figure, Figure 51, shows how the societal levels of all civilizations (except those in America and abortive civilizations) add to form the progress P(t) without taking account of the effects of modern technology. A straight line fit is a reasonable approximation to the overall growth of progress with time with a significant deficit after 1500 AD. The data for each civilization is based on the following:

- Egyptaic – as earlier in our discussion with a cutoff to zero at 500 AD.
- Syraic – as earlier
- Arab-Islamic – as earlier but with the Syraic part separated out to avoid double counting.
- Iranian-Islamic – as earlier but with the Syraic part separated out to avoid double counting.
- Japan – as earlier
- China – as earlier

The Life Cycle of Civilizations

- India – as earlier
- Hellenic – as earlier
- Minoan – standard shape with a startup in 2424 BC and a cutoff to zero in 757 BC.
- Western – as earlier but with Hellenic separated out to avoid double counting.
- Orthodox Main Body – as earlier but with Hellenic separated out to avoid double counting.
- Orthodox Russian – as earlier but with Hellenic separated out to avoid double counting.
- Sumeric-Babylonian - standard shape with a startup in 2824 BC and a cutoff to zero in 156 BC.
- Hittite - standard shape with a startup in 1556 BC and a cutoff to zero in 1088 BC.

The following figures in this section cumulatively add the societal values of each civilization year by year in a graphical manner to show the contributions of each to the overall total. For example in the year –1222 (1222 BC) four civilizations contributed to the overall total of 178:

$S = 51$ Egyptaic
$S = 44$ Minoan
$S = 42$ Sumeric-Babylonian
$S = \underline{41}$ Hittite
Total: 178

as can be seen visually in the following figure. The vertical order of the display of the civilizations has no particular meaning.

The straight line on the figure is meant to suggest a certain linearity that we will quantify later in this section.

The sharp breaks in Sumeric-Babylonian civilization at 200 BC and Egyptaic civilization at 500 AD that are seen in the following figures are imposed to prevent double counting of societal values as these societies are absorbed in successor civilizations.

The Life Cycle of Civilizations

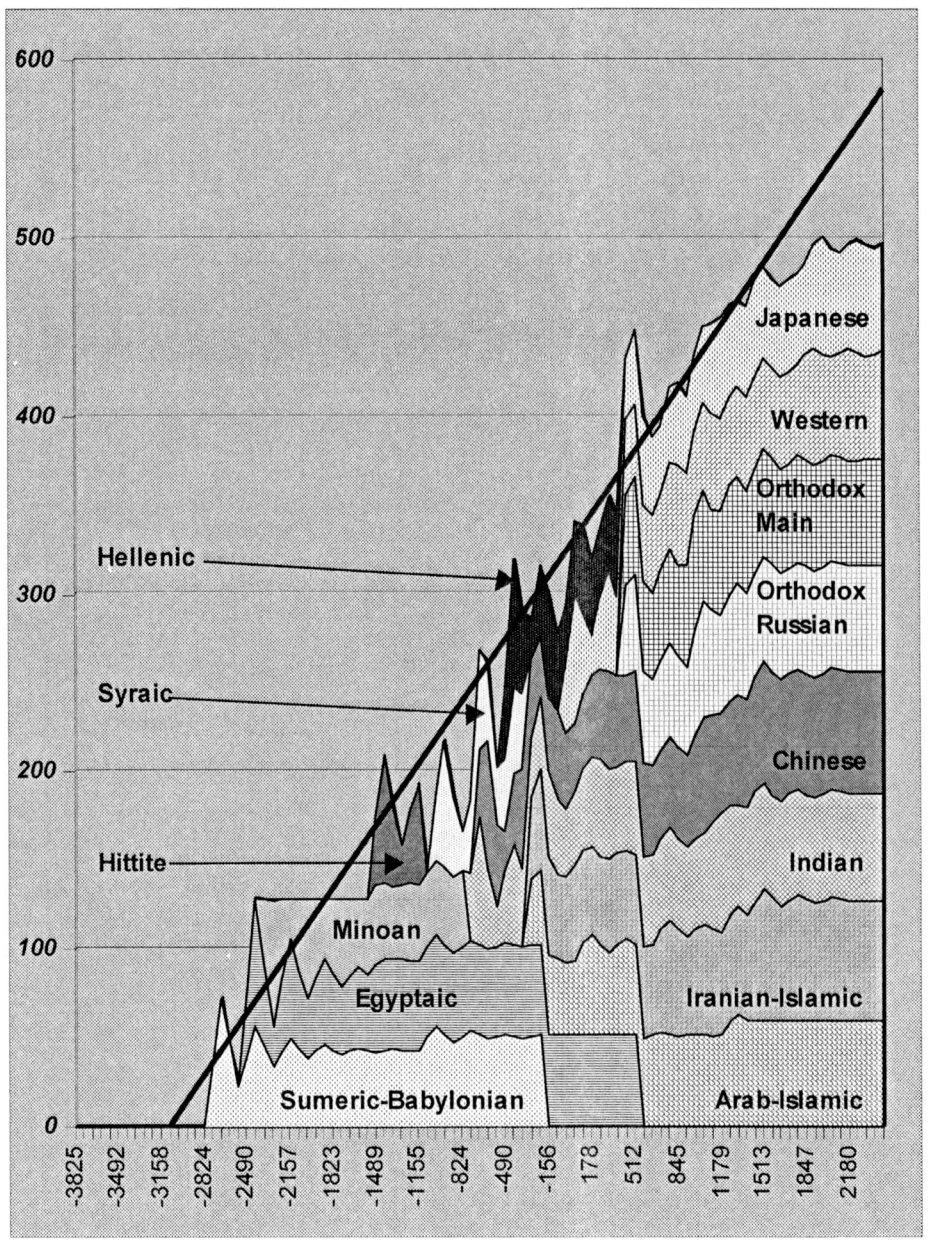

Figure 51. The progress of civilizations showing the progress of mankind without American civilizations or technical contributions.

The Life Cycle of Civilizations

The next figure, Figure 52, shows how the societal levels of all civilizations including the Andean and Mayan civilizations in America (excluding abortive civilizations) add to form the progress P(t), again ignoring the effects of modern technology. A straight line fit is a reasonable approximation to the overall growth of progress with time with a significant deficit still remaining after 1500 AD. The data for each civilization was based on the following:

- Mayan – standard shape with a startup in 223 BC and continuing to 2447 AD based on a continuing culture with a Western overlay until the present.
- Andean – standard shape with a startup in 912 AD and continuing to 2447 AD based on a continuing culture with a Western overlay until the present.
- Egyptaic – as earlier in our discussion with a cutoff to zero at 500 AD.
- Syraic – as earlier
- Arab-Islamic – as earlier but with the Syraic part separated out to avoid double counting.
- Iranian-Islamic – as earlier but with the Syraic part separated out to avoid double counting.
- Japan – as earlier
- China – as earlier
- India – as earlier
- Hellenic – as earlier
- Minoan – standard shape with a startup in 2424 BC and a cutoff to zero in 757 BC.
- Western – as earlier but with Hellenic separated out to avoid double counting.
- Orthodox Main Body – as earlier but with Hellenic separated out to avoid double counting.
- Orthodox Russian – as earlier but with Hellenic separated out to avoid double counting.
- Sumeric-Babylonian - standard shape with a startup in 2824 BC and a cutoff to zero in 156 BC.
- Hittite - standard shape with a startup in 1556 BC and a cutoff to zero in 1088 BC.

The Life Cycle of Civilizations

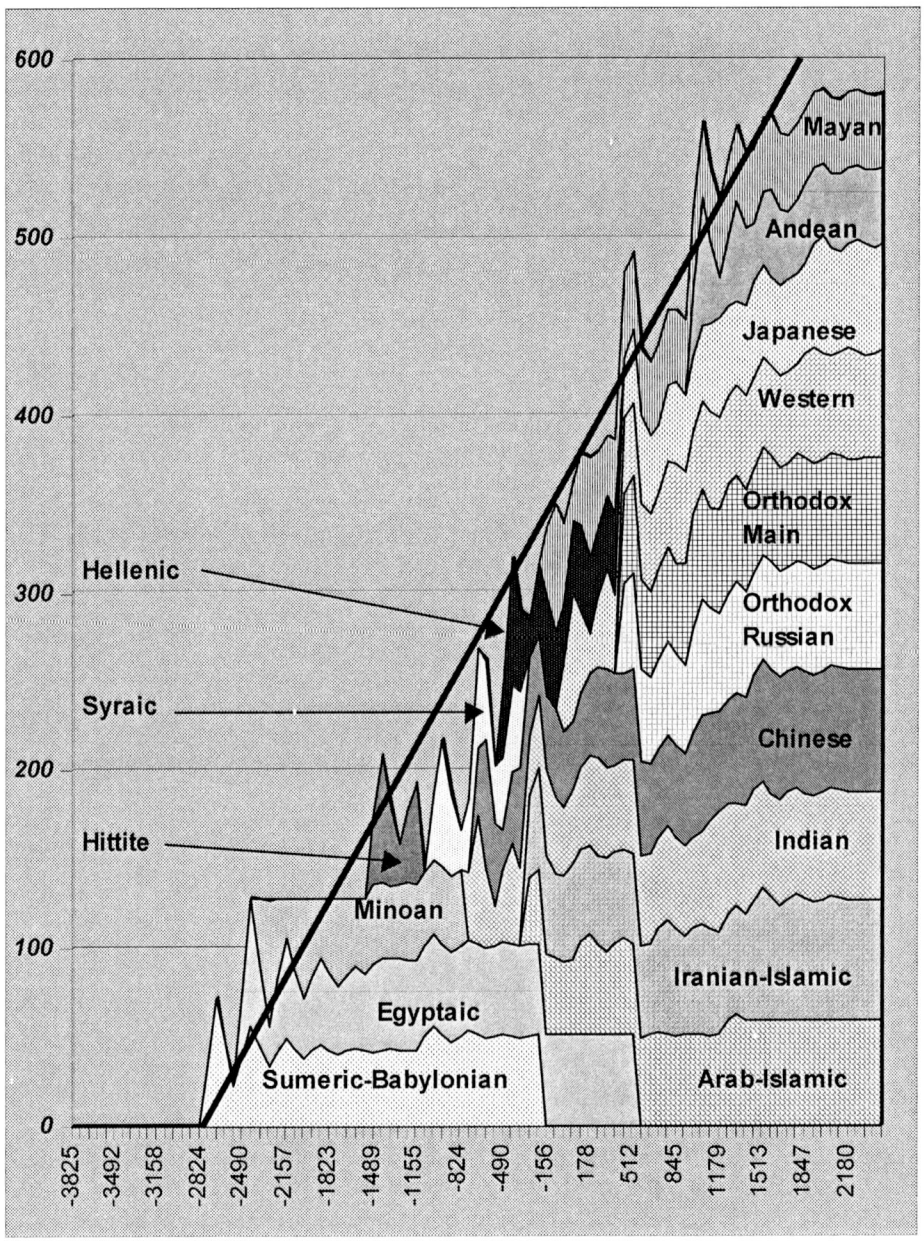

Figure 52. The progress of civilizations including American civilizations but without taking account of the effects of modern technology.

The Life Cycle of Civilizations

The next figure, Figure 53, shows how the societal levels of all civilizations including the Andean and Mayan civilizations in America (excluding abortive civilizations) add to form the progress P(t) taking account of an additional technological driving force for Western, Japanese, Indian, Chinese and Orthodox Russian civilizations. A straight line fit is a reasonable approximation to the overall growth of progress with time with the effect of the technological driving force eliminating the deficit after 1500 AD seen in the previous two figures. The technological driving force was assumed to be the bounded exponential force with parameters specified by equations (94) through (99). The starting year t_0 for the technological driving force is set individually for each civilization since technology took effective hold in these civilizations at different dates. The data for each civilization was based on the following:

- Mayan – standard shape with a startup in 223 BC and continuing to 2447 AD based on a continuing culture with a Western overlay until the present.
- Andean – standard shape with a startup in 912 AD and continuing to 2447 AD based on a continuing culture with a Western overlay until the present.
- Egyptaic – as earlier in our discussion with a cutoff to zero at 500 AD.
- Syraic – as earlier
- Arab-Islamic – as earlier but with the Syraic part separated out to avoid double counting.
- Iranian-Islamic – as earlier but with the Syraic part separated out to avoid double counting.
- Japan – as earlier but with the technological driving force starting in the year $t_0 = 1868$.
- China – as earlier but with the technological driving force starting in the year $t_0 = 1950$.
- India – as earlier but with the technological driving force starting in the year $t_0 = 1950$.
- Hellenic – as earlier
- Minoan – standard shape with a startup in 2424 BC and a cutoff to zero in 757 BC.
- Western – as earlier but with Hellenic separated out to avoid double counting and with the technological driving force starting in the year $t_0 = 1800$.
- Orthodox Main Body – as earlier but with Hellenic separated out to avoid double counting.
- Orthodox Russian – as earlier but with Hellenic separated out to avoid double counting and with the technological driving force starting in the year $t_0 = 1900$.

The Life Cycle of Civilizations

- Sumeric-Babylonian - standard shape with a startup in 2824 BC and a cutoff to zero in 156 BC.
- Hittite - standard shape with a startup in 1556 BC and a cutoff to zero in 1088 BC.

The Life Cycle of Civilizations

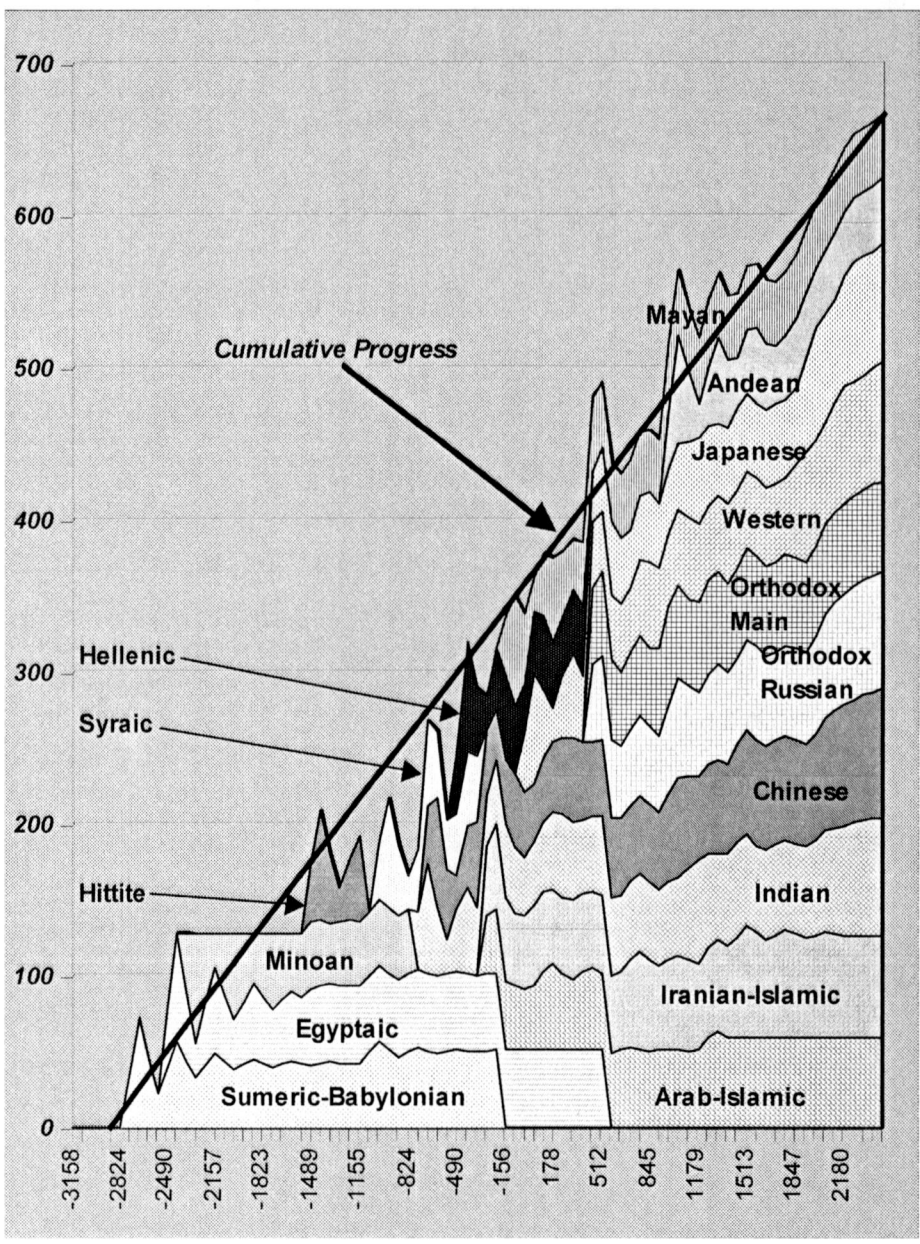

Figure 53. The progress of all known, non-abortive civilizations including the effects of technology.

A Formula for the Cumulative Progress of Mankind

Taking account of American civilizations (Mayan and Andean) and the recent impact of technology on civilizations we obtain the following approximate linear fit for progress from the preceding figure:

$$P(t) = 357 + 0.1265t \qquad (135)$$

Some representative values of P(t) are:

Year	−2824	−2000	−1000	0	1000	2000	3000
Actual P(t)	0	128	198	346	531	611	?
Calculated P(t)	0	104	231	357	484	610	737

The simple linearity of P(t) gives us reason to hope that P(t) may indeed may actually be a measure of the overall progress of human civilization.

A Human Supercivilization?

The preceding three figures strongly suggest a growth of human civilizations that appear at present to be joining together to become an eventual worldwide civilization that we will call a *supercivilization* since its components are civilizations. This phenomenon is called globalization in the press. It represents the coming together of world cultures through integrated communications, widespread travel and trade, integrated economies and a developing technologically based environment and culture. The linearity in time of the sum of civilizations that we seen in the preceding figure raise the question of whether we can treat the past five thousand years as the growth phase of a supercivilization with the dynamics that we have developed for an ordinary civilization.

Playing Devil's advocate we will construct the form of the societal curve of a supercivilization using our basic equations (13) and (15). We will use the flattening of the curve in recent times for civilizations (omitting technical effects) as a motivation to suggest that the supercivilization would have peaked without technology. Thus we would expect a breakdown point in recent history if modern technology had not come in to play. The year 1914 represents a major turning point in world history since it marked the beginning of the end of European world dominance. (It also marks a mid-point in the transition of contemporary civilizations from pre-technological to technological. Europe and North America entered the Industrial – Technological Age in the early 1800's. Asia entered a

The Life Cycle of Civilizations

technological phase around 1950 – 1970 with significant earlier industrial development as well.)

Therefore we will tentatively take 1914 as the point of breakdown, and 2824 BC as the beginning of a supercivilization. This time interval of 4,738 years is one-half of the period in this tentative theory. We will therefore take the period to be T = 9,500 using a convenient rounded-off number. From equation (15) we obtain b = 0.000661. We then fix the remaining parameter a by requiring S at the breakdown point of 1914 to equal the observed value of 581 assuming c_1 = 1 in equation (13) (as we have done throughout.) The result is a = .000849 and d = aT = 8.07 indicating a petrified civilization.

The following two figures show the curve for S compared to the actual sum of societal levels and P(t) calculated from equation (135). It also shows the curve for S shifted by 1,000 years to obtain a better fit of the S curve to the actual progress obtained by summing societal values of civilizations.

Although the shifted theoretical S curve fits the intermediate time periods fairly well it does not fit the early civilizations period well and is apparently inconsistent with technological effects in recent centuries. The T = 9500 year supercivilization theory does suggest that mankind might have entered into a global state of petrification if it were not for technology. We might have seen an increasingly populated earth sinking to a continually lower cultural and living standard.

Figures 54 and 55 suggest that the best fit to the actual progress calculated by summing the societal values of civilizations is the linear fit specified by equation (135). Based on this equation we can suggest that humanity is progressing upward linearly with time.

An integral part of the progress for the past two hundred years has been technology driven progress. In the absence of the driving force of technology the conjectured supercivilization might have peaked in 1914 and then declined into a static society similar to the petrified Chinese civilization of the Manchu Dynasty looking to the glories of the past rather than to the progress of the future. The large increase in the middle classes, the growth of wealth, and the uplifting of the working classes are based on the increased productivity and prosperity generated through technological progress.

We conclude that we have not yet seen the peak (breakdown point) of a potential human supercivilization and that its ultimate form, if it exists, remains to be determined. Instead, we appear to see a linearly rising Progress.

The Life Cycle of Civilizations

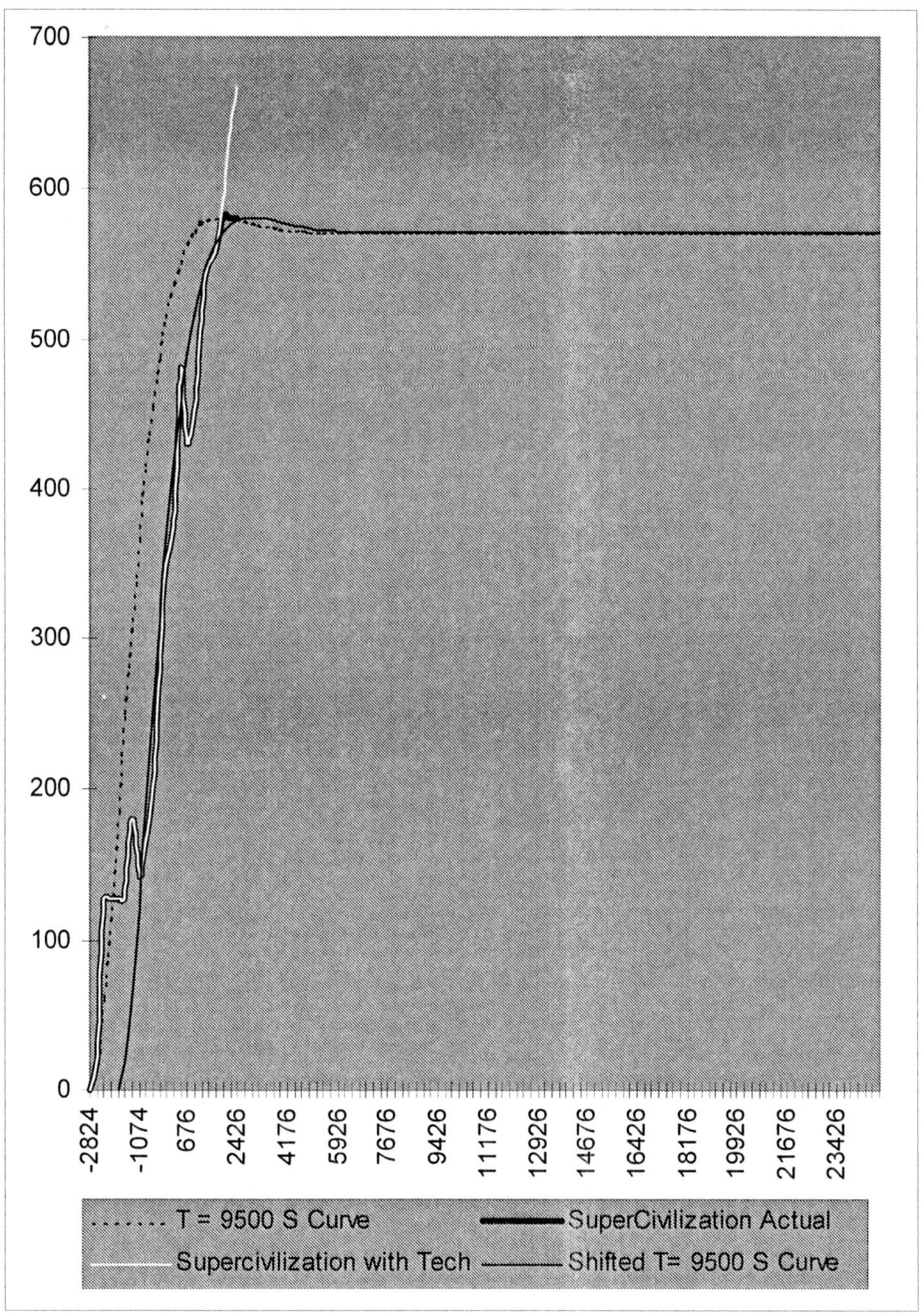

Figure 54. T = 9500 supercivilization compared to actual progress.

The Life Cycle of Civilizations

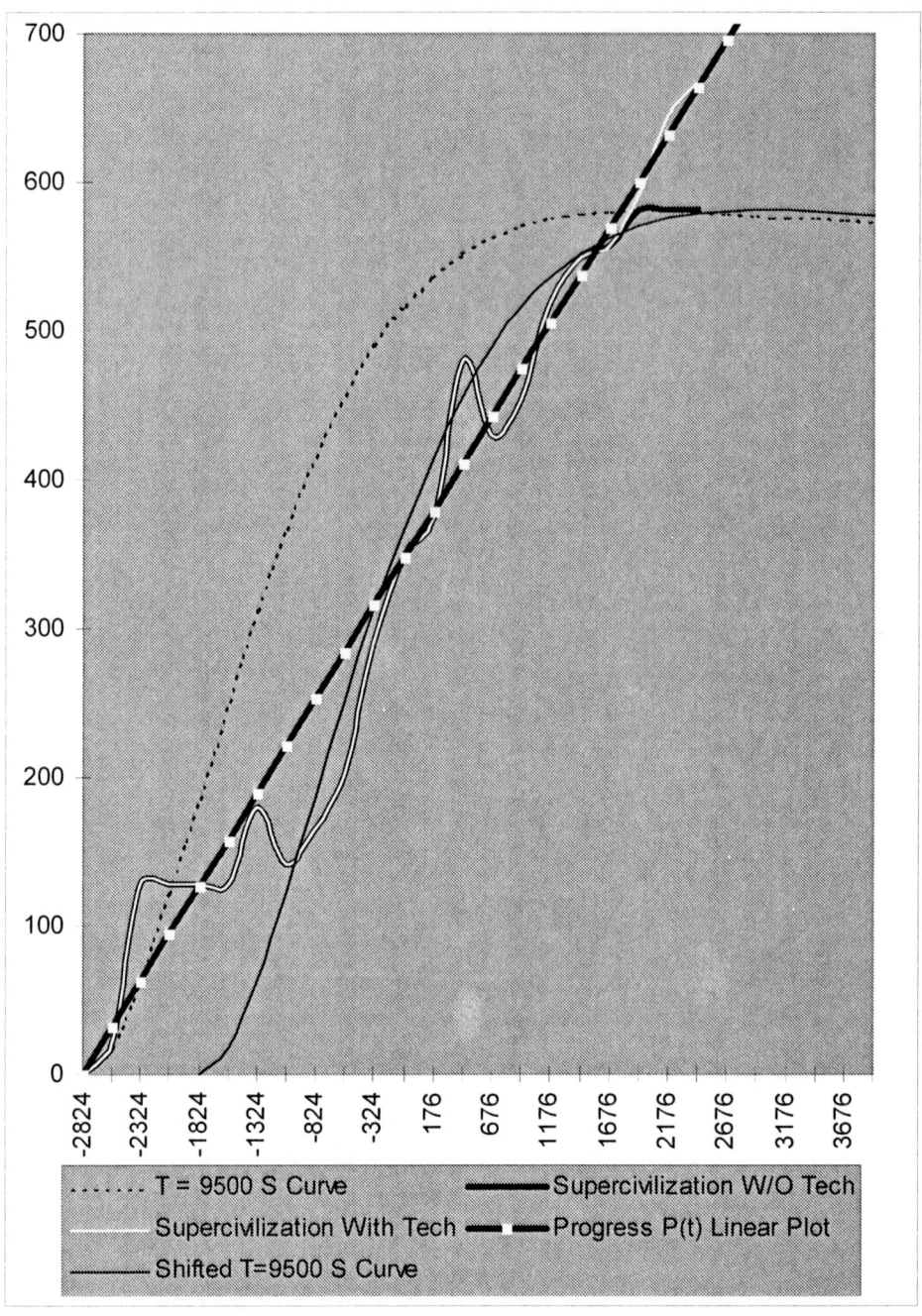

Figure 55. Close-up comparison of Progress and supercivilization curve.

17. The Mushroom of Civilizations

The Human Mushroom

The growth of civilizations is easy to picture. They seem to start from a small seed: a part of the Nile Valley or the Yangtze River and expand to larger areas as they evolve. Yet we cannot answer Banquo: "If you can look into the seeds of time, and say which grains will grow, and which will not, speak then to me." As Toynbee has pointed out it is difficult to see why a civilization developed in one setting and a civilization did not develop in another similar setting. We cannot look at the seeds of time and say which grains will grow into civilizations and which will not.

The cause eludes us. We can see that the earth has enjoyed very favorable climatic conditions in the past ten thousand years. We can see that a mutation approximately forty thousand years ago may have led to the development of the creative minorities that are so important in the growth of civilizations. The combination of the onset of favorable climatic conditions, and a venturesome mankind ready to grow, seems to have led to the rapid development of cities as early as 8,000 to 9,000 years ago and civilizations as early as 5,000 to 6,000 years ago. Very fast in comparison to the hundreds of thousands of years of slow development in the prior history of mankind.

The general theory of civilizations that we have developed provides a good macro description of the overall growth and disintegration of civilizations. However there is a need for a micro description of the growth and disintegration of civilizations based on a mathematical theory of population social dynamics. At the moment such a theory appears quite premature.

One important aspect of the evolution of civilizations is the importance of the frontier. Civilizations grow best on new land. The strongest part of a civilization often appears at the frontiers where the civilization is under attack by barbarians or other civilizations. In both cases the challenge of the environment – human or natural – seems to promote growth. "What does not destroy us strengthens us."

We can call this the *mushroom ring* effect. Civilizations grow outward in an expanding cultural and geographic ring. We have seen these rings of growth in the evolution of Chinese civilization from Sinic civilization, and the expansion of

The Life Cycle of Civilizations

Hellenic civilization from Greece to Asia Minor, Italy, Sicily, the shores of the Mediterranean, and on into India and eventually Europe and the Americas. Other civilizations such as Islamic civilization also show the mushroom ring effect.

The geographic expansion of a civilization is usually beneficial in the early phase of the growth of a civilization and contributes to the growth of the societal level. We see these benefits in the effects of the maritime expansion of the Greeks, particularly Athens, in early Hellenic civilization. When a civilization is in the disintegration phase the geographical expansion of a universal state can add more burdens on the populace and drain the resources of the state. The expansion of the Roman Empire into Babylonia illustrates this point. Realizing the drain on their resources the Romans voluntarily withdrew from Babylonia.

THE EXPANSION OF CIVILIZATIONS

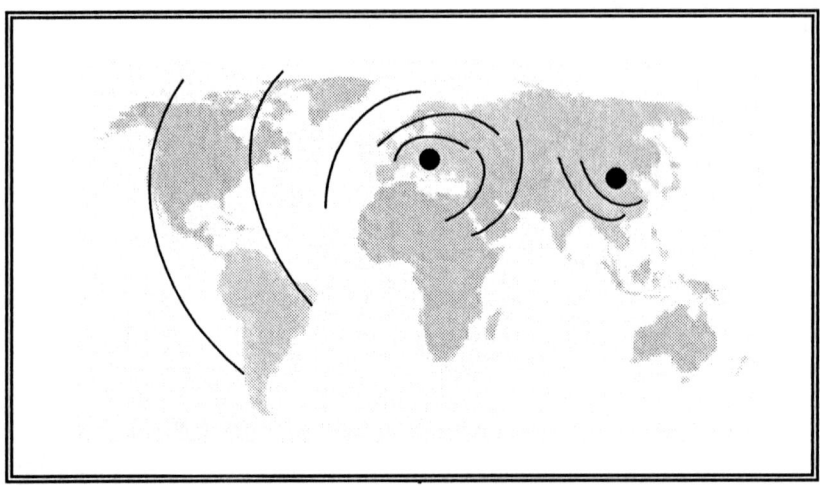

Figure 56. The spreading mushroom ring of civilizations. The expansion of the Western and Far Eastern civilizations is shown to illustrate the mushroom effect.

Global Civilization: The end of the mushroom?

Mankind has expanded to occupy the entire earth. There are no new Americas' or Australia's. The earth's resources are clearly being utilized to an extent that raises questions about mankind's long term survival.

The Life Cycle of Civilizations

We face global warming, pollution on a massive scale, and the over-utilization of natural resources. Under these circumstances it appears that we have reached the end of the earthly mushroom rings of civilizations.

It appears that a global amalgamation of civilizations is the next stage of the story of civilizations. A world civilization has some advantages, and some disadvantages and potential problems.

Firstly, our study of civilizations suggests that human civilizations by their very nature go through periods of growth and disintegration. The saving grace of multiple civilizations is that a decline in one civilization is often counterbalanced by growth in other civilizations. The overall linear growth of progress (previous chapter) reflects the balancing act of growth and disintegration in civilizations. In the period from roughly 2500 BC to 1500 BC the growth and decline of civilizations appear to have been in almost perfect balance as Figures 51 to 53 show. If the world's civilizations coalesce into one civilization we can expect to see massive world-wide periods of growth and decline that may lead to great suffering during a worldwide period of decline. Recent upheavals in the globalized financial industry are a premonition of the far greater upheavals that may be expected in a worldwide civilization.

Another significant danger for a global civilization is a homogenization of culture that can lead to a decline of growth. As an entity grows it becomes more stratified and less able to adapt and change. The least change can only happen through great effort and expense. A good example of this problem is the costly year 2000 computer industry problem caused by the practice of using two digits for the year rather than the four digits needed to distinguish between 20xx dates versus 19xx dates. The response to this challenge was very costly and deferred as long as possible.

Beehive-Earth

A reluctance to respond to challenges in a global civilization because of the large scope of the needed response can lead to a petrified civilization that might ultimately lead to Beehive-Earth. Given the earth's limited resources, which are already sorely pressed, a Beehive-Earth civilization will only lead to long term global decline.

The "end of the mushroom ring" picture that we have been presenting is not necessarily in the cards in the immediate future. Perhaps it is hundreds or thousands of years in the future. But it will occur unless mankind uses the escape valve that space travel represents, or unless mankind enters into a period of inner intellectual/spiritual growth that leads civilization away from material needs. The second possibility is both less likely and more remote than the first possibility. It is easier to make technical "gadgets" then it is to effect a significant change in the psyche of humanity. Thus it appears mankind must play the "space card."

18. The Importance of Being in Space

Perhaps the most important prospect for the future of mankind is in space. To some extent we are in a situation similar to the beginning of the exploration of the Americas. We can choose a large-scale movement into space, or we can be content with communications/weather satellites and science-oriented space stations.

The great problem of space travel is escaping from the confines of earth's gravity. The solution at the moment is prohibitively expensive rockets that restrict travel to a few essential personnel and equipment for satellite communications and scientific experiments.

Clearly an alternate approach to space travel is required. Undoubtedly the next step will be cheaper, "throw away" rockets. Nuclear rockets are ruled out by safety considerations.

Eventually travel from the earth may revert to a "space gun" approach of the Jules Verne type. However, instead of gunpowder or explosives, the primary propulsion mechanism may be magnetic fields that propel a shuttle along a deep, long (perhaps underground and/or perhaps up the side of a mountain) barrel to a speed necessary to reach space orbit or close to it. A "magnetic" shuttle could have enough on-board fuel for maneuvering and re-entry to earth.

After all, most of a rocket's fuel is expended on accelerating the fuel. With earth-based power propelling a shuttle into orbit, the fuel requirements and energy consumption would be much reduced. Once space stations and moon bases are established nuclear rockets could be used to travel to other planets.

Environmental Protection will Never Completely Work

There is a strong conservation movement in the United States and in other countries around the world. While this movement will achieve victories in the struggle to protect the environment from further deterioration, the shear size of earth's population makes it impossible to prevent environmental deterioration now and for the foreseeable future. Thus a major move into space and "new ground" is necessary for the advancement of civilization and to relieve the pressure on earth's resources. As Toynbee repeatedly points out civilizations grow best on new ground. Conservation by itself will result in an eventual static global civilization.

Proposal for a Tri-Planet Homeland for Humanity

The recent discovery of large amounts of water and frozen carbon dioxide on Mars gives hope to the possibility of transforming the Martian atmosphere into a thicker carbon dioxide atmosphere that eventually could be further transformed to contain sufficient oxygen for humans. There appear to be a number of feasible approaches. One approach might be to explode large hydrogen bombs to vaporize the Martian ice caps and create a thick atmosphere with carbon dioxide and water vapor. Introduction of plant life on a planetary scale could generate enough oxygen for a breathable atmosphere and a habitable planet in, perhaps, a few hundred years.

The transformation of Venus into a home for mankind also may be possible over a period of thousands of years. We must trap almost 99% of its (primarily) carbon dioxide atmosphere in the rock on the planet's surface creating an earth-like atmospheric pressure and reducing the greenhouse effect (perhaps through a nuclear winter or comet bombardment). Next we must generate an oxygen atmosphere and surface water (possibly through bombardment with diverted icy comets). The remaining issues: the slow rotation of Venus and the lack of a magnetic field create complications but they can also be overcome by an advanced society.

The accomplishment of these projects will give humanity three earth-like homes. If large extraterrestrial human colonies are established then a human space civilization will develop. *The size of the challenge confronting this future civilization is such that a successful response will create a civilization that may be an order of magnitude above current human civilizations.* The mushroom ring of civilization will then have expanded to the planets with a clear view towards the stars.

The United States is the only country with sufficient resources to lead the move into space. Rather than devote resources to war (and preparations for war) it should create a major presence in space. A militaristic role as world terrorist policeman will waste the resources of the United States. These resources could be better devoted to other purposes such as creating a major space colony—that would be to the United States as the United States was to Great Britain—the child that helped save the parent in two world wars.

The Life Cycle of Civilizations

Exhibit 26. Three planets home for humanity.

19. The Effect of Genetic Engineering, Mutations and Medical Advances on Civilizations

Genetic Engineering, Mutations and Medicine

The nature of mankind determines the evolution of civilizations. We have seen suggestive evidence that a mutation forty thousand years ago may have been a critical factor in the development of civilizations. Today we see the possibility of major changes in mankind due to genetic engineering and medical advances as well as naturally occurring mutations. Any, or all, of these sources of change can have major effects on the future development and evolution of civilizations. In this chapter we will explore some of the changes that might take place and their potential effect on civilizations.

Mankind and Civilizations Now

The civilizations that mankind created over the past six thousand years have been based on the social and physical characteristics of mankind. For example the period of a civilization T (which appears to be approximately 267 years for human civilizations) appears to be equal to the length of eight generations of approximately 33 years.

Some of the characteristics that determine the evolution of a civilization are related to the average life pattern and lifetime of the members of the civilization: the average lifetime of a person, the average age of the population, the average length of the "apprentice" part of a worker's life, the average length of the "mature" part of a worker's life, and the relative proportions of "apprentice" and "mature" workers. (We use workers in the general sense to mean the members of the civilization performing activities for the benefit of the civilization. Young children, the old and the infirm who may not contribute constitute the non-workers.)

The average lifetime of a person determines the length of a generation, which, in turn, affects the period T of a civilization.

The Life Cycle of Civilizations

The average age of the population affects the resistance to change in a number of ways. A youthful population is generally more accepting of change, more open to new ideas, and less tied to the "old" ways of doing things. Thus we would expect the resistance to change will be lower.

Similarly, the average length of the "apprentice" part of a worker's life, the average length of the "mature" part of a worker's life, and the relative proportions of "apprentice" and "mature" workers affect the resistance to change within the civilization.

Perhaps the most important determinant of the pattern of civilizations is the average lifetime of the population, which is usually measured as the life expectancy at birth. The following table and figure show the increase of life expectancy in both developed and undeveloped countries over the last two hundred years. In both cases life expectancy has roughly doubled primarily because of medical and hygienic advances. New medical discoveries and the exciting prospects of genetic engineering, of which we have only had a glimpse, suggest that the life expectancy of mankind will continue to increase.

Life Expectancy of	1800	1850	1900	1950	2000
More Developed Countries	35	43	50	65	77
Less Developed Countries	25	28	30	40	64

Figure 57. A table showing how the life expectancy of the populations of the less developed and more developed countries has changed over the past two hundred years.

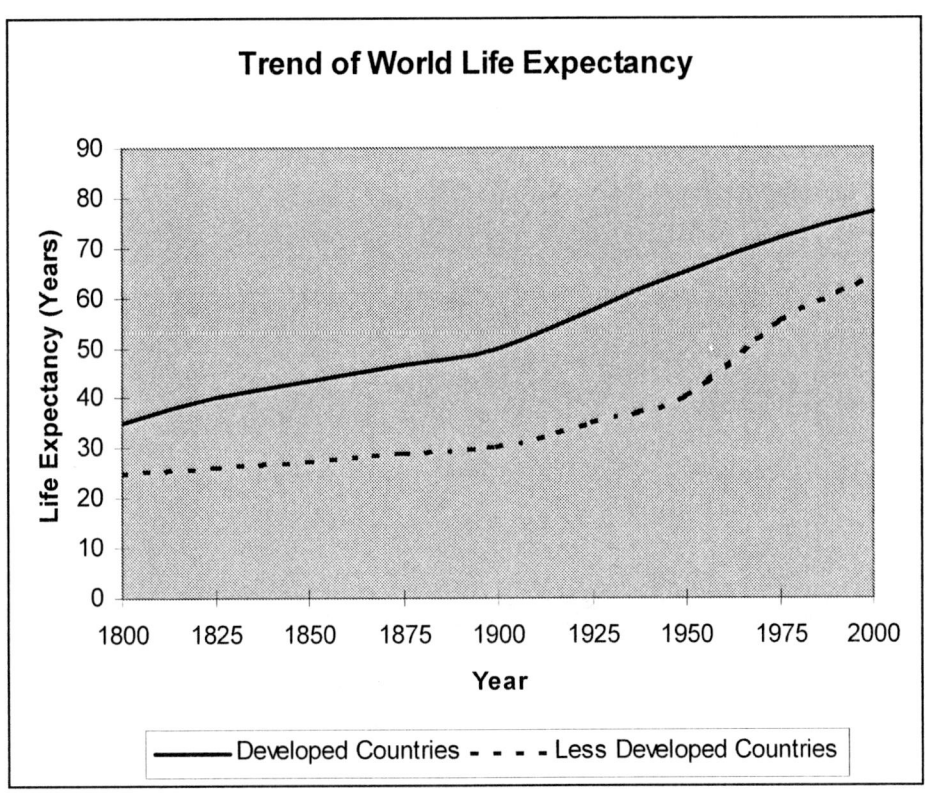

Figure 58. The trend of life expectancy over the past two hundred years.

Note the life expectancy of both more developed and less developed countries was around thirty years before 1800. This is roughly the length of time 33 years that we use for a generation.

Does the doubling of life expectancy since 1800 mean that the length of a generation and consequently the period T of contemporary civilizations has doubled? Probably not, because the doubling of life expectancy in the past two hundred years for the most part reflects the great decline in child mortality.

A more important indicator of the growth of mankind's lifetime is the rise in the maximum age at death. We are all familiar with the increasing number of individuals with ages over one hundred years. A recent study[9] on the changes in maximum age at death in Sweden, an advanced industrial country, suggest the

---

[9] J. R. Wilmoth, L. J. Deagan, H. Lundström, and S. Horuichi, Science **289**, 2366 (2000).

The Life Cycle of Civilizations

lifetime of mankind is increasing in advanced countries, and also suggests that a limit on the maximum lifetime may not exist (or may not be near). (Some experts have suggested that there is a maximum biologically determined age of 115 – 120 years for humans.[10])

Based on a careful examination of Swedish data on age Wilmoth et al states "Human progress is real somehow. We are changing the limits of the human life span over time."

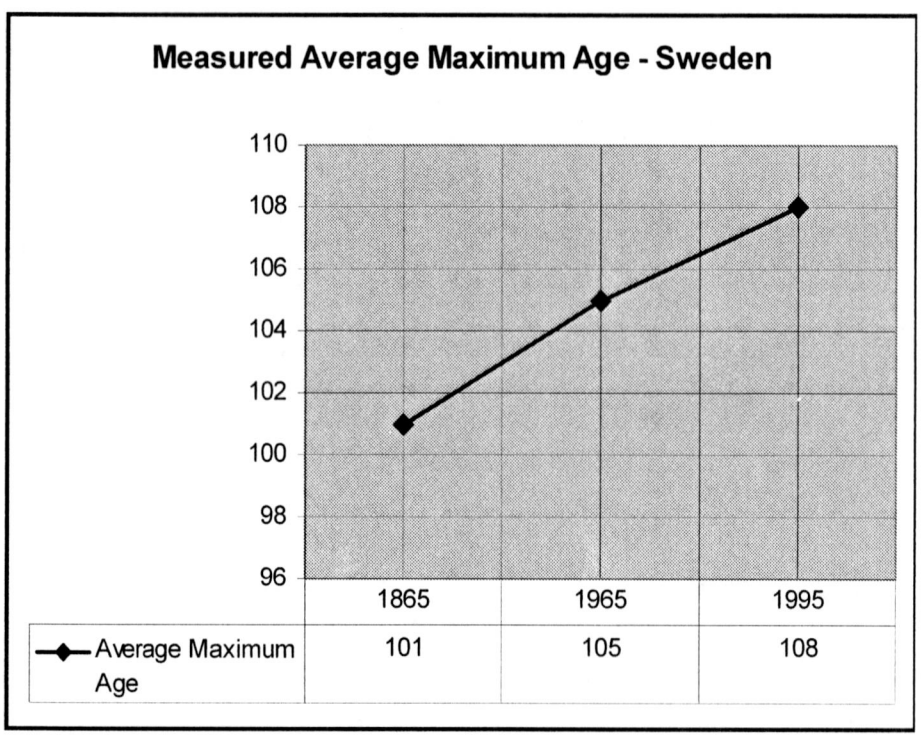

Figure 59. The measured average maximum age of the population in Sweden over a 130 year period.

Figure 59 shows the data Wilmoth and his colleagues have gathered in Sweden. The average maximum age is an average of the average maximum ages of people in Sweden at the three dates shown in the figure. The measured rate

---

[10] Professor Wilmoth has stated, "Those numbers are out of thin air. There is no scientific basis on which to estimate a fixed upper limit." in a University of California (Berkeley) Press Release dated 9/29/2000.

The Life Cycle of Civilizations

shows a rate of increase of one year in maximum age per each quarter century until roughly 1965. Between 1965 and 1995 the average maximum age increased by one year per decade due to the application of modern medical advances.

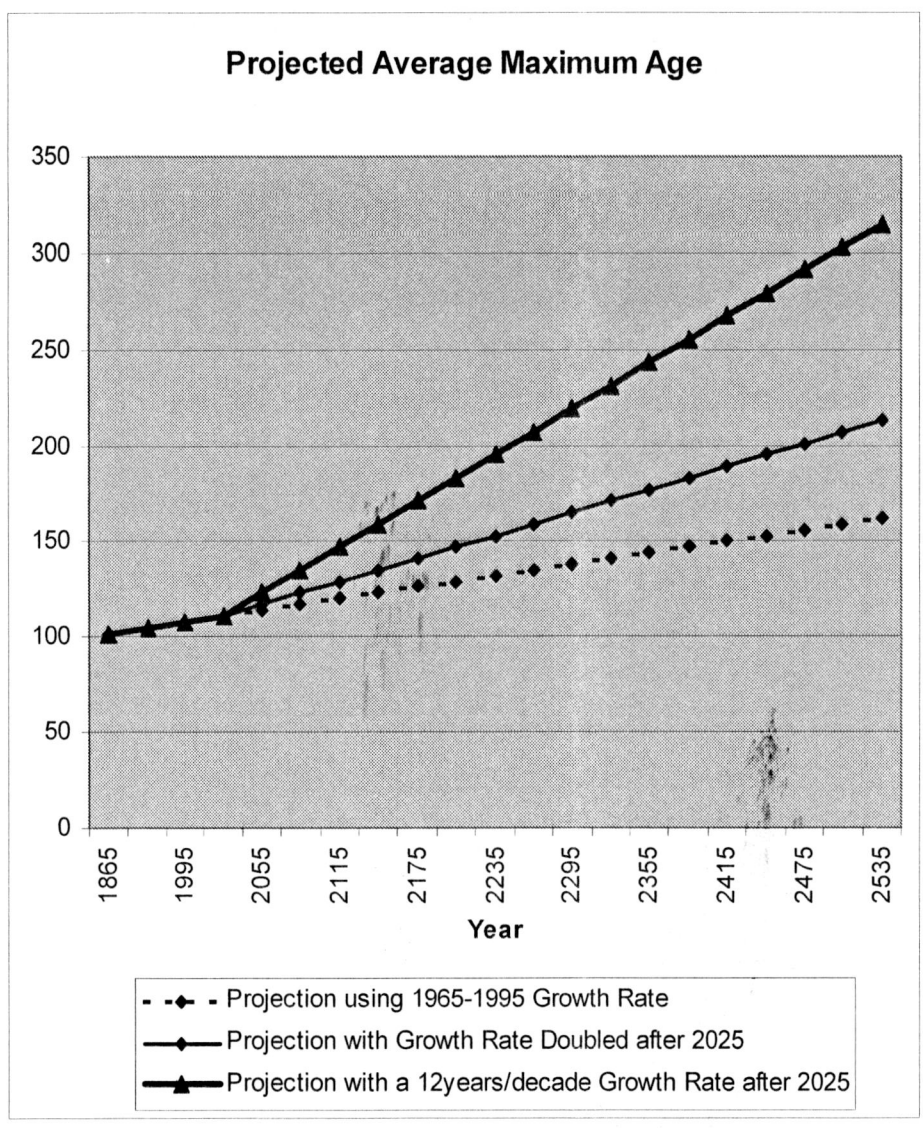

Figure 60. Projections of the average maximum age of people in advanced countries.

Figure 60 shows three projections into the future. Two of the projections are probably too conservative in the light of the rapid pace of recent medical and genetic advances. In one of these conservative projections we assume that the 1965 to 1995 rate of increase of the average maximum age of one year per decade continues indefinitely into the future. In the other conservative projection we assume that the 1965 – 1995 growth rate of the average maximum age doubles after 2025 to two years per decade. The third projection assumes a growth in the average maximum age of twelve years per decade. This rate may well be closer to the actual growth rate when current advances in genetic engineering and medicine move from the laboratory into everyday medical care.

The reasons for a lengthened life span appear to be better medical care and better public health measures that started when today's very old people were children together with much improved health care after age seventy due to recent medical advances.

Implications of Extending Mankind's Lifetime

The larger number of older people and the lengthening of the life span, in themselves, are not necessarily beneficial for civilizations. If the older segment of the population is a burden on society and not a source of creative progress then the older segment will constitute a drag or resisting force to the growth of a civilization.

A longer lifetime should imply a longer generation length. Since the period of a civilization T appears to be eight generations, the period should also increase if the length of generations increases.

But the effect of a longer life span is countered in a number of ways. It is countered at the present time by the higher proportion of young people in most less-developed countries (where most of the world's population resides).

A Larger older Population is a Potential Handicap

More importantly it is countered by the continuation of patterns of life that were based on a shorter life span in most developed and less developed countries. For example, most individuals in Western countries still plan to retire at age 65 as they did in 1900 when the life expectancy was 50 years. Most people in those countries start "slowing down" when they reach their fifties. As a result the majority of the "movers and shakers" in business and society tend to be concentrated in the 30 to 50 year old set as they were in the past. Thus the increases in life expectancy and life span do not translate directly into an equivalent increase in the length of a generation.

Required: A Youthful, Older Population

The increase of the length of a generation requires medical advances that make it possible for workers to continue working with the same strength and capabilities – both mental and physical – when they reach their fifties, sixties, and, possibly, their seventies as they did in their thirties and forties. In addition to maintaining physical and mental abilities into their seventies workers must have the psychological mindset to want to continue to work. Many workers become emotionally weary after many years of the "hard knocks" and experiences of life. Can the majority of people develop a long-term "youthful" attitude?

If a true increase in the length of an *active* generation can be accomplished with the preponderance of the population able to work, interested in continuing to learn, and wishing to continue to participate in the life and work of their civilization into their seventies or longer; then we may see a true increase in the period of a civilization. The consequences of such an increase are considered in the next section.

Structure of a Civilization for a Long Lived Mankind

In this section we consider an example of a new order of civilization for mankind in which the length of a generation has roughly doubled from 33 years to 67 years. We will see that the most important positive consequence of this doubling is the possibility of achieving a much higher societal level. On the negative side the possibility of a more static (or arrested) civilization increases. An older (on average) population will tend to remember the past when it approaches the problems of the future. The result might be an increased resistance to new creative thinking.

If we assume the length of a generation has doubled (approximately) to 67 years and the period T is eight generations as it was in our earlier discussions we obtain a period of $T = 533$ years and a value for the constant $b = .0118$. This doubling leads to a time of troubles lasting 800 years and a universal state lasting 800 years in our standard approach (using equations (13) through (16).)

The parameter a, which is proportional to r the resistance to change, still remains to be determined. If the psychology of the older segment of the long-lived population remains youthful and flexible then the resistance, and thus a, may very well remain the same as it has been for the past six thousand years. On the other hand if the older part of the population has the more rigid, less changeable temperament that we see in the older segments of contemporary (and past) civilizations then the overall resistance can be expected to be larger in a civilization with a long lived population. In the following figure we display the case where the resistance, and thus a, are 50% greater than in contemporary and past civilizations ($a = .00422$). We also consider the case where the resistance,

The Life Cycle of Civilizations

and a, are the same as we have seen in contemporary and past civilizations, namely a = .00281.

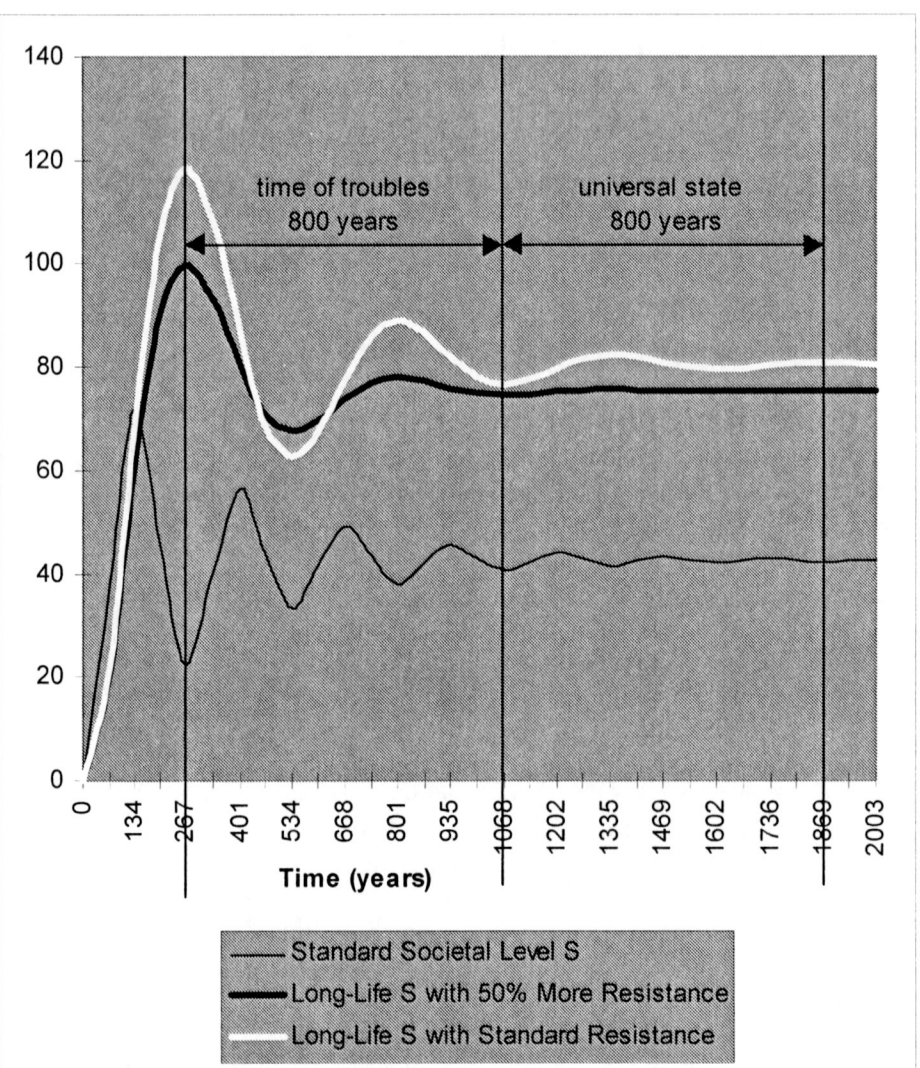

Figure 61. A comparison of societal levels of a civilization with a long-lived population with the standard civilization of three and a half beats.

Figure 61 considers the case of a "long-lived" civilization (the white line) with the *standard* resistance represented by a = .00281 that we have used in all previous cases (except arrested civilizations). It also shows the S curve of a long-lived civilization (the black line) with the resistance increased by 50% to a = .00422. In both cases the value of b was chosen to be .0118, which corresponds to a doubled generation length of 67 years and thus a doubled time of troubles length and a doubled universal state length to 800 years.

Features of a Civilization with a Long Lived Population

A civilization with a long-lived population would have a number of advantages relative to civilizations that we have seen in the past six thousand years. It would also have a number of potential disadvantages. The S curves in Figure 61 reflect these advantages and disadvantages to some extent.

The advantages of a civilization with a long-lived population in which the population would remain youthful and flexible into their 80's or 90's are:

> 1. The population would develop a longer and deeper experience of society and life that would help them to avoid making the decisions that lead to civil strife and war. In our current civilizations we have seen repetitive patterns of war every few generations that are in part due to the ignorance of war of new generations that grow up without a first-hand knowledge of its horrors. Similarly internal political dissension might be better handled by a long-lived people with a long experience of political affairs.

> 2. The Arts and Sciences would possibly benefit from a long professional lifetime *with youthful vigor*. The growth of knowledge and culture has lengthened the time required for individuals to acquire a mature knowledge of their fields in many areas. Often an individual's powers start to decline not long after they have reached maturity in their field of activity. As a result we frequently see long "apprenticeships" to acquire knowledge and skills followed by rather short professional lives. Societies may thus devote a disproportionate amount of resources to education relative to the amount of return on the societies' investment. We remember the great artists and scientists who died at an early age before their "pen has gleaned ... [their] teeming brain" (Keats for example). A long creative lifetime appears to have manifold benefits for a civilization by strengthening its Arts and Sciences.

The Life Cycle of Civilizations

3. The creative minority of a civilization would be able to develop a deeper knowledge and experience that should help them better meet the challenges the civilization will encounter.

Figure 61 reflects the advantages expected of a long-lived population by showing a much higher societal level after the startup phase then past civilizations. It also shows that a "youthful" long-lived civilization, which we take to be the one with the standard resistance, has a generally higher societal level than a long-lived civilization with a higher resistance, which we assume reflects a population that has a longer life span but does not have a proportionate increase in the length of the individual's creative life.

It is interesting to note that the long-lived civilization with a significantly increased resistance has an S curve that is closer to that of an arrested civilization than to a vibrant three and a half beat "living" civilization.

The disadvantages of a long-lived civilization are:

1. The potential dominance of the "old of heart". The American post-World War II baby boom graphically demonstrated that the relative proportions of young and old have a strong impact on society. In past civilizations the dominance of the older segment of society was lessened by the smaller numbers of old people due to disease, accidents and the other events associated with aging. In a long-lived civilization with a large population of older people the potential exists for a slowdown in the growth of the civilization. A dominant older generation can stifle creativity and the search for new solutions to societal challenges. If the long-lived civilization has been able to infuse a continuing youthfulness and creativity in the older components of the population then this disadvantage would be eliminated. The S curve for the civilization with increased resistance in Figure 61 reflects the potential retarding effects of a non-creative segment of older population. This curve is similar to the curve of a static arrested civilization.

2. A long-lived civilization may have its resources diverted to maintain and care for a large older population segment. We see this problem emerging today in Japan and America where an increasingly large population of elderly is straining pension plans, social security and medical care. If the older segment of a long-lived civilization absorbs too much of the resources of the civilization then the civilization will become essentially an arrested civilization like the Eskimos – not because of a harsh external environment but because of internal social/medical demands on the civilization's resources. Figure 61 shows

the S curve of a civilization with increased resistance which presumably corresponds to a long-lived civilization with an older population segment that is not youthful. This civilization's S curve is closer to the S curve of an arrested civilization.

Therefore we can conclude that attempts to prolong life must be matched with attempts to lengthen the youthful, creative period of life. Otherwise the result will be an increased, perhaps stifling burden on civilizations.

Postscript – Implications of a History with Patterns

Relation to the Philosophy of History

There are two branches to the philosophy of history: substantive—the past as seen from a universal viewpoint and considered with the view of uncovering the overall nature and direction of the historical process; and analytical—the study of the procedure followed by historians in investigating the past and of the fundamental concepts of historical thought.

The substantive branch of the philosophy of history has been in disfavor for most of the twentieth-century. The most recent major efforts in support of this direction were by Toynbee and Sorokin. This book represents an effort to develop a quantitative approach based on a physical sciences model. Similar attempts have been made in economics and a new sub-field – Econophysics – has appeared as a result. The theory we have developed might be called the "Sociophysics of history".

Types of Patterns

There appear to be four possible overall forms of History:

1. The history of Mankind reflects a continuing decline from Paradise or a Golden Age. This view is represented by the Bible, and Hesiod's *Works and Days* (Early Greek).

2. The history of Mankind reflects an overall continuing advance from savagery to high civilization. This view was advanced by the French Philosophes of the Enlightenment (such as Condorcet in his *Sketch for a Historical Picture of the Progress of the Human Mind*); and nineteenth-century thinkers such as Comte, de Saint-Simon, and Marx as well as religious thinkers such as Augustine (*The City of God*) and Bossuet (in his *Discourse on Universal History*).

3. The history of Mankind is cyclic – rising and falling in a recurring cycle. This view was espoused by Greek and Roman philosophers, and some modern philosophers.

4. The history of Mankind has no discernible patterns. The events of History are meaningless.

This book presents a theory that supports the view that History has an overall pattern that combines forms 2 and 3 above. The historical development of Mankind proceeds through a series of waves of civilization. Each civilization starts with a "big wave" that diminishes with time but still represents an upward movement. The continuing series of civilizations combine to produce a continuing advance of Mankind into the future. Two complementary pictures of this theory come to mind:

> 1. Mankind is in a relay race of sorts with civilizations competing with each other and urging each other on just as relay runners. At certain points each relay runner passes the baton to another runner who carries the race forward with new energy.

> 2. History is cyclic with civilizations cycling into the future. Each civilization constitutes a cycle in an upward spiral of Mankind advancing into the future.

In our view the conflict between Western Civilization and Islamic Civilization, that is reemerging after an interlude of several hundred years, is part of the ongoing advance of Mankind. We find it difficult to appreciate that fact because of the turmoil and suffering associated with the historical process.

The End of "The End of History"

Some authors have suggested that the overwhelming predominance of the United States in 1990 due to the collapse of communism has produced an "End of History". While the 1990's were something of a vacation from the large-scale conflicts that have been the hallmark of the twentieth century, the early days of the twenty-first century have brought us back to the view that History will continue. Mankind is far from united and major conflicts are likely to occur into the foreseeable future. These conflicts at the national and international level are reflections of the conflicts between civilizations at a deeper level. The theory of continental drift offers an apt analogy: The continents slowly move across the surface of the earth sometimes crashing into each other. Their movement is governed by processes deep within the earth's crust that cause the movement of the plates upon which the continents reside.

Thus the conflict between Western civilization and Islam will not be quickly resolved. It is likely to take centuries for its resolution. In addition a conflict between Western civilization and Chinese civilization may not be far off as China grows to become the second power in the world. The competition for control of the central Asian oil states is a potential source of conflict as NATO and China both expand into this area. A continuing conflict between a resurgent India (Indian civilization) and China is also likely for control of Southeast Asia, and due to overlapping border claims. A conflict between Russia and China for Siberia, and its mineral wealth, is also possible.

Thus the world has sufficient fuel for an "exciting" future history.

How would a Pattern Arise?

Patterns can arise through a combination of any or all of three mechanisms:

1. Divine Guidance – God has a plan for Mankind and we are going through the stages of that plan.

2. Genetic Imperative – Mankind follows a general pattern in the progress of history that results from traits embedded in the genetic makeup of Mankind.

3. Environmental Determinism – Mankind is following a pattern of history due to gross, and subtle, environmental effects such as climate changes and/or cyclic processes in the environment. The environment could also affect the course of history by exerting natural selection pressures on the genetic makeup of Mankind. Just as the daily cycle of day and night has had an effect on our genetic makeup, longer environmental cycles could also have induced corresponding social cycles in Mankind's history that are subtly encoded at the genetic level.

Are We the Pawns of Mindless Genetics?

If the broader drift of history contains patterns that are repeated over and over again such as we suggest is true for civilizations, then can we transcend this recurrent pattern – rise above the mindless genetics that may be embedded within us, and establish a more rational evolution of Mankind's history? Unconsciously, we have been trying to do this through the League of Nations and, more recently, the United Nations. Both institutions represent attempts to replace war with the resolution of conflicts through peaceful means. Whether the United Nations or a similar future organization will achieve this goal remains uncertain. The alternative seems to be "mindless armies fighting in the night" for transitory and fleeting goals.

Appendix A. Qualitative Theory of Civilizations

If you want to win, you've got to know the rules.
V. Sperandeo

Dow Theory

The stock markets are human phenomena that display trends, peaks and valleys. They are influenced by all sorts of events in the outside world. Charles Dow created a theory of the New York stock market at the beginning of the twentieth century. Dow theory was further developed by Peter Hamilton and Robert Rhea in the following forty years.

Dow theory is based on trends and fluctuations in indexes of the same name: the Dow Jones Average, the Dow Transportation Average and the Dow Utilities Average. Each average is a weighted average of the prices of a selection of key stocks. The most prominent index is the Dow Jones Industrial Average.

Civilizations also have trends, peaks and valleys. However the time scale of these changes is not measured in weeks, months or years. The time scale for changes in civilizations are measured in generations. Trends take hundreds of years, and the lifetime of a civilization is of the order of a thousand years usually. Whereas Charles Dow developed a major part of Dow theory based on five years of observation of the stock market 1895-1900 Toynbee and others examined almost six thousand years of history of twenty-six civilizations to develop an understanding of civilizations.

Dow's observations proved to be remarkably accurate although they were based on the very limited period of five years of observation. We hope that the historians' observations based on "only" twenty-six civilizations may prove to be similarly accurate.

Toynbee's work is described in the twelve volumes of his *A Study of History*. The observations that he made from his study of history are remarkably similar *in style* to the observations (theorems) that constitute Dow Theory. For example, one of the observations (or theorems) of Dow Theory may be stated as "A primary movement in the market is a broad fundamental trend (a bull market or bear market) that extends over a period of time varying from less than one year up to several years." Another observation (or theorem) is "A bear market has three phases: in the first phase the hopes upon which stocks were bought at inflated prices are abandoned; in the second phase declining earnings and business activity stimulate selling; and in the third phase solid stocks are forced to be sold by those who need to raise cash (to meet margin calls and so on)."

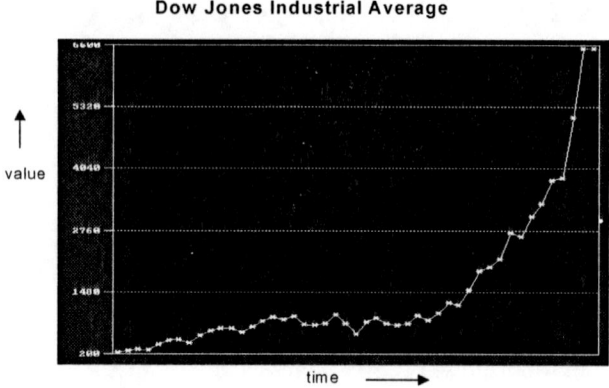

Figure 62. A fifty year picture of the Dow Jones Industrial Average.

A Qualitative Theory of Civilizations

The cumulative works of the historians contain a large number of observations and conclusions that can be used as a basis to create a qualitative "Dow Theory" of civilizations. The theorems of our Dow-like Theory of Civilizations are:

1. Societies of mankind exist that form intelligible units that we can call civilizations. Civilizations normally have a significant population and geographical extent. Civilizations are socially united by a common leadership although they may not have an all-encompassing central government.

2. Civilizations originate as a successful response to a challenge. Civilizations tend to be born in difficult environments that have the potential to support a prosperous society after sufficient effort. The first generation of human civilizations originates as a successful response to physical, environmental challenges. The following generations of civilizations arise as successful responses to social challenges (and sometimes physical challenges), and are built on the ashes of prior civilization(s).

3. A civilization may expend all its energy in making a successful response to a challenge and enter a "perpetual" static state. These civilizations are called *arrested civilizations*. An arrested civilization is a civilization that successfully responded to a challenge whose severity placed it on the borderline of the impossible. An arrested civilization, after a breakdown in growth, can persist for a long period of time in a no growth state that is called *petrifaction*. It need not disintegrate.

4. All known arrested civilizations appear to have two features: a caste system and a high degree of specialization. Individuals are constrained to a specific social and economic role in the society. The civilization is highly adapted to a specific environment like an anthill or a beehive. By abandoning the infinite possibilities of humanity they have lost their capacity for growth and become static.

5. A civilization that develops under adverse conditions will be all the stronger for developing in adversity if it does not expend all its energy. An adverse environment can be a stimulus towards the growth of civilization. An "easy" environment may be inimical to the growth of civilizations.

6. New ground is more stimulating for the development and growth of civilizations than "old ground." Significant growth in a civilization often comes from its periphery or frontier regions where no civilization existed previously. The growth of a civilization generally appears to be similar to the growth of a mushroom ring.

7. Civilizations grow by successfully meeting challenges. The change or growth is not geographical or in physical wealth but in the fabric of the society and the inner development of the individual members of the society. This process of inner growth is called *etherialization*.

8. Etherialization, the true growth of a civilization, is in the development of the inner life of the individual. This inner development radiates outward into the development of social institutions and the unity of the civilization. As a civilization grows the focus shifts from the external environment to the inner development of the society.

9. A civilization has three groups that play a role in its evolution: a *creative minority* (that can transform into a *dominant minority*), an *internal proletariat*, and an *external proletariat*.

10. The creative minority consists of a group of individuals who are able to break the mold of custom and forge creative advances in a civilization through a bold, adventurous spirit, genius, and outstanding personal characteristics. Part of these attributes may have a recent origin as a genetic mutation. The other people of the civilization, the internal proletariat, imitate the actions and ideas of the creative minority in a process called *mimesis*. Mimesis requires an act of will on the part of the members of the internal proletariat and a willingness of the internal proletariat to play the role of good followers.

11. Change takes place in growing societies through mimesis. The internal proletariat imitates the creative minority particularly in the growth resulting from successful responses to challenges.

12. The external proletariat is the group of individuals outside the civilization (often called the barbarians) who engage in interactions with the civilization: warfare, trade, travel and the exchange of ideas.

13. The creative minority has two possible sources of failure: 1) the creative minority may itself succumb to the process of mimesis and lose its creativity by opting to maintain the *status quo* thus ending the growth phase of the civilization; or 2) the creative minority may cease to lead by mimesis and attempt to rule by force thus alienating the internal proletariat, destroying the mimesis-based unity of society and perhaps causing rebellion and anarchy.

14. When a civilization fails to successfully meet a significant challenge it undergoes a breakdown. The creative minority that previously ruled by virtue of its success in meeting challenges transforms into a dominant minority that rules through force and coercion. The *breakdown* of a civilization is the point where the growth of the civilization ends.

15. When a civilization undergoes a breakdown its social and intellectual fabric is rent and the civilization begins to disintegrate. The mimesis-based unity of the civilization disintegrates as the dominant minority now rules by oppression and the internal proletariat responds by developing a desire to secede.

16. During the period of disintegration the civilization may be united for a time in a universal state and/or undergo geographical expansion. These events mask or temporarily halt the process of disintegration. The creation of a universal state is a symptom of a disintegrating civilization.

The Life Cycle of Civilizations

17. A civilization may encounter a challenge of such a magnitude that it causes the collapse of the civilization. If the challenge and collapse occurs in a "young" civilization it is called an *abortive civilization*.

18. The breakdown of a civilization marks the beginning of a time of troubles during which the civilization endures devastating events such as wars and social strife. Times of trouble typically last approximately four hundred years.

19. A civilization may encounter sudden blows of a military or environmental nature. If the civilization is in the growth stage and survives the blow (even if it loses much) it will normally emerge stronger. A remarkable challenge can evoke a remarkably creative response. On the other hand, if the blow is too strong the civilization may be destroyed.

20. A civilization, which is under constant pressure from outside forces (or from the environment), will normally be strengthened by its successful resistance. The most enterprising parts of a civilization are the parts in closest proximity to (on the frontiers of) the external pressure. If the pressure is too strong the civilization may eventually disappear.

21. There is a range of stimuli that promote optimal growth in a civilization. An optimal challenge not only provokes a successful response but also generates a forward momentum towards new challenges that promote further growth. Healthy growth stimulates an atmosphere that promotes further healthy growth.

22. If a civilization establishes a fixed border with external barbarians, the barbarians will begin to acquire the military and other superior skills of the civilization. Eventually the barbarians will use these acquired skills, and the knowledge that the civilization is weakening, to successfully invade the civilization's territories. A civilization succeeds against barbarians by continually pushing them back. What does not grow, declines.

23. Nomadic barbarians will invade a civilization for two reasons: their grazing lands have become unable to support the nomadic population for reasons such as desiccation, or a social vacuum has developed in the nearby regions of the civilization that entices a nomadic invasion for conquest and booty. The duration of nomadic empires resulting from these incursions is about three generations (about 120 years) on the average. The nomadic conquerors are then either expelled or assimilated. (The sole exception is the Ottoman Empire that lasted for 400 years.)

24. Improving technology has not necessarily been a source of growth in civilizations. Technology is not necessarily an accurate measure of social growth or the social level of a civilization.

25. Technological advances can survive the disintegration of civilizations.

26. Technological progress is governed by the law of "progressive simplification." Large, complex, expensive technology tends to be replaced with simpler, more compact, easier to use, cheaper technology. Simplification is based on sophistication.

27. As a civilization develops it tends to differentiate itself from other civilizations and develops a distinctive character of its own.

28. Civilizations, like individuals, are born, develop and eventually die. Civilizations progress through a comparable series of stages although chance historical and environmental events introduce variability in the history of each individual civilization. Superimposed on this cycle of life and death of individual civilizations is a major trend of progress in the development of the human race.

29. The breakdown and disintegration of a civilization is the result of an internal breakdown in the social fabric of the civilization usually combined with a breakdown in the psyche of the people of the civilization ("a loss of nerve").

30. The fundamental cause of the breakdown of a civilization is the appearance of internal social discords. Discords can be between geographically separated parts of the civilization, or between different social classes or political parties within the civilization.

31. A civilization can totally disintegrate, and after an intervening interregnum, be reborn as part of a new civilization creating a relationship called *Apparentation and Affiliation*. Alternately, a civilization can also be absorbed by one of its contemporaries preserving some continuity in its social fabric and perhaps becoming a contributing element of the absorbing civilization. The absorbed civilization may completely lose its identity.

32. An assault on a civilization by an alien society (the "barbarians") normally has a stimulating effect on the growth of the civilization unless it overwhelms the civilization as usually happens in the last stages of a civilization's disintegration. In this case the "barbarians" administer the *coup de grâce* to the civilization.

33. A revolution is an act of mimesis that has been delayed or retarded, and which therefore explodes with a force proportionate to the delay.

34. Whenever the current social structure of a civilization is challenged by a new social pressure there are three possible responses: 1) a peaceful, gradual adjustment of the social structure to the pressure; 2) a revolution causing a sudden change; or 3) a calamity representing a breakdown of the civilization.

35. If a civilization discovers a technique, either social or technological, which is highly successful, it risks being locked in by the very success of the technique. It then may fail to achieve a further advance. Its rivals may seize the lead by making further advances. Success breeds complacency.
36. Militarism saps the strength of a civilization. It often accompanies the disintegration process.

37. An increasing control of the physical environment appears to be associated with the disintegration process and not the growth phase.

38. The disintegration of a civilization leads to the creation of three factions: a dominant minority that may create a universal state as a response to the disintegration process; an internal proletariat that may create a universal church as a response to its alienation from the dominant minority; and an external proletariat that may create barbarian war-bands to plunder the wealth of the disintegrating civilization. In some cases an alien society may impose a universal state on a civilization.

39. During the disintegration of a civilization the dominant minority tends to become vulgarized by adopting the ways of the internal proletariat and to become barbarized by emulating the physical actions, manners and warlike nature of the external proletariat.

40. The establishment of a universal church by an internal proletariat is accomplished by a creative minority that develops within the internal proletariat. The remainder of the internal proletariat becomes the laity of the church.

41. Creative persons will continually arise during the history of a civilization. In the disintegrating phase of a civilization creative persons will form a creative minority (group) within the internal proletariat and also perhaps within the external proletariat.

The Life Cycle of Civilizations

42. After establishing a universal state a dominant minority will often produce a governing class of administrators who administer the state in a fair, just, and efficient manner.

43. The members of the internal proletariat are not identifiable by their wealth or poverty or social status. Rather they are members by virtue of being conscious (and resenting) of the loss of their ancestral position in the civilization and/or of their present role as followers.

44. The internal proletariat of a civilization can be augmented by the incorporation of aliens (people from outside the civilization) into the civilization. An important component of this alien contingent is a group that can be called the *intelligentsia*. This group learns the ways of the civilization and uses that knowledge to help the alien group to adapt to the ways of the civilization. Historically, an intelligentsia begins with military figures, then includes merchants who facilitate trade and commerce, and then broadens to the other aspects of society such as government, education and the skilled workers and professions. An intelligentsia is normally hated by the alien group of which it is a part because it represents the domineering civilization. An intelligentsia is normally despised by the civilization that it serves.

45. An external proletariat begins by following the creative minority of the adjacent civilization, and acquiring the ways and techniques of the civilization through mimesis. In this stage the civilization does not have a fixed border but is, in fact, expanding into the surrounding regions. When a fixed border develops, as it does in the disintegration phase of the civilization, the external proletariat crystallizes as a group. This group no longer engages in mimesis but rather realizes its separateness from the civilization and assumes an independent stance as an external proletariat. The civilization rules part of the external proletariat by force. The free remainder of the external proletariat becomes the enemy.

46. Indigenous universal states have a greater continuing popularity with the people of a civilization than an alien universal state. Alien universal states tend to become less popular with time.

47. Barbarian invaders who have not been influenced by another civilization tend to be more acceptable to the dominant minority of an invaded civilization. Those invaders who have been influenced by another civilization must either purge themselves of that influence or face inevitable ejection or elimination.

48. The disintegration of a civilization takes place in part in the psyches of the members of the civilization. The psyches of the members can make a limited variety of choices. These choices can be characterized as active or passive. The passive choice centers on the abandonment of a sense of responsibility and standards. The passive choice involves "letting oneself go", spontaneity, giving free rein to one's appetites, intellectual and artistic promiscuity, a sense of drift, and a return to the freedom and creativity of nature. The active choice centers on discipline, restraint and self-mastery.

49. In a disintegrating civilization attempts are made to halt the disintegration by looking to an idyllic past state of the civilization (*archaism*) or by looking to an idyllic future state of the civilization (*futurism*). In both cases philosophers develop Utopias without the troubles of the present.

50. Archaism can change to detachment from the troubles of the world when men realize that a violent reversion to an idyllic past is not possible. Then they may seek to avoid the pain of the present through detachment. Archaism and detachment tend to appeal to the dominant minority. Detachment represents a complete loss of hope.

51. Futurism can change to a religious attitude of transfiguration with a concern for the divine world rather than the present or future world of troubles. Futurism and transfiguration tend to appeal to the proletariat. Transfiguration represents deferred hope.

52. On a stabilized border of military importance the normal course of events is to have a civilization's armies initially staffed by citizen-soldier conscripts and then by professional volunteer soldiers. Over the course of time the staffing of the army will transition from members of the dominant minority to members of the internal proletariat to a mix of members of the external and internal proletariats. The barbarians eventually become an integral part of the civilization's armies. In time the barbarians may assume a leadership role and become self-confident in their barbarian culture abandoning attempts to emulate the style and customs of the civilization.

53. After penetrating a civilization's armies the barbarians will tend to penetrate business and commerce as well as other institutions of the civilization.

54. As a civilization disintegrates the dominant minority tends to adopt the manners and style of the internal proletariat while the internal proletariat becomes enfranchised adopting a leadership role. This joint tendency may reach

The Life Cycle of Civilizations

a point where the dominant minority is effectively merged into the internal proletariat.

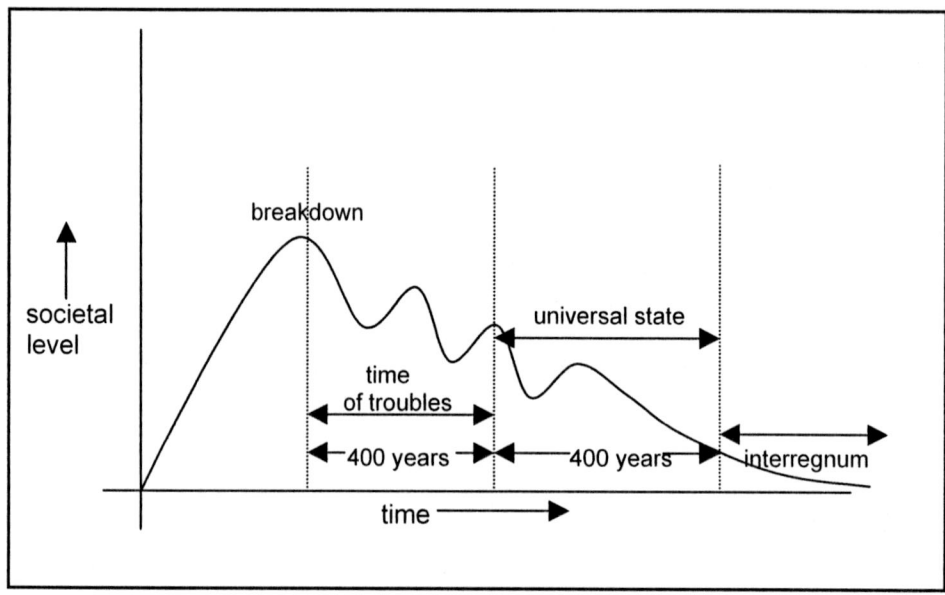

Figure 63. The typical pattern of evolution of a civilization.

55. The vulgarization of the dominant minority combined with the entry of the culture of the barbarians can lead to a decline in the quality and style of the civilization. This decline can take place in the arts, in language and in social manners. Religions may amalgamate or affect each other's beliefs, rites, and gods. Rival philosophies may be similarly affected.

56. The pattern of evolution of a typical civilization appears to be: birth, growth, a breakdown in growth, a time of troubles (a rout), a rally during the time of troubles, another rout, the creation of a universal state (a rally), a rout during the existence of the universal state, a rally in the latter history of the universal state, and the interregnum after the destruction of the universal state (a rout). The pattern has three and a half beats: rout, rally, rout, rally, rout, rally, rout. A graphical visualization of this progression is (400 year time frames are typically seen):

57. Variations from the three and a half beat pattern can occur. For example a two and a half beat pattern or a four and a half beat pattern. A civilization may not complete the three and a half beat pattern because it is absorbed by a neighbor.

58. Growing civilizations display a tendency towards diversity and differentiation. Disintegrating civilizations display a tendency towards a uniformity of roles for the three groups: the dominant minority (generating philosophies and universal states), the internal proletariat (creating higher religions), and the external proletariat (developing warrior bands and epic heroic ages). The individuals in a disintegrating civilization also display uniformity in psyche and behavior.

59. The remnants of a disintegrated civilization may combine with alien features of other contemporary civilizations to produce a new civilization after an interregnum.

60. A universal state created by the members of a civilization will tend to be increasingly regarded as an absolute necessity for civilization. If the universal state is very strong, or endures for a long period of time, it assumes the cloak of immortality. When it falls the psychological shock can be devastating.

61. Over time the outer parts of a universal state will lose their local leadership. As a result the central government will take increasing control of the "provinces" with the end result being total control being placed in the hands of a central, hierarchical bureaucracy.

62. The internal proletariat makes effective use of the unity and peace of a universal state to propagate its higher religion.

63. The extinction of a civilization is usually accomplished either through conquest by barbarians, or through occupation by a group from another culture or civilization, or through both.

64. It is possible for a civilization whose universal state has been prematurely ended by invaders to hibernate for centuries and to revive its universal state after expelling the invaders.

65. If a civilization attempts to destroy and absorb another civilization there are two possible outcomes: the attempt may be successful but it may require

The Life Cycle of Civilizations

hundreds of years to accomplish, or the attempt may fail over the short term or the long term due to a resurgence of the partially destroyed civilization.

66. Universal states tend to move or build their capital cities near the most dangerous frontier of the civilization.

67. The leadership of a universal state will eventually tend to come from regions near the most dangerous frontiers.

68. In the absence of modern technology, the expansion of universal states relies on roads and cleared fields to a great extent. Dense forests and other natural barriers tend to become the borders of universal states.

69. A hostile frontier between a civilization and barbarians is like a dam that keeps the barbarians out but also has the effect of building up a pressure in the barbarians to overflow/break the dam and to flood the civilization. A frontier acts to limit and distort the "radiation" of the civilization's culture to the barbarians. Eventually the radiation degenerates to trade and war, and perhaps the adoption of a modified form of a higher religion created by the civilization's internal proletariat.

70. After the barbarians succeed in overcoming a civilization they tend to lose the unity and discipline derived from opposition to the civilization. Barbarian successor states have short lifetimes because they are not able to create the institutions necessary for a continuing government.

71. Universal churches may be a distinct and separate "social species" from civilizations. They may have a symbiotic relationship with civilizations as each proceeds through their respective life cycles.

72. A universal church tends to be born during a time of troubles.

73. Successful religions emerge from the proletariat.

74. Attempts by rulers or dominant minorities to impose a religion on their people are usually unsuccessful over the long term although they may have some success in the short term.

75. An alien universal religion can achieve success in a civilization if it adapts its message and rituals to the traditional ways of the civilization both in external rites and representations, and in its internal beliefs.

76. An alien tinge in a higher religion helps the religion win converts because it offers a new source of authority to an internal proletariat that has rejected the authority of the dominant minority.

77. As a civilization disintegrates rival religions may amalgamate and/or exchange beliefs, rites and gods. They may also be strongly affected by philosophies. An alien or proletarian religion can put on the cloak of a civilization's philosophy.

78. Philosophies are the creation of a civilization's creative minority or dominant minority.

79. When a higher religion enters into a conflict with a philosophy the religion will rise and the philosophy will decline. If the philosophy develops religious attributes it will tend to decline into superstition because philosophies lack spiritual vitality to appeal to the masses.

80. During an interregnum a universal church may provide the seed around which a new civilization may crystallize. A universal church may interleave two successive civilizations providing continuity from the old civilization to the new civilization.

81. A universal church can serve as a source of creativity, and as a channel for the energy of the people, during the interregnum prior to the appearance of a new civilization. It also will naturally attract talented men who may not have a place available in the secular sphere.

82. A religion seems to be an important part of the social apparatus of a new civilization whether it is of a first generation civilization or succeeding generations.

83. A church draws on the vitality of the civilization in which it is born, and gives vitality to the cultural, political and economic spheres of the new civilization that emerges after an interregnum.

84. Regions where three or more civilizations intersect tend to be the locale for the generation of several higher religions.

85. The history of religion shows a trend to higher levels of spirituality.

86. The higher religions have significant similarities.

87. High points in religious history tend to correspond with low points in secular history.

88. The discovery of a "new world" such as America, or India (by the Macedonians and the Portuguese in different times) gives a civilization an exhilarating boost that promotes the expansion of its intellectual horizon.

89. A superior science and philosophy will radiate to nearby civilizations under appropriate circumstances.

90. Civilizations that come into contact are more likely to war with each than to engage in peaceful exchanges. In some cases a civilization will attempt to isolate itself from an intruding civilization.

91. A successful aggression by one civilization on another opens up the aggressor's civilization to the culture of the victim civilization possibly accentuating difficulties within the aggressor's civilization.

92. A cultural or social element that is harmless in one civilization may prove to have a major impact on a civilization that imports it. If a civilization imports a cultural or social element from another civilization it is likely that it will import additional elements from the exporting civilization. It is difficult to limit a cultural invasion once it has begun.

93. A cultural transmission from one civilization to another that takes place through the transmittal of pieces separately is apt to be reassembled into a cultural pattern similar to that in the transmitting civilization.

94. When a civilization has been unable to prevent the transmission of one or more elements from another civilization then it may be able to successfully respond by wholeheartedly accepting the inflow of elements of the transmitting civilization.

95. A renaissance is a cultural infusion into a civilization from the culture of a period in its parent civilization. A renaissance can only occur if a civilization reaches the same cultural level as the period of its parent when the parent civilization was developing the cultural achievements that the civilization is reviving.

96. There is a cyclic pattern in the history of civilizations reflecting the struggle between the forward momentum of the civilization and a long run tendency of the civilization to wind down in alternate rallies and routs.

97. It appears to require three generations to achieve a significant social change and four generations to achieve a significant change in international politics.

98. The time of troubles and the universal state phases of the life of a civilization seem to total to approximately eight hundred to a thousand years.

99. The disintegration phase of civilizations appears to be similar in pattern and timing for most civilizations.

100. The growth phase of civilizations does not show a recognizable pattern of routs and rallies or the like. It appears as a short time interval of major progress.

101. The rate of cultural change in civilizations is variable—sometimes accelerating and sometimes decelerating.

102. Fratricidal warfare is the commonest cause of the breakdown of civilizations.
103. Productive, creative leisure is the source of much of the cultural growth of civilizations.

104. Human history is only in its initial stages. The succession of civilizations on earth appears to be part of a process leading humanity to a higher (yet earthly) plane of consciousness and socialization— etherialization.

Appendix B. Reconstructing Prehistoric and Unknown Civilizations

Reconstructing Forgotten Civilizations

When we developed our theory of civilizations and applied it to known civilizations we found that the historical data suggested that additional civilizations existed that had not hitherto been recognized. This situation is not uncommon in science. After a theory has been developed for a set of phenomena, a reexamination of the accumulated data often leads to the recognition that, what appeared to be random data, is in fact structured in a way that the theory describes. A good theory gives focus to our eyes. We see patterns, forms and structures where previously we only saw randomness.

After examining the Japanese branch of Far Eastern civilization we found it made sense to view the roughly thousand year period before the start of Japanese Far Eastern civilization in 1048 AD as containing an earlier civilization that we called Early Japanese that began in 58 BC. An important confirmation of this suggestion was the match between two "bad" emperors with a low societal level and a "good" emperor with a high societal level. A more detailed confirmation is not presently possible because of uncertainties in the history of that period.

We also found the placement of a civilization between Hellenic civilization and Orthodox Christian (main body) made sense when we examined events in the Eastern Roman (Byzantine) Empire. We called this new civilization Byzantine civilization.

Similarly the placement of a civilization between Syraic civilization and Iranian Islamic civilization also seemed to make sense and be in accord with historical data. This new civilization which we call Iranic civilization started in 312 BC and was based on a fusion of Hellenic and Iranian culture. Its historical events matched the routs and rallies in the societal level as we showed.

In addition we found historical support for a new civilization in Palestine starting in 107 AD that we call JudaeoPalestinic civilization, an Early Hindu civilization starting in 80 AD, and a New Sinic civilization starting in 172 AD.

The Life Cycle of Civilizations

All of these civilizations show a pattern of historical events that follows the routs and rallies of our theoretical societal levels.

The major impact of technology on civilizations in the past two hundred years led us to propose a number of new technologically based civilizations. Again, recent historical events seem to agree with the calculated societal levels.

So we have recognized the pattern of civilization in historical periods where civilizations had not previously been identified. Our theory sharpens our view of the historical record and gives us new eyes. We have found the following sequences of human civilizations (with our NEW proposed civilizations indicated):

Hellenic-Western civilizations:
    565 BC – 378 AD   Hellenic civilization
    717 AD – 1650 AD   Western civilization
    1781 AD – 2715? AD   Technic civilization (NEW)

Hellenic-Orthodox Christian (main body) civilizations:
    565 BC – 378 AD   Hellenic civilization
    364 AD – 840 AD   Byzantine civilization (NEW)
    840 AD – 1768 AD   Orthodox Christian (main body)

Hellenic-Orthodox Christian (Russian) civilizations:
    565 BC – 378 AD   Hellenic civilization
    364 AD – 840 AD   Byzantine civilization (NEW)
    941 AD – 1881 AD   Orthodox Christian (Russian)
    1917 AD – 2851 AD   RussoTechnic (NEW)

Syraic-Palestinian civilizations:
    1060 BC – 332 BC   Syraic civilization
    107 AD – 969 AD   JudaeoPalestinic civilization (NEW)
    1209 AD – 2172? AD   Arab Islamic civilization
    1950 AD – 2884? AD   PetroIslamic civilization (NEW)

Syraic-Iranian civilizations:
    1060 BC – 332 BC   Syraic civilization
    312 BC – 641 AD   Iranic civilization (NEW)
    641 AD – present   Iranian Islamic (with interregnum)
    1950 AD – 2884? AD   PetroIslamic civilization (NEW)

The Life Cycle of Civilizations

Indian civilizations:
    855 BC – 80 AD   Indic civilization
    80 AD – 1011 AD   Early Hindic civilization (NEW)
    1011 AD – 1947 AD   Hindu civilization
    1950 AD – 2884 AD   IndoTechnic (NEW)

Chinese civilizations:
    768 BC – 172 AD   Sinic
    172 AD – 878 AD   New Sinic (NEW)
    878 AD – 1853 AD   Far Eastern (main body)
    1950 AD – 2884? AD   SinoTechnic (NEW)

Japanese civilizations:
    58 BC – 876 AD   Early Japanese (NEW)
    1048 AD – 1868 AD   Far Eastern (Japan)
    1868 AD – 2802 AD   JapoTechnic (NEW)

The preceding civilizations, both known and new, all have fairly well developed historical records with which to compare our theory. We would now like to turn our attention to possible prehistoric civilizations to see if our theory can give some structure to sketchy periods of prehistory.

Prehistoric Civilizations

The first generation civilizations, that Toynbee was aware of, have had the good fortune to have a written language in which their history has been at least partially recorded. We think particularly of the Sumeric, Egyptaic and Sinic civilizations in this regard.

Both the Egyptaic and the Sinic civilizations have writings referring to an earlier stage in their civilizations, or a predecessor civilization, that existed prior to the known civilizations with which we are familiar. These periods were more or less prior to the development of writing in the respective civilizations.

Some Egyptian and Greek historical records describe a period of civilization with a united Egypt under the Pharaoh Menes in 3000 BC. While we often think of Egyptaic civilization as suddenly flowering from nothing, and then immediately building pyramids, there is a long prior period during which the Nile Valley was brought into cultivation, and societies and governments developed. This prior period encompassed the 0th and 1st Dynasties. It included the legendary kings:

    Ka
    Narmer

Aha
Djer
Djet
Den
Anedjub
Semerkhet
Qa'a

King Narmer appears to be the King who united Upper and Lower Egypt based primarily on a shield-shaped sculpture called the Narmer Palette that has been dated to 3150 – 3125 BC. The front side of the Narmer Palette shows Narmer wearing the White Crown of Upper Egypt in the act of striking an enemy from the marshlands. The rear side shows Narmer wearing the Red Crown of Lower Egypt (the Nile delta) as he inspects the bodies of headless enemies.

Front   Rear

Exhibit 27. The Narmer Palette. J. E. Quibell discovered the Palette while excavating royal residences of early Egyptian kings at Hierakonpolis in Upper Egypt in 1898. Narmer's name appears in the serekh sign at the top.

The Life Cycle of Civilizations

In the period from 3500 BC to 2600 BC, Egypt evolved from two separate regions, Upper Egypt with strong African influences and Lower Egypt (the Nile delta region) with strong Libyan and Middle Eastern influences, into one united kingdom. The building of the great pyramids that followed reflected the wealth and power of a united Egypt. This later Egypt was the Egypt of Egyptaic civilization.

But the prior one thousand years contained an Egypt of various states created during and after the taming of the Nile Valley. It also developed a universal state that existed for about four hundred years before the beginning of Egyptaic civilization (which we have set for good reason at 2557 BC.)

The only other important "known facts" of the thousand years of prehistory are:

- A major (unspecified) calamity took place in the reign of King Semerkhet around 2800 BC,
- An upheaval appears to have happened during the reign of King Qa'a,
- A major rivalry existed between the cults of Set and Horus around 2725 BC.

Although the data on Egyptian prehistory is somewhat sketchy we can use our theory of civilizations to develop a picture of that civilization based on any one of the following dates:

1. The beginning of the time of troubles
2. The end of the time of troubles
3. The beginning of a universal state
4. The end of a universal state

Any one of these data items fixes the S curve for the civilization. Any other information that we have on the civilization can then be used to check the routs and rallies of the S curve to confirm its validity.

Similarly we can examine the information in early Chinese writings referring to prehistoric dynasties and empires from the period before the recognized beginning of Sinic civilization. Again only one date is necessary to fix the S curve for a possible pre-Sinic civilization.

We do not expect that many more unknown civilizations will be uncovered in view of the beginning of climatic conditions favorable for civilizations only 10,000 years ago and the need for some time after that point for the growth of agriculture and the growth of population levels necessary for civilization. However, if evidence of additional civilizations is found, then our theory offers a way to set up a time framework for the evolution of a civilization with minimal data input: namely one of the above mentioned four dates.

The Life Cycle of Civilizations

A Prehistoric, Unrecognized Egyptian Civilization?

The Narmer palette showing Narmer wearing the White Crown of Upper Egypt and the Red Crown of Lower Egypt is believed to indicate that Narmer united Upper and Lower Egypt into a universal state. Other historical data indicates his central importance. Since the Narmer Palette has been dated to 3150 – 3125 BC we have chosen 3157 BC as the beginning of the universal state of a prehistoric civilization that we will call *Nile River civilization*.

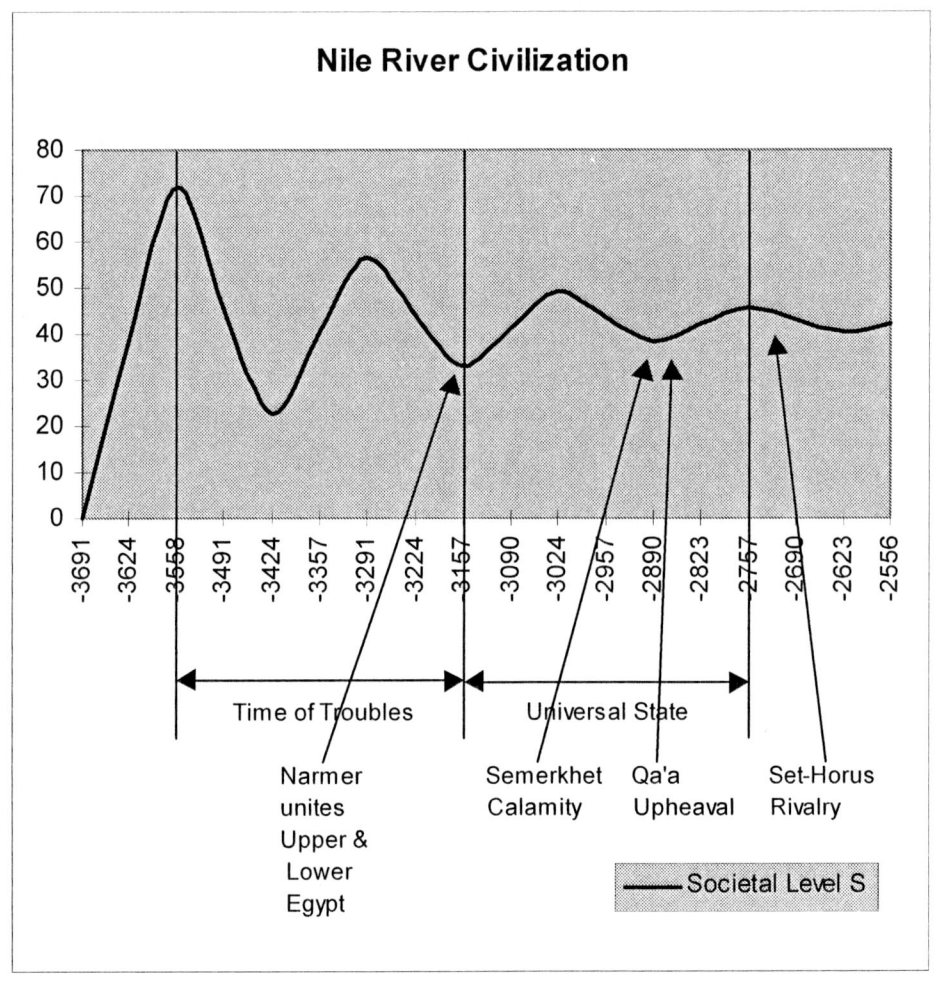

Figure 64. Societal Level curve of Nile River civilization.

The Life Cycle of Civilizations

Allotting 400 years for a time of troubles and 134 years for a Startup phase we arrive at a beginning date of Nile River civilization of 3691 BC. We use the standard theory of a civilization to obtain the societal curve shown in Figure 64.

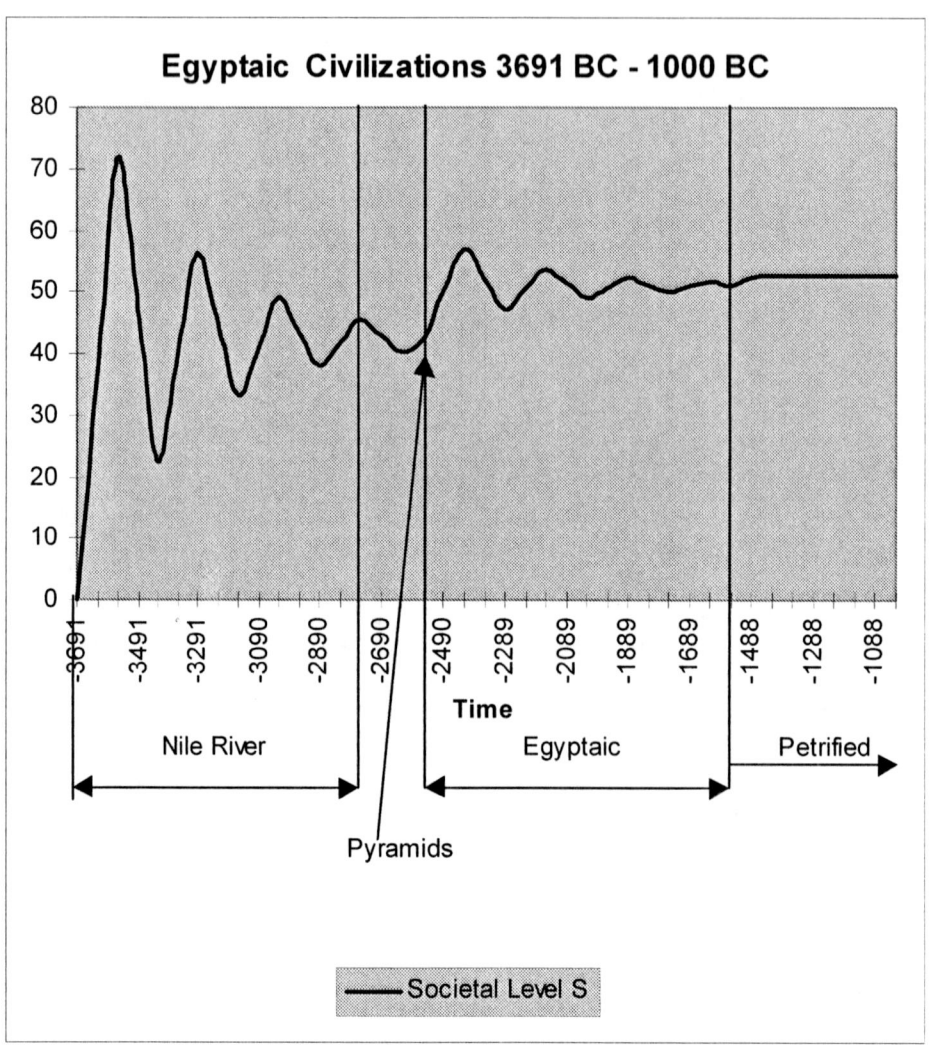

Figure 65. The Nile River and Egyptaic civilizations 3691 BC – 1000 BC.

The societal level of the Nile River civilization is

$$S_{NRC}(t) = S(t + 3691) \qquad (136)$$

where S(t) is specified by equation (20).

The Semerkhet Calamity and the Qa'a Upheaval appear at a low point of the theoretical societal level. Also, the rivalry between the Set and Horus cults appears on the slope of a downturn in the societal level. Thus there is a correlation between known historical events, and the routs and rallies of the societal curve. As further archaeological data surfaces, more detailed tests of the S curve of the Nile River civilization will be possible.

The complete societal curve of the sequence of Egyptian civilizations is given in Figure 65. It is calculated from the following expression using equation (29) and our consistent theoretical approach:

$$\begin{aligned} S_{Egypt} = \; & S_{NRC}(t) + g_1 \theta(t + 2557.5) S(t + 2557.5, r) + \\ & + g_2 \theta(t + 1580) S(t + 1580, 6.67r) \end{aligned} \qquad (137)$$

where r is specified by d = .75 and where

$$g_1 = g_2 = 1/5 \qquad (138)$$

A Prehistoric Unrecognized Chinese Civilization?

Chinese writing matured during the waning years of the Shang Dynasty around 1400 BC to 1200 BC. Prior to that time we have pictographs and early Chinese characters—many of which are not known, or imprecisely known, in terms of modern equivalents.

Chinese prehistory is not well documented. Some Chinese classics describe legendary figures and historical events of the period before 1000 BC. Some of these works appear to contain passages that are forgeries from later times. Generally Western historians have viewed historical accounts of these early times with suspicion.

Hints of an Early Chinese Civilization

However, recent archaeological finds have been changing the view of western historians. The Shang Dynasty period from 1766 BC to 1123 BC was viewed as mythical until recent archaeological discoveries confirmed the existence of this dynasty and its place in the history of China. The earlier Hsia Dynasty (usually thought to last from 2205 BC to 1766 BC with some proposing

The Life Cycle of Civilizations

the alternate period of 1994 BC to 1523 BC) has been radiocarbon-dated to 2100 BC to 1800 BC in relatively recent archaeological studies of its capitol city.

An examination of the culture and events of China between 3000 BC and 1000 BC suggests that a civilization existed in the Yellow River region which we will call the *Yellow River civilization*. The sophistication of the *Shih Ching* (the "Book of Songs") which dates to before 1000 BC confirms the existence of a lengthy, previous cultural tradition. We will now summarize the known events and features of the period before 1000 BC that suggest an unrecognized civilization existed in that period.

Chinese History from 3000 BC to 2205BC

Chinese history in this period has a mythological flavor but probably is based, at least in part, on historical fact. There are two phases in this period: the period of the three cultural heroes and the period of the three sage kings. The center of cultural development was the Yellow River valley. The climate of the valley at this time was warmer and more moist then the present climate of this region. Swamps and lakes were more common.

The three cultural heroes were three great kings who were prominent in a period of significant cultural development. They were accorded credit for the cultural and technological progress of the period. These great kings who lived between 2800BC and 2600 BC are:

- Fu Hsi – He taught men how to hunt, fish, and cook.

- Shen Nung – He developed the cultivation of the five grains, invented the plow, and established markets (a mercantile economy).

- Huang Ti – He invented boats, oars, and the fire drill. He cleared the plains with fire so crops and cattle could be raised. He encouraged his court to cultivate music.

The three sage kings of this period were Yao, Shun, and Yu. These kings were celebrated for their wisdom and virtue. The approximate date of their activity is:

- Yao – 2350 BC

- Shun – 2250 BC

- Yu – 2205 BC

Emperor Yu, who drained the land so that it could be cultivated, is reputed to have created the mountains and founded the Hsia Dynasty in 2205. Most western historians view the period up to the founding of the Hsia Dynasty as mythological. Yet the fact remains it was a period of major cultural growth as well as major advances in agriculture.

Chinese History from 2205 BC to 768 BC

This period can be viewed as composed of three parts: the Hsia Dynasty (2205 BC – 1766 BC, or alternately 1994 BC – 1523 BC), the Shang Dynasty (1766 BC – 1123 BC, or alternately 1523 BC – 1027 BC), and an interregnum (1123 BC – 768 BC, or alternately 1027 BC – 768 BC) started by a successful invasion of King Wu of Chou (the leading march (frontier) state).

The Hsia Dynasty was founded by the sage Emperor Yu in 2205 BC in an inland portion of the Yellow River valley. Historians had viewed this dynasty as mythological until excavations in 1959 in the city of Yanshi uncovered what appears to be the capitol of the Hsia Dynasty. Radiocarbon dating of artifacts at the site showed they dated from 2100 BC to 1800 BC.

The Hsia Dynasty existed until the reign of Emperor Chieh, reputedly a decadent emperor, who was overthrown by the wise and virtuous Emperor T'ang who founded the Shang Dynasty in 1766 BC.

The Shang Dynasty is noted for the invention of Chinese writing. Some of the noteworthy events and features of the Shang Dynasty are:

- The Dynasty had a number of capitols until Emperor Pan moved the capitol permanently to Yin (near modern Anyang) in 1401.

- The Dynasty developed a highly organized bureaucracy.

- Bronze casting reached a peak of perfection during the later years of the Dynasty.

- The religion of this period combined ancestor worship with the worship of a supreme god Shang Ti ("Lord on High") who presided over the lesser gods.

- Between roughly 1500 BC and 1100 BC Chinese writing underwent a transition from pictographic writing (pictures representing words) to Chinese characters similar to modern Chinese characters. Many of the Chinese characters of those times are not known today.

The Life Cycle of Civilizations

- The boundaries of the Shang Empire at its peak were the Pacific Ocean on the East, Shensi on the West, southern Hopeh on the North and the Yangtze on the South.

The Shang Dynasty ended in 1123 BC. There was a great drought in the reign of the last Shang emperor, Ti-hsin, that probably weakened the dynasty significantly. King Wu of the leading march state, a vassal on the frontiers of the empire, staged a successful revolt and invasion in 1123 BC conquering the empire. Wu started the Chou Dynasty that also appears at the beginning of the Sinic civilization.

The period between the fall of the Shang Dynasty (1123 BC) and the beginning of the Sinic civilization (768 BC) was an interregnum. This period contained about 1773 feudal fiefs engaged in constant warfare. It is similar in character to the feudal period of European history.

A Yellow River Civilization

The Hsia Dynasty lasted for approximately 400 years. The Shang Dynasty lasted for approximately 600 years. The length of these periods and the advanced state of their culture strongly suggest that a significant civilization existed.

We will apply our standard theory of civilizations to the Yellow River civilization using equation (20) and set the end of the civilization's universal state to the end of the Shang Dynasty in 1123 BC. With this choice the beginning of the civilization (the startup) is 2057 BC – a date that is consistent with the radiocarbon dating of the Hsia Dynasty to 2100 BC. Using these dates the societal level of the Yellow River civilization is

$$S_{YRC}(t) = S(t + 2057) \qquad (139)$$

where S(t) is specified by equation (20). $S_{YRC}(t)$ is plotted in Figure 66.

Remarkably the beginning of the universal state is 1553 BC and the time of troubles period lasts from 1924 BC to 1523 BC – these dates are remarkably similar to the dates that some modern scholars specify for the Hsia Dynasty (1994 BC to 1523 BC) and the Shang Dynasty (1523 BC to 1027 BC). With a Startup date of 2057 the dates are consistent with radiocarbon dating of the Hsia capitol artifacts at Yanshi.

The complete societal curve of the sequence of Chinese civilizations is given in Figure 67 if the new prehistoric civilization is accepted. It is calculated from the following expression using equation (38) and our consistent theoretical approach:

The Life Cycle of Civilizations

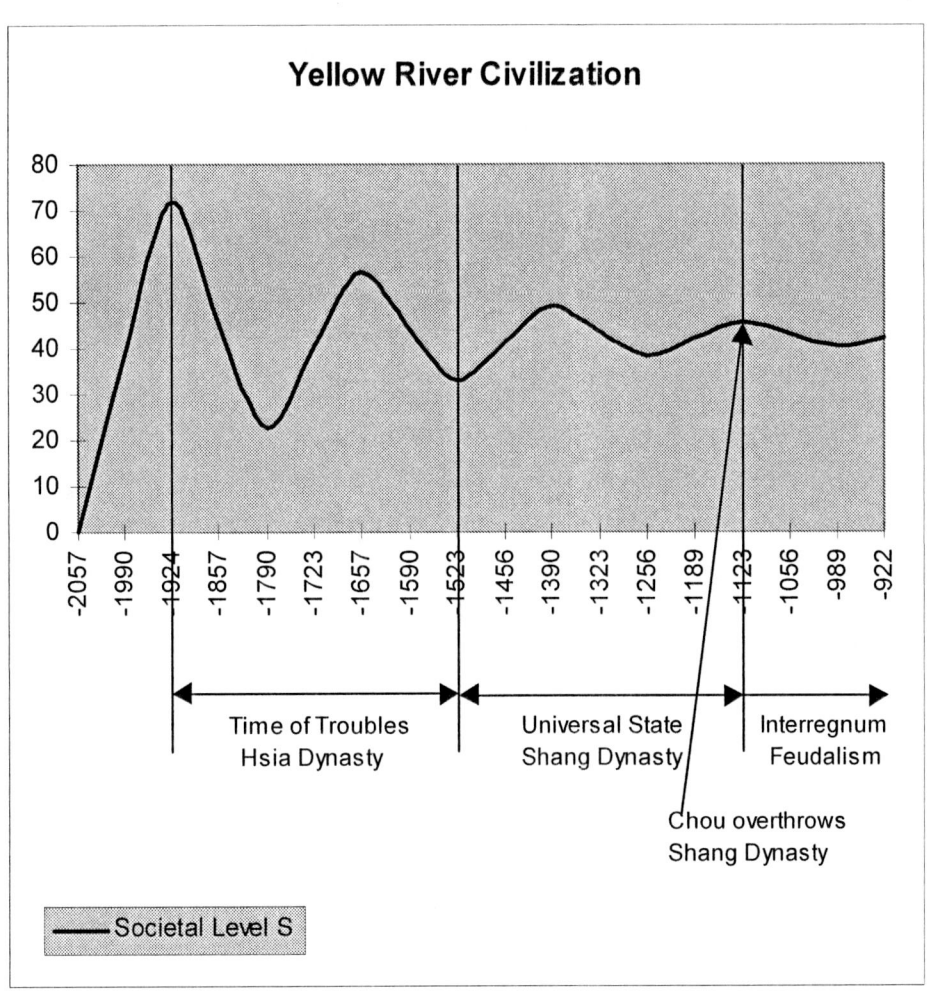

Figure 66. Societal Level curve of Yellow River civilization.

$$\begin{aligned}
S_{China} = \ & S_{YRC}(t) + g_1 \theta(t+768)S(t+768, r) + \\
& + g_2 \theta(t-172)S(t-172, r) + \\
& + g_3 \theta(t-878)S(t-878, r) + \\
& + g_4 \theta(t-1368) S(t-1368, 6.67r) \\
& + S_{tech}(t) \hspace{4cm} (140)
\end{aligned}$$

The Life Cycle of Civilizations

where r is specified by d = .75, S_{tech} is specified by equation (95) with t_0 = 1950, and where

$$g_1 = g_2 = g_3 = g_4 = 1/5 \qquad (141)$$

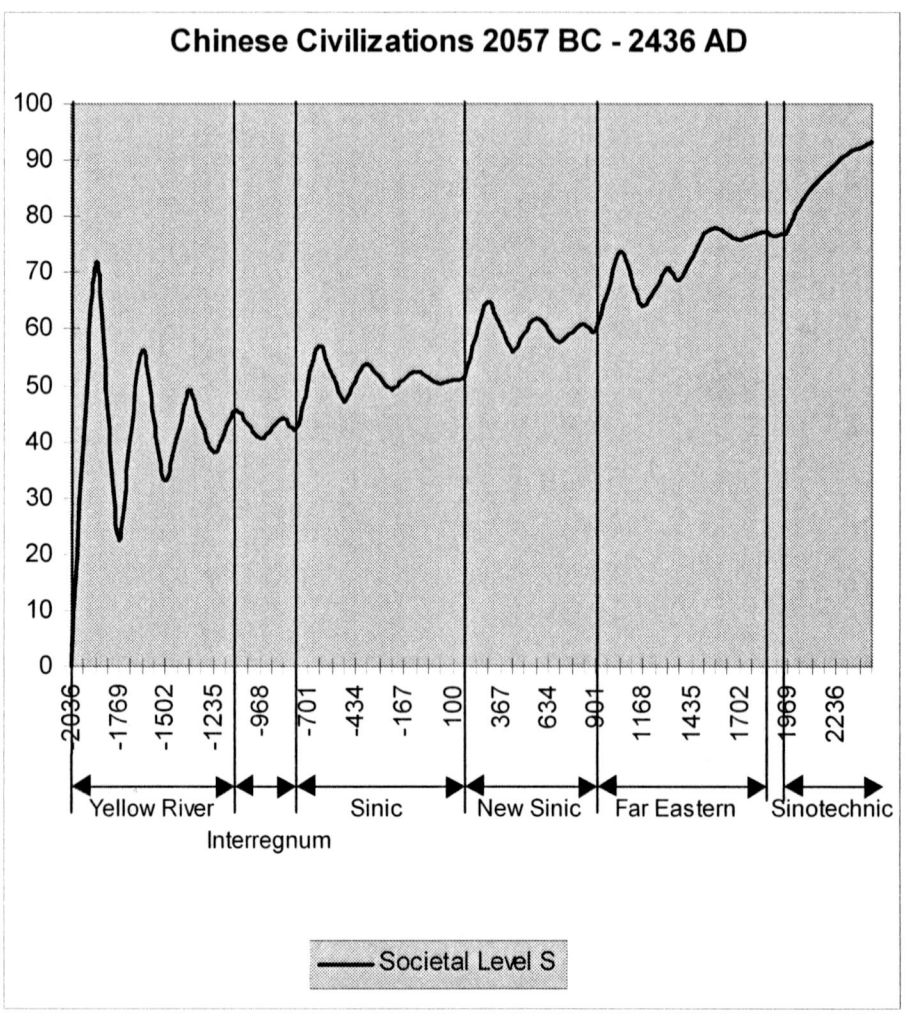

Figure 67. The civilizations of China including a prehistoric civilization and recent technological effects.

A New View of Chinese and Egyptian Civilizations?

The analysis we have performed on prehistoric Egypt and China strongly suggests that unrecognized prehistoric civilizations existed in those countries. In our view the list of Egyptian and Chinese civilizations is:

Chinese civilizations:

2057 BC – 1123 BC	Yellow River (NEW)
768 BC – 172 AD	Sinic
172 AD – 878 AD	New Sinic (NEW)
878 AD – 1853 AD	Far Eastern (main body)
1950 AD – 2884 AD	SinoTechnic (NEW)

Egyptian civilizations:

3691 BC – 2757 BC	Nile River (NEW)
2557 BC – 500 AD	Egyptaic

The application of our theory to other potential lost civilizations, that may be uncovered as archaeology progresses, can help to expand our understanding of these forgotten civilizations.

The Effect on the Cumulative Progress

The addition of the Nile River civilization and the Yellow River civilization to the roster of civilizations changes the Progress line in Figure 53 that we developed earlier. A linear fit to the Progress with time is still a good approximation. The addition of the new prehistoric Egyptian and Chinese civilizations modifies equation (135) slightly to

$$P(t) = 377 + 0.122t \qquad (142)$$

where t is measured in years. Figure 68 shows this new linear fit to the expanded data. The net effect of the addition of newly found prehistoric civilizations is to lower the slope of the line of Progress.

The Life Cycle of Civilizations

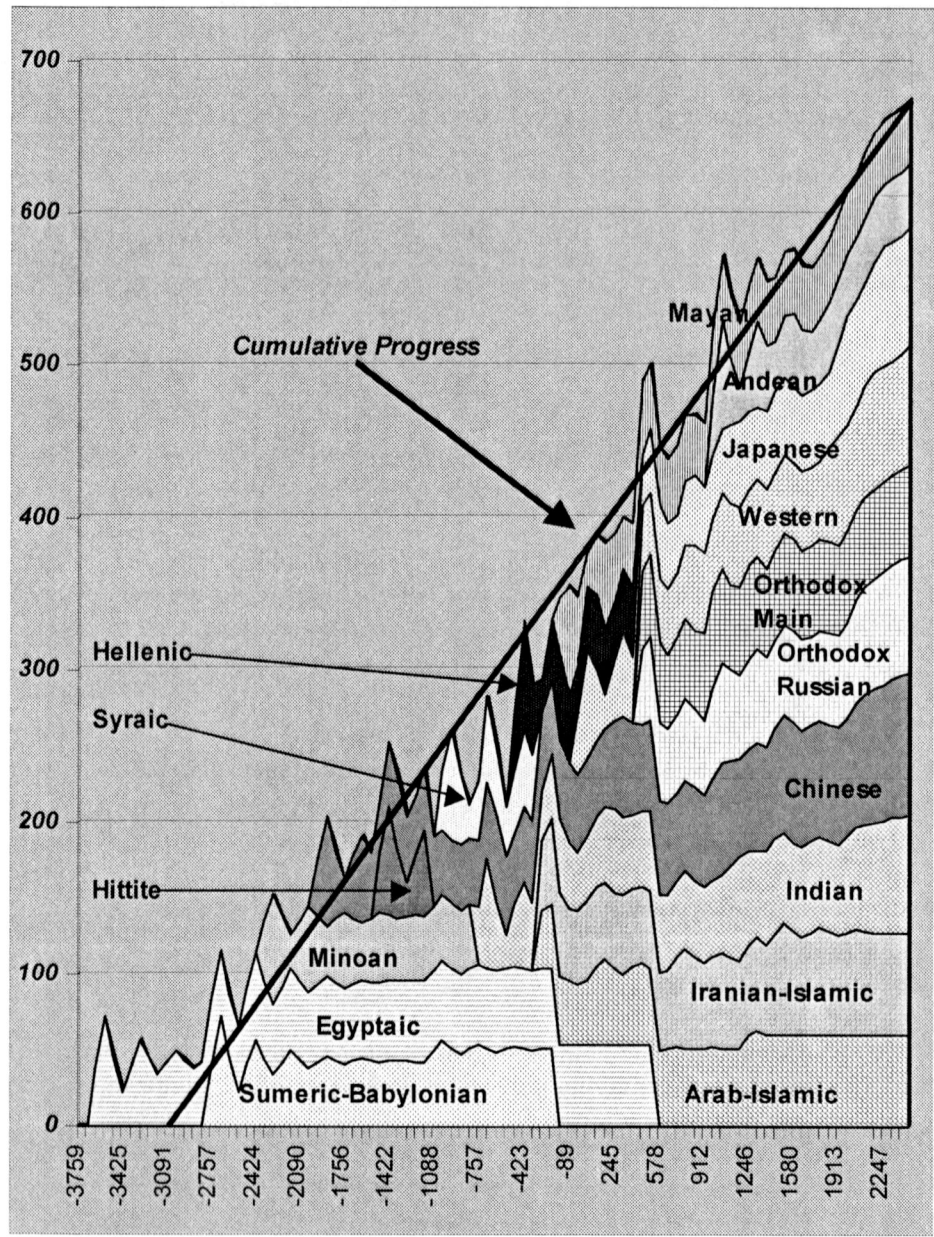

Figure 68. The cumulative progress of civilizations modified to include the Nile River and Yellow River civilizations (together with recent technological effects.)

Appendix C. Reconstructing Mayan Civilization

Recently new Mayan hieroglyphics were accidentally found in Dos Pilas, Guatemala that describe a series of events and wars between the Mayan "superpowers" Tikal and Calakmul.[11] These historical findings appear to support our new mathematical theory of civilizations. Previously Mayan history was viewed as a collection of random wars between city-states that ended around 900 AD in a mass exodus from the cities. It now appears that Mayan civilization was undergoing a pattern of development that is similar to the pattern of development of Eurasian civilizations.

Theory Compared to Mayan History

If we apply the Standard S Curve to Mayan civilization we need to set only one parameter – the point where the civilization began its rise. Previously we set the beginning of Mayan civilization to 223 BC and so we have:

$$S_{Mayan}(t) = S(t + 223) \qquad (143)$$

where $S_{Mayan}(t)$ is the curve for Mayan civilization. ($t = -223$ or $t = 223$ BC is the beginning year of the civilization; prior to that year we view the Mayan society as largely static.) BC years are specified as negative numbers. Exhibit 28 shows the plot of $S_{Mayan}(t)$ as a red line. Known events of Mayan history (including the new hieroglyphic data) are identified in the Exhibit and show good agreement with the ups and downs of $S_{Mayan}(t)$. The graph is superimposed on a photograph of an impressive Mayan Temple.

---

[11] Williams, A. R., "A New Chapter in Maya History: All-out War, Shifting Alliances, Bloody Sacrifices", National Geographic Magazine **202**, no. 4 (October, 2002).

The Life Cycle of Civilizations

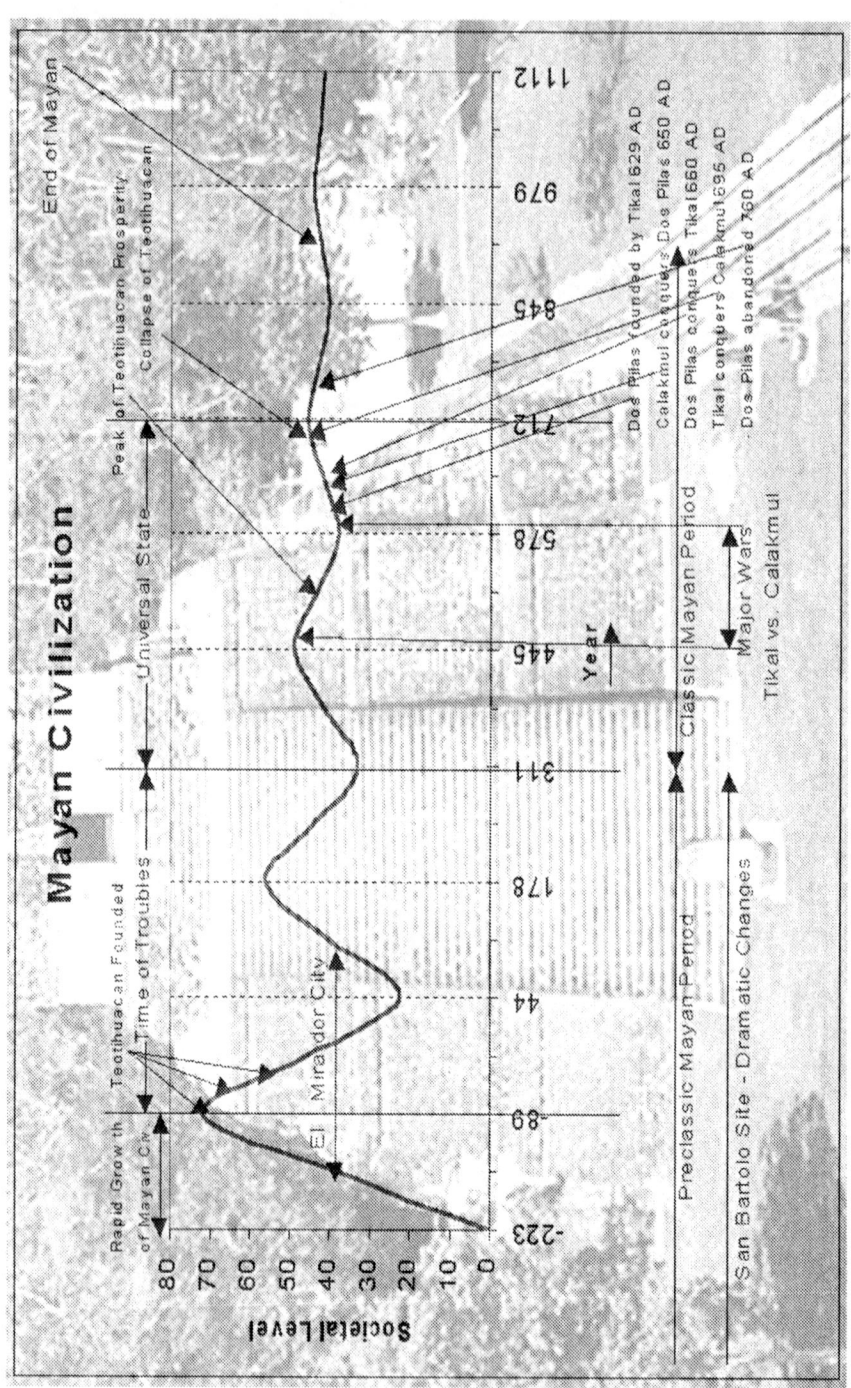

Exhibit 28. The pattern of Mayan civilization.

Mayan Civilization World War

A series of major wars between Tikal and Calakmul, Mayan superpowers, in the fifth through seventh centuries appears to have brought Mayan civilization to its knees. Recently unearthed hieroglyphics describe phases of this war such as the founding of an important military outpost (stronghold) Dos Pilas by Tikal in 629, its conquest by Calakmul around 650, its emergence as a powerful state that conquered its founder Tikal around 660, and its eventual abandonment in 760. Thus a sequence of what originally appeared to be local conflicts between 600 and 700 were, in reality, a continuation of a "world war" between Tikal and Calakmul that culminated in the conquest of Calakmul in 695 by Tikal.

The roughly 250 years of warfare between Tikal and Calakmul lasting from the fifth through seventh centuries corresponds to the 267 year cycle found in Western civilization, and Middle Eastern and Asian civilizations, and embodied in our theory.

Mayan civilization began with a roughly 134 year period of major growth starting around 223 BC. Great cities were built such as El Mirador. Teotihuacan was also founded in the first century BC. Mayan civilization then went through three and a half cycles of ups and downs just like Eurasian civilizations. The last cycle was dominated by constant wars between Tikal and Calakmul that culminated in the decline of Mayan civilization. Tikal's conquest of Calakmul around 700 AD started the last stage of decline that ended in the complete abandonment of the Mayan cities around 900 AD. The last stages of the decline of the Mayans can be compared to the last stages of the decline of Rome: constant warfare with Barbarian invaders culminating in the conquest of Rome and the reduction of Rome to a small agricultural village among splendid ruins.

Thus the spectacle afforded by Mayan history compares with that of European and Asian civilizations, and confirms the evolution of civilizations is based on our common human nature.

Exhibit 28 shows a chart of the ups and downs of the history of Mayan civilization from its beginning around 223 BC until its end around 900 AD according to the Theory of Civilizations. The red line is a plot of the "societal level" – the inherent strength (health) of the overall civilization.

As can be seen in the period from 445 – 575 AD, overwhelming fratricidal warfare between states weakened the strength of the civilization. The period between 580 and 700 shows an upturn in the civilization that is probably due to a lower level of conflict that allowed the civilization to begin growing again. The settlement at Dos Pilas in 629 and its growth into a major power support the notion that the Seventh Century was a period of growth.

The Life Cycle of Civilizations

The emergence of a "winner" – Tikal – in 695 with the conquest and destruction of Calakmul roughly marks the high point of the period as shown in Exhibit 28.

The period denoted "Time of Troubles" was probably a period of fierce conflict between the city-states. In Eurasian civilizations it is normally a period of ruinous conflict.

The period denoted "Universal State" normally is a time in the life of a civilization where the civilization is dominated by an empire. In the case of Mayan civilization this time may actually have been a time dominated by a confederation of states that often had internal wars. It may have been analogous to the Parthian Empire, which consisted of loosely united, more or less independent provinces.

The history of Teotihuacan appears to follow the general pattern of Mayan civilization. It was founded during the period of great initial growth, reached its peak shortly after a peak in Mayan civilization and collapsed at roughly the same time as Calakmul was conquered.

Appendix D. Comparison to Toynbee

This work is based in large part on observations made by Toynbee (and other historians before him as well). There are also a number of new concepts that appeared to the author to be natural within the framework of this quantitative theory. In this appendix we summarize the content from Toynbee and other historians, and the new content within our theory.

Concepts Developed by Toynbee and Others

The quantitative theory of civilizations described herein is based on the following historical observations of Toynbee and others:

1. Civilizations appear to have a lifetime of approximately one thousand years.

2. Civilizations typically begin with a growth phase, which ends in a breakdown (meaning an end of growth). They then normally have a four hundred year, "Time of Troubles", followed by a four hundred year "Universal State".

3. The Time of Troubles phase quite often contains a growth phase within its overall trend of decline. The Universal State phase often has a significant dip ("bad times").

4. Civilizations have successor civilizations.

5. The up and down trends typically last for four generations or roughly 130 years.

The qualitative theory of civilizations that is described in Appendix A is a set of "laws" that we constructed from observations and conclusions embodied in the work of Toynbee and other historians.

New Concepts Developed in the Quantitative Theory of Civilizations

The quantitative theory of civilizations that we have developed contains a number of features that are not evident in Toynbee's work although they are not inconsistent with it. Some of these features are:

1. There is a measure associated with each civilization that measures its state. We call this measure the Societal Level.

2. The overall shape of the Societal Level as a function of time is that of a damped harmonic oscillator with a period of 267 years.

3. The curve of the Standard Societal Level is the solution of the damped harmonic oscillator differential equation in which a "social" restoring force term and "social friction" term appear.

4. Sudden major shocks to a civilization: environmental disasters such as a major volcanic eruption, or a major sudden, overwhelming barbarian invasion can be approximated as Dirac delta-function "hammer blows".

5. The longer-term interaction between two civilizations and the interaction between a civilization and a barbarian society can be modeled using coupled differential equations.

6. The series of civilizations in a sizable region with a continuing large population are interrelated through apparentation and are represented by a superposition (a sum) of the civilizations standard S curves.

7. A civilization subject to a sudden *major* external shock (hammer blow) may restart with the order of the Time of Troubles and Universal State reversed.

8. The period of oscillation (denoted b in the equations) and the measure of decline in a civilization (denoted a in the equations) appear to be the same for almost all civilizations except for arrested or abortive civilizations.

9. The strength of the interaction between a civilization and another society, and the strength of a reaction to a hammer blow appears to be about 1/5 in most cases.

10. The fact that the theory appears to apply to the Roman Catholic Church as well as civilizations provides strong support for the notion that its basis is within human nature and thus genetic in origin.

11. Technological progress appears to have a significant impact on a civilization's Societal Level.

REFERENCES

1. Bernal, J. D., *The World, the Flesh and the Devil* (Indiana University Press, Bloomington, IN, 1929)
2. Braudel, F., *A History of Civilizations* (Penguin Books, New York, NY, 1993)
3. Coulborn, R., *The Origin of Civilized Societies* (Princeton University Press, Princeton, NJ 1959, 1969)
4. Huntington, S. P., *The Clash of Civilizations and the Remaking of World Order* (Simon & Schuster, New York, NY, 1996)
5. Joos, G., *Theoretical Physics* (Hafner Publishing, New York, 1950) or any good second year college Mechanics textbook.
6. Kroeber, A. L., *Configurations of Culture Growth* (University of California Press, Berkeley, CA, 1944)
7. Melko, M., *The Nature of Civilizations* (Porter Sargent Publishers, Boston, MA, 1969)
8. Melko, M. and Scott, L. R. (eds), *The Boundaries of Civilizations in Space and Time* (University Press of America, Lantham, MD, 1987)
9. Richardson, L. F., *Arms and Insecurity* (Quadrangle Books, Chicago, IL, 1960)
10. Shklovskii, I. S., and Sagan, C., *Intelligent Life in the Universe* (Dell Publishing Co., New York, NY, 1966).
11. Sorokin, Pitirim, *Social and Cultural Dynamics* (four volumes, Porter Sargent Publishers, Boston, MA, 1937-41)
12. Sorokin, Pitirim, *Social and Cultural Dynamics* (Abridged, Porter Sargent Publishers, Boston, MA, 1957)
13. Spengler, O., *The Decline of the West* (Oxford University Press, Oxford, UK, 1991)
14. Sperandeo, V., *Methods of a Wall Street Master* (John Wiley & Sons, New York, 1991)
15. Toynbee, A. J., *A Study of History* (twelve volumes, Oxford University Press, Oxford, UK, 1934-61)
16. Toynbee, A. J. and Somervell, D. C., *A Study of History (Abridgement of Volumes I-VI)* (Oxford University Press, Oxford, UK, 1987)
17. Toynbee, A. J. and Somervell, D. C., *A Study of History (Abridgement of Volumes VII-X)* (Oxford University Press, Oxford, UK, 1987)

INDEX

A

Abbasid Caliphate, 95
abortive civilization, 215
acceleration, 45, 46, 47
ADHD, 38
Adrianople, 102
affiliated civilizations, 70
Afghan, 128
Africa, 2, 38, 82, 125
Aha, Pharaoh, 229
al Qaeda, 4, 128, 129
Alexander the Great, 87, 94
Alexandria, 136
alienation, 217
American Revolution, 88
Anatolia, 102
Anatolian Plateau, 37
Andean civilization, 16, 31, 81, 182, 184, 187
Anedjub, Pharaoh, 229
Antonines, 26
Apparentation and Affiliation, 216
Arab Abbasid Caliphate, 95
Arab Islamic civilization, 92, 94, 108, 227
Arabia, 1, 92
Arafat, 9
archaism, 219
Archimedes, 136
Arctic, 39
Armenia, 102
Arnold, Matthew, 48
arrested civilization, 39, 40, 67, 68, 203, 207, 213
Asia Minor, 192
Asimov, Isaac, 42, 43, 161
Athens, 49, 177, 192
Augustine, 208
Augustus Caesar, 153
average maximum age, 200, 201, 202
Aztecs, 20

B

Babylonia, 192
Babylonian civilization, 17, 180
Balkan provinces, 102
Banquo, xiii, 191
barbarian invaders, 218
barbarian successor states, 222
barbarians, xv, 7, 8, 18, 20, 24, 29, 30, 31, 43, 44, 45, 80, 112, 116, 129, 145, 146, 168, 175, 191, 214, 215, 216, 219, 220, 221, 222
bear market, 211
Beehive-Earth, 193
bell clapper, 49
Black-Scholes Model, 43
blade technology, 37
boats, invention, 234
Book of Songs, 234
border, effect of, 7, 129, 130, 215, 218, 219
Bossuet, 208
breakdown, 18, 20, 24, 25, 26, 27, 28, 29, 31, 44, 50, 60, 64, 66, 80, 82, 88, 92, 94, 100, 114, 116, 117, 125, 126, 127, 128, 129, 130, 131, 187, 213, 214, 215, 216, 217, 220, 225
Brutus, 113
Buddhism, 13, 16, 32, 118
Buhei, 29
Bulgars, 105
Buretsu, Emperor, 78
burning mirrors, Archimedes, 136
Byzantine civilization, 103, 105, 108, 226, 227
Byzantine Empire, 102, 105

C

Calakmul, 241, 243, 244
Canton, 83
Carolingian Renaissance, 88

Cassius, 113
central banks, 6
central government, 28, 212, 221
Charlemagne, 88
Chieh, Emperor, 235
China, 12, 76, 81, 82, 83, 107, 126, 129, 130, 144, 151, 179, 182, 184, 210
Chinese, 2, 11, 12, 85, 107, 116, 126, 151, 184, 188, 191
Chinese characters, 233, 235
Chou Dynasty, 236
Christianity, 13, 16, 32, 118
Cimbri, tribe of, 147
civilization, 14
civilization, extinction of, 221
civilizations, first generation, 31, 32, 64, 116, 135
civilizations, hibernating, 221
Cleopatra, 152
climate, xiv, 25, 33, 34, 39, 40, 116
climatic conditions, favorable, 39, 191
Cold War, 21, 125
Communist World, 1
Communists, 126
Comte, 208
Condorcet, 208
cosmic senescence, 44, 112
coupling constants, 135
creative minority, xiv, 22, 24, 25, 27, 28, 30, 33, 38, 39, 40, 213, 214, 217, 218, 223
cultural invasion, 224
cultural transmission, 224
culture, 1, 14, 21, 35, 37, 39, 50, 66, 76, 81, 94, 95, 107, 116, 125, 126, 127, 145, 146, 147, 148, 149, 150, 151, 174, 177, 182, 184, 187, 219, 220, 221, 222, 224
culture, homogenization of, 193
cycles, weather, 122
cyclicity, 48

D

d parameter, 67, 107
Dark Ages, 87, 88, 174
data compression, 166
David, King, 116
de Saint-Simon, 208
decline, of West, 125
Den, Pharaoh, 229
desiccation, 215
detachment, 219
Dirac delta-function, 72, 73, 76, 132, 133
Discourse on Universal History, 208
disintegration phase, xiv, xv, 16, 17, 18, 24, 25, 28, 29, 30, 31, 41, 42, 46, 50, 52, 66, 107, 145, 146, 177, 191, 192, 193, 214, 216, 217, 218, 219, 225
Divine Guidance, 210
Djer, Pharaoh, 229
Djet, Pharaoh, 229
dog sledges, 39
domestication, plants, 37
dominant minority, 22, 24, 25, 26, 27, 28, 29, 30, 31, 213, 214, 217, 218, 219, 220, 221, 223
Dos Pilas, 241, 243
Dover Beach, 48
Dow Theory, xiv, 41, 43, 211, 212, 226, 228, 241
Dow Theory of Civilizations, xiv
Dow, Charles, 211
DRD4 gene, 37, 38
dynamics, societal, 42

E

Early Hindic civilization, 102, 109, 228
Early Japanese civilization, 78, 107, 109, 226, 228
earth civilization, 150, 166, 168, 169, 172, 173, 174, 175
Eastern Roman Empire, 7, 102
econometric models, 122
Econophysics, 208
Egypt, 1, 9, 14, 21, 28, 41, 80, 81, 83, 116, 136, 152, 157
Egyptaic civilization, 13, 16, 18, 25, 28, 31, 32, 39, 60, 62, 64, 70, 71, 72, 73, 74, 75, 76, 78, 85, 116, 132, 152, 153, 154, 155, 156, 157, 173, 174, 179, 180, 182, 184
Electrodynamics, 44
Electromagnetism, 44
Elliott wave theory, 57
End of History, 209
Environmental Determinism, 210
epic heroic ages, 221
Eskimo, 39, 67
etherialization, 213, 225

Europe, 2, 8, 41, 87, 88, 102, 125, 130, 136, 192
external proletariat, 18, 22, 24, 30, 31, 213, 214, 217, 218, 221
extraterrestrial civilization, xv, 150, 160, 161, 166, 167, 168, 169, 170, 171, 172, 173, 174, 175
extraterrestrial civilizations, xv, 159, 161, 162, 163, 164, 165, 166, 173, 175

F

Far Eastern civilization, xiv, 6, 11, 12, 17, 76, 78, 79, 81, 82, 83, 86, 107, 109, 192, 226, 228, 239
Faraday, 44
farming, 37
feudal period, Chinese, 236
Fibonnacci numbers, 57
five grains, invention, 234
forces, 1, 45, 46, 47, 48, 76, 92, 95, 100, 139, 144, 146, 167, 177, 215
Foundation SF novels, 42, 161
France, 20, 136
French Enlightenment, 88
French Revolution, 88
friction, societal, 49
frontier, 7, 24, 191, 213, 222
Fu Hsi, 234
Fujiwara clan, 76
futurism, 219

G

g constant, 74, 80, 107, 120, 133, 135, 141, 142, 151, 153, 154, 155, 156, 157, 233
Galactic Empire, 161
generations, 15, 65, 113, 116, 117, 118, 126, 153, 160, 161, 178, 211, 212, 215, 223, 225
generations, of civilizations, 109
genetic engineering, 197, 198, 202
Genetic Imperative, 210
German, 20, 102, 145
Germanic culture, 147, 148, 149
Germanic tribes, 147
Ghana, 1
Ghuzz Turkmen, 95

Gibbon, Edward, 26, 28, 29, 145
global warming, 33, 123, 130, 193
globalization, 187
Golden Age, 208
Goths, 4
governing class, 218
gravity, problem of, 194
Great Britain, 126, 136
Greek Diaspora, 87
growth phase, xiv, 114, 116, 125, 127, 128, 129, 130, 133, 187, 214, 217, 225
Guatemala, 241
Gupta Empire, 100

H

Hamilton, Peter, 211
Han Dynasty, 82
Hangchow, 83
harmonic oscillator, damped, 48, 49, 57
health care, 130, 202
Hellenic breakdown, 60
Hellenic civilization, 14, 21, 25, 28, 29, 44, 60, 61, 64, 87, 88, 92, 94, 102, 108, 129, 146, 147, 148, 149, 152, 153, 157, 192, 226, 227
Hesiod, 208
hieroglyphics, 241, 243
Hindu civilization, 17, 100, 101, 102, 108, 109, 228
Hindu fundamentalist sub-society, 130
Hinduism, 13, 16, 32, 118
history, model of, 122
Hittite civilization, 17, 81, 180, 182, 185
Hopeh, 236
Horus cult, 230, 233
Hsia Dynasty, 233, 235, 236
Huang Ti, 234
Huchow, 83
Hung Kou canal, 64
Hyksos, 60, 71, 73, 75, 78, 83, 132, 133, 145, 173

I

Ice Age, 39, 40
Iconoclasm movement, 103, 105
Imhotep, 136

The Life Cycle of Civilizations

immigration, 4, 8, 125, 129, 130
Inagaki Hiroshi, 29
India, 94, 126, 127, 130, 144, 180, 182, 184, 192, 210, 224
Indic civilization, 17, 81, 100, 101, 102, 108, 109, 228
Indonesia, 128
IndoTechnic civilization, 109, 127, 130, 228
Indus river, 95
Industrial Revolution, 20, 88, 136, 141
intelligentsia, 218
internal proletariat, 18, 22, 23, 24, 25, 27, 30, 31, 33, 213, 214, 217, 218, 219, 221, 222, 223
Internet, 1, 9
interregnum, 28, 95, 108, 127, 216, 220, 221, 223, 227
interstellar travel, 159
Iran, 4, 6, 9, 47, 95
Iranian culture, 95
Iranian Islamic civilization, 81, 94, 95, 97, 98, 108, 226, 227
Iranic civilization, 97, 108, 179, 226, 227
Iraq, 1, 4, 6, 9, 95, 128
Iraqi Gulf War, 3
Islam, 1, 2, 4, 6, 8, 9, 13, 16, 32, 118, 127, 128, 129
Islamic civilization, xiii, xiv, 2, 3, 4, 9, 11, 12, 92, 94, 95, 127, 128, 129, 179
Ismail I, Shah, 95
Israel, 2, 4, 8, 9, 127, 128
Israeli-Palestinian conflict, 4
Italy, 102, 152, 192

J

Japan, 21, 76, 78, 79, 80, 81, 107, 109, 116, 125, 126, 129, 174, 179, 182, 184, 228
Japanese, xiv, 2, 29, 76, 78, 85, 125, 129, 144, 174, 184, 228
JapoTechnic civilization, 109, 228
Jewish, 8, 9, 92
Jewish revolts, 92
Jovian satellites, 158, 166
Jovian, Peace of, 102
Jupiter, 166

K

K'ai-feng, 83
Ka, King, 228
kayaks, 39
Keats, 205
Knossos, 133
Kondratieff cycle, 122
Korea, 76

L

League of Nations, 210
leisure, creative, 225
liberalism, 88
Library of Alexandria, ii, 136
life expectancy, 198, 199, 202
lifetime, maximum, 200
lifetimes, of species, 88, 160, 222
Ligeti, Paul, 116
light, speed of, 159, 166
long-lived population, 203, 204, 205, 206
looms, 140
loss of nerve, 44, 113, 216
Lower Egypt, 229, 230, 231
Luddites, 140

M

Macedonians, 224
magnetic propulsion, 194
Maine, 34
Manchu Dynasty, 126, 188
Manchu manners, adoption of, 126, 151
Marcus Aurelius, 26
Mark Anthony, 152
Mars, 158, 166, 195
Martian atmosphere, 195
Marx, 208
mass, 6, 9, 24, 44, 45, 48, 82, 109, 111
Massachusetts, 34
Maxwell, 44
Mayan, 241
Mayan civilization, 16, 81, 182, 184, 187
medical advances, 160, 197, 201, 202, 203
Meiji Restoration, 76, 78, 125, 174
Melko, M., 32, 248
Menes, Pharaoh, 228

merchants, 24, 218
Mesopotamia, 92
Michael III, 102
middle class, 22, 24, 136, 188
Middle East, 21, 35, 37, 41, 87, 92, 94, 127
Militarism, 217
military, 2, 11, 22, 82, 125, 128, 129, 136, 147, 174, 215, 218, 219
mimesis, 22, 24, 214, 217, 218
Minamoto clan, 76
mindless armies, 131, 177
Minoan civilization, xv, 39, 132, 133, 134
Mohammed, 8, 92, 95
Mongol, 41, 83, 95, 145
multi-generation, 117
multi-generation social cycles, 122
Museum, of Alexandria, 136
mushroom ring, xv, 191, 192, 193, 195, 213
Muslim, 2, 4, 6, 7, 8, 9, 92, 95, 129
mutation, xiv, 33, 35, 37, 38, 39, 191, 214
mutations, 197

N

Napoleon, 123
Narmer Palette, 229, 231
Narmer, Pharaoh, 228, 229, 231
NATO, 210
Neandertals, 35, 36, 38
New Kingdom, 76, 132
New Sinic civilization, 82, 109, 226, 228, 239
Newton's force law, 45, 46, 77, 85, 90, 94, 97, 100, 103, 105, 120
Nigeria, 128
Nile, 13, 16, 25, 115, 191
Nile River civilization, 231, 233, 239
Nintoku, Emperor, 78
nomadic empires, 215
Nomads, 67
Noreia, battle of, 147
nuclear destruction, 125
nuclear proliferation, 9, 125
nuclear rockets, 194

O

Ockham's Razor, 43, 178

Octavius Caesar, 152
oil, 4, 6, 9, 94, 127, 129
Oprah, 1
Orthodox Christian civilization, 102, 103, 104, 105, 106, 108, 127, 226, 227
Osama bin Laden, 4
oscillation, 51, 113, 116, 118, 160
Osmanli conquests, 92
Ostrogoths, 102
Ottoman Empire, 92, 215

P

Palestine, 41, 92
Palestinian state, 8
Palestinic civilization, 92, 108, 226, 227
Pan Islamic Movement, 127
Pan, Emperor, 235
Paradise, 208
Parthian Empire, 94
Parthians, 102
peaks, 26, 51, 59, 74, 80, 88, 107, 112, 114, 120, 162, 211
Peloponnesian League, 64
Peloponnesian War, 27, 29, 88
pendulums, 48
Pepin the Short, 88
Periclean Age, 116
period, 2, 11, 18, 27, 28, 29, 30, 31, 34, 35, 36, 37, 38, 39, 42, 50, 57, 64, 65, 66, 67, 74, 76, 78, 80, 82, 83, 90, 95, 97, 100, 103, 105, 107, 113, 114, 116, 117, 118, 120, 122, 125, 126, 131, 132, 140, 143, 145, 147, 149, 152, 153, 160, 161, 162, 163, 164, 165, 166, 168, 173, 174, 188, 193, 211, 213, 214, 221, 224
Persia, 1, 94, 102
Persian invasion, 116
petrifaction, 83, 213
petrification, global, 188
petrified civilization, 67, 71, 76, 80, 109, 153, 162, 174, 175, 188, 193
PetroIslamic civilization, 94, 97, 108, 127
Philippines, 128
philosophies, 30, 220, 221, 223
physical environment, 16, 217
pictographs, Chinese, 233
Pisistratus, 64
plow, invention, 234

plumbing, Egyptian origin, 157
Polynesian civilization, 67
population social dynamics, 191
Portuguese, 224
progress, xiv, 2, 6, 21, 22, 35, 36, 113, 125, 127, 136, 138, 139, 141, 172, 174, 177, 178, 179, 181, 182, 183, 184, 186, 187, 188, 189, 190, 193, 216
psyche, 44, 216, 221
Ptolemaic Dynasty, 136, 152
pyramids, 28, 39, 64, 116, 117, 136

Q

Qa'a, Pharaoh, 229, 230, 233
Qa'a Upheaval, 233
quantum communications, 159
quantum entanglement, 159
Quantum Mechanics, 112
quantum teleportation, 159

R

rally, 44, 66, 113, 116, 117, 125, 129, 220
Red Crown of Lower Egypt, 231
religion, 2, 18, 20, 24, 28, 30, 31, 116, 118, 220, 221, 222, 223
renaissance, 95, 224
Republica Christiana, 90
resistance, 47, 67, 73, 109, 140, 146, 215
resistance to change, 47, 109, 140, 146
revolution, 127, 138, 140, 217
Rhea, Robert, 211
Richardson, Lewis F., 42, 44, 248
Roman Catholic Church, xv, 117, 118, 120, 121
Roman Empire, 6, 7, 18, 25, 26, 29, 44, 92, 102, 112, 129, 145, 151, 152, 153, 157, 192
Roman military power, 147
Romano-Jewish Wars, 92
Rome, 4, 25, 29, 44, 94, 129, 147, 152
Rosetta stone, 172
rout, 44, 66, 113, 116, 117, 125, 144, 220
Russia, 76, 125, 128, 129, 130
Russian Revolution, 127
Russians, 105
Russo-Japanese War, 125

RussoTechnic civilization, 108, 128, 227

S

S curve, 135, 157, 188
Sagan, Carl, 158, 248
sage kings, three, 234
Samurai Banners, 29
Santorini volcano, 133
Sarajevo, 88
Sasanian Empire, 95, 102
Saturn, 166
Saudi Arabia, 8, 9
science, 20, 22, 128, 129, 136, 166, 177, 194, 224
Selden, Hari, 42, 43
Seleucid Empire, 94
Seleucus, 94, 95
Semerkhet Calamity, 233
Semerkhet, Pharaoh, 229, 230, 233
Set, 230, 233
SETI, Project, 159, 168
Shah, 47, 95
Shahruhk, 95
Shang Dynasty, 233, 235, 236
Shang Ti, 235
Sharia, 2
Shelley, P. B., 48
Shen Nung, 234
Shensi, 236
Shih Ching, 234
Shintoism, 118
Shotoku, Prince, 78
Shun, King, 234
Siberia, 130, 210
Sicily, 192
silk trade, 6
Sinic civilization, 16, 17, 18, 60, 63, 64, 70, 81, 82, 86, 107, 109, 191, 228, 230, 236, 239
SinoTechnic, 239
SinoTechnic civilization, 109, 126, 129, 228
Sketch for a Historical Picture of the Progress of the Human Mind, 208
skilled workers, 218
smelting, 136
Smuts, General, 33
social discords, 216
social pressure, 217

societal level, 44, 45, 46, 50, 57, 59, 65, 66, 67, 68, 74, 76, 77, 85, 89, 90, 92, 94, 96, 97, 100, 103, 105, 113, 114, 118, 120, 129, 132, 133, 135, 136, 138, 139, 140, 141, 144, 146, 150, 151, 153, 157, 160, 168, 173, 179, 192
Sociophysics, 208
Solomon, 92, 116
Soochow, 83
Sophocles, 48
Sorokin, 208
space, xv, 12, 126, 128, 129, 130, 144, 193, 194
space civilization, 195
Spencer, Herbert, 18
Spengler, Oswald, 18, 32, 66, 248
Spock, 43
standard curve for S, 57
Star Trek, 43
Startup phase, 9, 50, 64, 76, 78, 80, 81, 82, 83, 88, 92, 94, 95, 100, 102, 105, 107, 111, 118, 120, 125, 126, 127, 128, 132, 138, 144, 153, 161, 174, 180, 182, 184, 185
steam boiler, 136
step function, 73, 135, 139, 140, 141
Stock Market, xiv
Sudan, 128
Sumeric civilization, 16, 17, 18, 32, 39, 81, 180, 182, 185
Sung dynasty, 83
supercivilization, 187, 188, 189, 190
Sweden, 199, 200
Syracuse, 136, 1
Syraic civilization, 17, 92, 93, 94, 95, 97, 98, 108, 116, 179, 182, 184, 226, 227

T

Taliban, 128
Tamerlane, 95
Technic civilization, 90, 108, 125, 129, 136, 138, 160, 166, 167, 168, 170, 171, 172, 173, 174, 227
technologic, xiv
technological force, 138, 139, 140, 141, 142, 143, 184
technology, societal benefits, xiii, xv, 1, 2, 7, 20, 21, 22, 39, 76, 94, 125, 126, 127, 129, 130, 136, 138, 140, 141, 142, 143, 144, 166, 177, 178, 179, 184, 186, 187, 188, 216
Temple Mount, 8
Teotihuacan, 243, 244
terrorism, 2, 4, 8, 128, 129
Teutones, tribe of, 147
The World's Great Age, 48
Theran volcano, xv
Third World, xiii, 125, 128, 130
three and a half beat, 41, 44, 45, 47, 50, 52, 59, 64, 71, 107, 118, 221
Ti-hsin, Emperor, 236
Tikal, 241, 243, 244
time of troubles, 9, 12, 18, 28, 29, 50, 78, 80, 82, 83, 88, 90, 94, 95, 100, 107, 113, 114, 116, 120, 125, 126, 127, 129, 131, 132, 215, 220, 222, 225
Togrul the Turkman, 95
Toynbee, Arnold, xiv, 1, 12, 13, 15, 16, 18, 19, 20, 22, 24, 26, 27, 28, 29, 30, 31, 32, 33, 34, 38, 41, 42, 43, 44, 47, 58, 74, 76, 108, 113, 114, 115, 116, 117, 122, 131, 174, 177, 191, 211, 248
transfiguration, 219
Turks, 95

U

United Nations, 210
United States, 1, 2, 3, 4, 8, 20, 113, 117, 125, 128, 130, 136
universal church, 217, 222, 223
universal state, 1, 18, 28, 29, 50, 71, 74, 76, 78, 81, 82, 83, 90, 95, 100, 107, 113, 114, 127, 132, 161, 192, 214, 217, 218, 220, 221, 222, 225
universal states, expansion of, 191, 192, 222, 224
Upper Egypt, 230, 231
Upper Paleolithic Explosion, 35, 37
USSR, 128
Utopias, 219

V

Vedic period, 100
Venus, 195

Verne, Jules, 194
Visigoths, 102, 147

W

war, 2, 3, 4, 7, 8, 9, 22, 24, 27, 31, 38, 43, 88, 102, 125, 128, 130, 131, 145, 152, 214, 217, 222, 224, 225
warrior bands, 221
waves, 112, 172
Western civilization, xiii, xiv, 1, 3, 4, 9, 10, 11, 87, 88, 90, 108, 128, 129, 136, 138, 160, 174, 188, 227
White Crown of Upper Egypt, 231
Works and Days, 208
world history, model of, 122
World Trade Center, 4, 113
World War I, 11, 21, 88, 125, 130
World War II, 2, 9, 21, 126, 144

Wu, King of Chou, 235, 236

Y

Yangtze River, 191, 236
Yanshi (city), 235, 236
Yao, King, 234
Yellow River (China), 234, 235, 236, 237
Yellow River civilization, 234, 236, 237, 239
Yu, Emperor, 234, 235
Yuryaku, Emperor, 78

Z

Zeno, Emperor, 102

About the Author

Stephen Blaha is an internationally known physicist with extensive interests in Science, the Arts and Technology. He has written a highly regarded book on physics, consciousness and philosophy – Cosmos and Consciousness, a book on Science and Religion entitled The Reluctant Prophets, and books on Java and C++ programming. He has had faculty positions at Cornell University, Yale University, Syracuse University and Williams College. He was also a Member of the Technical Staff at Bell Laboratories. He has been an Associate of the Harvard University Physics Department for nineteen years. Dr. Blaha is noted for contributions to elementary particle theory and solid state physics theory as well as contributions to Computer Science.

Printed in the United States
797700002B